Praise for *God's Favorite Place on Earth*

"Frank Viola's *God's Favorite Place on Earth* is a fast-moving, ground-breaking look at the Christian's struggle against legalism, discouragement, doubt, rejection, and spiritual complacency. A masterfully engaging book."

Mark Batterson, author and pastor

"A lot of people write books; Frank writes stories, and in this one we once again see why he's such a master. Honored to call him a friend, excited to call him an author I love to read."

Jon Acuff, author and blogger

"Frank Viola's pen and voice are consistently both penetrating and trustworthy."

Jack Hayford, renowned pastor and author

"Frank continues to challenge the church-at-large with a powerful mind, an impassioned voice, and a love for the Bride of Christ."

Ed Stetzer, author and speaker

"*God's Favorite Place on Earth* realigned my heart toward Jesus and His mysterious, confounding, surprising, beautiful ways. It's not often I learn something new when reading a book, but Frank Viola's sharp storytelling and insightful interpretation made me hunger for more of the real Jesus. Pick up this book if you need a reversal in your Christian life; it will not disappoint."

Mary DeMuth, author and blogger

"The best thing I can say about Frank Viola is this: When I read his books—and I read them all—I don't think much about Frank Viola. I think about Jesus. And I learn to love Him more. This book is no different. Read it, and you'll find yourself thinking, if you're like me, 'I knew Jesus was great, but . . . Wow!' And that, at least from me, is as good as it gets."

and radio personality

"As masterly as a C ___ re, Frank Viola surpasses himself in hi ___ e, soaring magnificence. Part novel, pa ___ Bible study, Frank's imaginative touch an ___ prose haiku leaves the reader resolved more than ever to be a Bethany—God's favorite place on earth."

Leonard Sweet, author, seminary professor, speaker

"Combining masterful storytelling, historical knowledge, biblical insight, and practical wisdom, Frank artfully uses the Gospels' depiction of Lazarus and the small town of Bethany to lay out a beautiful and compelling vision of a God who longs to make every human heart and every church 'His favorite place.' This is a beautifully written, timely, prophetic work all would benefit from reading!"

Greg Boyd, pastor and author

"*God's Favorite Place on Earth* beautifully creates a powerful and moving portrait of the humanness of Jesus and His dearest relationships. Taking a story well told, Frank Viola engages the voice and view of Lazarus to bring a new perspective and moving relatability to Jesus' life on earth. Incredibly thoughtful and moving."

Jenni Catron, author and leadership consultant

"Few authors challenge me in my faith like Frank Viola. This book and the stories it contains will force you to face the myth of religion and instead adopt a life of deeper dedication to God, to find your own Bethany. It sure did for me."

Jeff Goins, author and blogger

Praise for *From Eternity to Here*

"Frank's *From Eternity to Here* is a masterpiece. . . . It reads like a movie on paper."

Dr. Myles Munroe, author and speaker

"When you're as old as I am, you don't hear new stuff. You can hardly say anything about religion that I haven't heard several times. But what's in *From Eternity to Here* is so new to me."

Steve Brown, author and talk-radio show host

"A great work of narrative theology."

Alan Hirsch, author and speaker

"Dissent is a gift to the church. It is the imagination of the prophets that continually calls us back to our identity as the peculiar people of God. May Viola's words challenge us to become the change that we want to see in the church."

Shane Claiborne, author and activist

"I just finished *From Eternity to Here*. I'm in process of reading it again. It has moved into my top ten books. Brilliant."

Derwin Gray, pastor and author

Praise for *Jesus Manifesto*

"There cannot be enough books written about the majesties and excellencies of Christ. I am grateful that Frank and Leonard Sweet put *Jesus Manifesto* in the lap of so many."

Matt Chandler, pastor and author

"Whether you are a seminary professor or someone seeking answers about Christ for the first time, *Jesus Manifesto* promises to illuminate the truth about the greatest personality to ever walk the earth."

Ed Young, pastor and author

"If we follow the Spirit, Christ can become as real to us as the world was when we were sinners. *Jesus Manifesto* is a compass pointing toward this holy pursuit."

Francis Frangipane, pastor and author

"*Jesus Manifesto* is a passionate invitation to fall head over heels in love with the Son of God. Prepare to be shaken. Prepare to be awakened. And prepare to answer the call to follow Jesus with wholehearted abandon. After reading this book, you'll never be the same."

Margaret Feinberg, author and speaker

"*Jesus Manifesto* is the most powerful work on Christ I have read in recent years. The Christ of the Empty Tomb is back among us. Sweet and Viola have beckoned us to return to Olivet and renew our souls. I was hushed by its welcome authority. I found a lump in my throat as I read through page after page of biblical witness to the one and only, incomparable Christ in whom alone is our Salvation. You must read this book. All of us must, and then we must believe in this book, rise, and advance on our culture with the truth we have lately backed away from in our faulty attempt to play fair at the cost of our God-given mission."

Calvin Miller, author and professor

"Brilliant, refreshing, soaring—and that's just the first chapter! This book is destined to be a classic devotional volume that will inspire generations of

Jesus-followers. The line from the song goes, 'You can have all this world, but give me Jesus.' This book does just that."

Reggie McNeal, author and missional specialist

Praise for *The Day I Met Jesus*

"What a treasure this diary-style book—*The Day I Met Jesus*—is!"

Lysa TerKeurst, author and speaker

"Jesus, from the very beginning, has been 'good news for women.' One reads of His encounters with the women described in *The Day I Met Jesus* with a sense of wonder that these interactions took place two thousand years ago. He is good news for women still."

John Ortberg, pastor and author

"I thought I knew the women in these stories well, but in this beautiful book—*The Day I Met Jesus*—I met each one in a fresh, personal, and profound way."

Sheila Walsh, author and speaker

"We all long to lift the veil of history and catch a glimpse of the real story— the one that makes our hearts pound, our faith grow, and our lives change. You will never look at Scripture or God's work in your own heart the same way again after you close the final page."

Holley Gerth, author

"An amazing new book that will give you a glimpse of Jesus that you probably never saw before. This is a very unique book."

Dr. Michael Brown, author, speaker, radio personality

"It's one thing to skim a story about women meeting Jesus; it's another one to dive deeply into their hearts. *The Day I Met Jesus* shines the light on desperate lives and Jesus' powerful intervention. These stories made me think about my own transformation by the One I love. If you want to love Jesus more, this is the book for you. Scholarly and accurate, but also tender and beckoning, it's a book you won't want to miss!"

Tricia Goyer, author and blogger

INSURGENCE

INSURGENCE

Reclaiming the
GOSPEL OF THE KINGDOM

FRANK VIOLA

BakerBooks

a division of Baker Publishing Group
Grand Rapids, Michigan

© 2018 by Frank Viola

Published by Baker Books
a division of Baker Publishing Group
PO Box 6287, Grand Rapids, MI 49516-6287
www.bakerbooks.com

Printed in the United States of America

ISBN 978-0-8010-7701-2

Library of Congress Cataloging-in-Publication Control Number: 2017055468

Scripture quotations labeled ASV are from the American Standard Version of the Bible.

Scripture quotations labeled BLB are from The Holy Bible, Berean Literal Bible. Copyright ©2016 by Bible Hub. Used by Permission. All Rights Reserved.

Scripture quotations labeled BSB are from The Holy Bible, Berean Study Bible. Copyright ©2016 by Bible Hub. Used by Permission. All Rights Reserved Worldwide.

Scripture quotations labeled ERV are from The Holy Bible: Easy-to-Read Version.

Scripture quotations labeled ESV are from The Holy Bible, English Standard Version® (ESV®), copyright © 2001 by Crossway, a publishing ministry of Good News Publishers. Used by permission. All rights reserved. ESV Text Edition: 2011

Scripture quotations labeled GW are from GOD'S WORD®. © 1995 God's Word to the Nations. Used by permission of Baker Publishing Group.

Scripture quotations labeled HCSB are from the Holman Christian Standard Bible®, copyright © 1999, 2000, 2002, 2003, 2009 by Holman Bible Publishers. Used by permission. Holman Christian Standard Bible®, Holman CSB®, and HCSB® are federally registered trademarks of Holman Bible Publishers.

Scripture quotations labeled KJV are from the King James Version of the Bible.

Scripture quotations labeled NASB are from the New American Standard Bible®, copyright © 1960, 1962, 1963, 1968, 1971, 1972, 1973, 1975, 1977, 1995 by The Lockman Foundation. Used by permission. (www.Lockman.org)

Scripture quotations labeled NKJV are from the New King James Version®. Copyright © 1982 by Thomas Nelson, Inc. Used by permission. All rights reserved.

Scripture quotations labeled NIV are from the Holy Bible, New International Version®. NIV®. Copyright © 1973, 1978, 1984, 2011 by Biblica, Inc.™ Used by permission of Zondervan. All rights reserved worldwide. www.zondervan.com

Scripture quotations labeled NLT are from the Holy Bible, New Living Translation, copyright © 1996, 2004, 2015 by Tyndale House Foundation. Used by permission of Tyndale House Publishers, Inc., Carol Stream, Illinois 60188. All rights reserved.

Scripture quotations labeled NTE are from the New Testament For Everyone.

Scripture quotations labeled MNT are from the Moffatt New Translation.

Scripture quotations labeled Weymouth are from Weymouth New Testament.

Scripture quotations labeled YLT are from Young's Literal Translation Bible. Copyright 1898. Baker Book House.

Emphasis added by author in Scripture references indicated by italics or all caps.

Some names and details have been changed to protect the privacy of the individuals involved.

18   19   20   21   22   23   24   7   6   5   4   3   2   1

Contents

Introduction   11

A Warning Before You Read Further   15

What Is the Insurgence?   19

PART I   THREE DIFFERENT GOSPELS   23

PART II   UNVEILING THE KING'S BEAUTY   43

PART III THE GOSPEL OF THE KINGDOM   81

PART IV ENTERING AND ENJOYING THE KINGDOM   149

PART V   OUR GLORIOUS LIBERTY   209

PART VI ADVANCING THE KINGDOM   297

Notes   433

Acknowledgments   439

Introduction

Now after John had been taken into custody, Jesus came into Galilee, preaching the gospel of God, and saying, "The time is fulfilled, and the kingdom of God is at hand; repent and believe in the gospel."

Mark 1:14–15 NASB

The book you hold in your hands contains a revolutionary message. One that has shaken nations, toppled kingdoms, altered lives, and set countless people free.

That message radically changed my own life. And it's still challenging me, stretching me, probing me, transforming me, and (on occasion) scaring me, even as I pen these words.

I've been a Christian for over thirty-five years. Throughout that time, I've heard countless sermons, read countless books, and traveled the world. Based on my experience and observation, the message I will be presenting in this book is rarely preached today.

I wish I had heard it when I first became a believer. It would have spared me so many problems. Unfortunately, the revolutionary message I will share with you has been replaced by two "lesser" messages. The sober confession of one young man sums up the fruit of one of these:

When I first got saved, I really wanted to please God. So I sat under convicting preaching and read convicting books. I did everything I was told. I worked very hard at trying to serve God and did my best to build His kingdom. But I eventually burned out. And looking back, I didn't see much impact from my efforts. Later my eyes were opened that my main motivation I was operating from was guilt and fear. Fear of having God upset with me because I wasn't doing enough for Him. Guilt (which I called "conviction") because I didn't measure up, despite my best efforts.

Another confession from a young woman describes the fruit of the other lesser message:

> When I received Jesus, I rejoiced that I was forgiven of all my sins. I was told that my personal life didn't matter much to God because He loves me despite what I do. I'm under grace, and God is primarily interested in justice and helping the poor. For years, my life was focused on raising my children, sending them to college when they grow up, and someday having grandchildren. I went to church once a week, read my Bible, and prayed. I was hungry for justice in the world and supported several causes that promoted it. Looking back, I discovered that Jesus was really just a supplement to my already busy life. Christ wasn't the reason why I breathed. I was living for other things, even good things like raising a family and working for justice, but they weren't my Lord Jesus.

Interestingly, the New Testament takes dead aim at these two lesser messages and the fruit they produce. In fact, most of Paul's letters—which make up the majority of the New Testament—were provoked because the churches he planted embraced one of these two messages.

Sadly, countless Christians today have never been exposed to any other message. Especially the groundbreaking message that we find all throughout the New Testament and that I will seek to unveil in these pages.

This book is divided up into six parts:

Part I   Three Different Gospels

Part II   Unveiling the King's Beauty

Part III   The Gospel of the Kingdom

Part IV Entering and Enjoying the Kingdom

Part V   Our Glorious Liberty

Part VI Advancing the Kingdom

Each part builds on the previous one. And they all contain short chapters for ease of reading. Also, some of the questions that will arise in your mind while reading will be answered later in the book.

If I developed every theme in this volume, it would be more than 1,000 pages. Consequently, I've included footnotes and endnotes that contain source material and supplemental resources that delve deeper into the themes. You can obtain these resources at InsurgenceBook.com.

God's Eternal Purpose

For the last two decades, my main focus, burden, and passion has been God's eternal purpose. It is the thread that runs through all my work.

As I have argued in detail elsewhere, the eternal purpose of God is the grand narrative of the entire Bible.[1]

The kingdom of God is at the heart of God's eternal purpose. In fact, in recent years, I've come to realize that the kingdom of God is just another term for the eternal purpose. In this respect, John Bright was correct when he wrote,

> The concept of the Kingdom of God involves, in a real sense, the total message of the Bible. . . . The Bible is *one* book. Had we to give that book a title, we might with justice call it "The Book of the Coming Kingdom of God." That is, indeed, its central theme.[2]

The kingdom of God explains and sums up the meaning and purpose of Jesus. The kingdom points to the universal glory, fullness, and rule of Jesus Christ and the exercise of God's image and authority through human beings—the central features of the eternal purpose.

I want to make clear at the outset that I'm not writing this book for scholars or theologians. Yet I believe scholars and theologians will benefit from it.

I'm instead writing so that a teenager in high school who is familiar with the basics of the Bible will be able to understand and gain value from it.

My Hope

My hope in writing this book is that its message will deliver you from every other version of the gospel except the gospel of the kingdom—a gospel that has been virtually lost to us today.

When properly understood and received, I am convinced that the gospel of the kingdom will capture your heart and ruin you for the Lord Jesus Christ and the insurgence He launched on the day of His resurrection.

It's that powerful.

A Warning Before You Read Further

If you dare to read this entire book, you may be infuriated by some of the things I write. And you will probably become defensive over certain parts of it. (So make sure no one is around if you decide to fling the book across the room. Neither I nor the publisher are responsible if you take out an eye! If you're reading the book on your Kindle or Nook, it may be even more dangerous, given that those devices weigh more than a paperback.)

All humor aside, this book is not your typical "Christian" work. Some of the statements I make are admittedly extreme. But they are no less extreme than those made by Jesus and Paul.

Given the explosive content of the book, I interrupt some of the chapters with heartfelt prayers. I encourage you to read those prayers and not skip over them.

So yes, you may get agitated while reading. But holster your weapons and consider whether or not your anger is directed at what I've said or what Jesus or Paul said.

To be candid, I'm writing to strike at your heart. Consequently, if you have a spiritual pulse, I believe you'll be deeply challenged and stirred. And you'll take action.

Being forewarned is being forearmed. And my warning is simple. *You will be distracted from finishing this book*. You will also be distracted from taking action on it.

What follows is my strong encouragement before you turn to the next chapter:

1. Decide right now that you're going to act on the message. The goal of reading this book isn't just to persuade you to change. It's to navigate you through *what* to change.

   For this reason, I've added a "Taking Action" section following each part of the book. This section contains steps on how to practically apply the message of the kingdom to your life.

2. If you're going to invest the valuable asset of time to begin this book, make it productive and decide to finish it come hell or high water.

   I suggest that you set a clear goal (with a date) as to when you will finish. And create a reading plan where you commit to reading a certain number of chapters each week.

   Finishing the book is important, because the threads laid out in previous parts will be pulled out and expanded in later parts. So unless you read every part of the book, you will likely come away with a misunderstanding.

3. If you consider yourself to be a Christian, saved by Christ, I would encourage you to do something you may find strange at first. *Read this book as if you were never saved.* Come to it as a person who is hearing the gospel for the first time.

   The truth is that virtually all Christians have heard the gospel of salvation, but not many have heard the gospel of the kingdom. And in the first century, the two weren't separated like they are today. This book seeks to present the full gospel to you for the very first time. So it is to your benefit to prepare your heart and hear it as if it were the first time.

4. In each part of the book, I introduce you to individuals whom I know have obeyed the gospel of the kingdom. Because they are "unsung heroes" in my eyes—ordinary souls, mostly obscure and unknown—I believe their stories will inspire you with confidence that you too can live out the message of this book.

   In that regard, I love these words attributed to Dr. Joseph R. Sizoo:

   > It is what the unimportant do that really counts and determines the course of history. The greatest forces in the universe are never spectacular. Summer showers are more effective than hurricanes, but they get no publicity. The world would soon die but for the fidelity, *loyalty* and consecration of those whose names are unhonored and unsung.[1]

5. This book isn't just about you or for you. It's also about and for the people you know. So the single best thing you can do after finishing is to give your copy to someone else. Or better, buy them their own copy. I don't say this because I want to sell books; I have no personal need for that.

    But I believe in the message. It changed my life and the lives of those I've shared it with. In fact, to gain the most value from the book, I suggest you read it with a friend or a group.

6. Due to space limitations, we had to move some of the chapters in the original manuscript to InsurgenceBook.com as online articles. Therefore, I encourage you to read each article when you are prompted to in the footnotes.

7. Despite its comprehensive nature, I am not presumptuous enough to think that this book is the final word on the kingdom of God. I regard it as a robust exploration of the subject. I've spoken and written more about the kingdom elsewhere, and so have others whom I mention in the footnotes and endnotes. And many of them are listed on InsurgenceBook.com, a website dedicated to those who wish to delve deeper into the content.

    All told, when you finish this volume, you will be equipped to take your place in the divine insurgence that launched 2,000 years ago. An insurgence that will set you free from everything else except Jesus Christ and His glorious kingdom.

· insurgence

noun

An organized opposition intended to change or overthrow existing authority:
insurgency, insurrection, revolt, revolution, sedition, uprising

What Is the Insurgence?

During the last weekend of July 2017, I spoke at a conference in Central Florida. People attended from all over the United States, Australia, New Zealand, China, Norway, Denmark, Sweden, the UK, UAE, and Canada.

The conference was marked by great diversity.

Racial diversity, diversity in age, culture, social status, and so forth. It was a microcosm of God's kingdom.

What took place that weekend was remarkable. A piece of heaven broke through to all of us.

During the conference, I did my dead-level best to unleash the titanic, explosive, cataclysmic, earth-shaking, life-altering gospel of the kingdom that was preached by all the apostles in the first century and that turned the world into a mad rage.

The second night of the conference, something incredible happened. A number of people pulled me aside after the meeting and said things like, "I've not been so shaken by the Lord through a message." Another said, "What took place was electric. Something very special happened in that room that I can't fully describe." Others said they were deeply stirred and rocked by what took place.

We didn't plan this nor foresee it, but the next morning, a number of people expressed their desire to be baptized. So I asked a brother and a sister in Christ to baptize anyone who wanted to respond to the gospel of the kingdom. Those who responded were baptized in the hotel pool where the conference was held.

Each person being baptized gave a moving testimonial about severing their ties with the world system and making their entrance into the glorious kingdom of God. More than half the conference attendees came out to witness the baptisms and rejoice. (At a public hotel pool!) I was on the tenth floor observing the entire event, and I could hear the clapping and singing from there. The sight brought me to tears.

The next day, I returned home humbled and profoundly thankful. To my mind, the weekend was historical. Many who attended wrote me testimonials of how their lives were turned upside down.

Here is the moving testimony of a woman named Ruth. She wrote it, then read it aloud to everyone just before she was baptized Saturday afternoon.

Thirty-four years ago I responded to a very weak and inaccurate gospel message that I had been taught all of my life. It was a message that was mixed with half truth and half lies. It was a perverted "gospel message" based on works and fueled by fear. I was baptized into that system of control. It's important for me to be re-baptized today to declare my renunciation with that system and my commitment to the real, true gospel and to our Lord Jesus Christ. So today I do this before you as witnesses, God, and all the heavenly beings, both holy and the demonic beings, because they need to hear my renunciation and proclamation:

By my baptism today, I publicly declare my intentions to completely break ties of loyalty to and come away from this world's systems and all of its entanglements, distractions, and counterfeits. I choose to forsake all that gets in the way of me fully coming into the kingdom of God—into the Lord Jesus Himself. I repent of being baptized into a legalistic system that taught my acceptance by Him was based on my performance in addition to what Jesus did for me. I renounce any agreement with the fear that this belief produced in me if I didn't measure up. Although I believed I would go to heaven, I did not know then what it meant to forsake all and to fully enter His kingdom; to "come follow Him."

I sever my ties to a mixture of lies and half truth, which resulted in a lack of seeing the power of the pure gospel's effect in my life. I repent of not receiving the fullness of the power of the resurrected Christ in my heart, but instead followed a lie of Him still on the cross. I choose to live by the power of the resurrected Christ and by His grace to appropriate my full inheritance that He paid for, to be a radical laid-down lover of Jesus who will bring this kingdom everywhere I go, to be the royal mature bride that my Beloved deserves and to impact the world with His love.

By His grace, I have counted the cost as best as I know, and I choose to be "all in" toward Him and all out of the world today and forever. I go under the water so that I might die to myself and everything that has tentacles around me, including compromising the gospel. I come up in newness of life, into His glorious light, putting to death all known or unknown agreements to darkness or to living by my flesh or man's systems. I will be a new creation, a new citizen who is fully immersed in God's kingdom! I will live by Jesus' gospel, not any version of man's invention. Today is a new day, a new start!

~Ruth

What I've described above is an example of the insurgence that I will be discussing throughout this book. The insurgence is no less than the recovery of the radical gospel of the kingdom of God—a gospel that I believe will once again shake this earth.

A Prayer for the Insurgence

This is the prayer that was in my heart when I began penning this book. Please read it now and agree with me before the Lord:

Lord, I ask that You push back the limits of Your mercy. I confess that the message in this book is beyond me. I'm totally incapable of delivering Your Word within these pages, so I lean hard on You as I craft each sentence.

Give every person who reads this volume a deeper comprehension into Your eternal purpose and everlasting kingdom. Motivate and inspire each one to complete this book and take action on its challenging, yet liberating message. And out of it, gain a people for Yourself who will raise a new standard in the earth of what it means to obey the gospel of the kingdom.

Make them a witness and a testimony of the present—yet ancient—insurgence.

Amen.

Part I
THREE DIFFERENT GOSPELS

Three "gospels" dominate the Christian world today. Two of them are diluted at best or false at worst. The third is the one that fully liberates. We will begin to explore all three now.

The Crisis of Our Times

As I write these words, the Christian faith is in crisis. The impact that the body of Christ has on the world is meager.

The reason for much of this problem has to do with an insipid allegiance to the Lord Jesus Christ among Christians and a profound misunderstanding of His kingdom. In fact, I'm convinced that our understanding of "allegiance" to Jesus is warped at best.

By and large, Christians seem to fall into one of two camps when it comes to following Jesus.

Camp 1 consists of those whose relationship to Jesus is understood to be an allegiance to external rule-keeping. These people may not realize it, but they are in bondage to religious duty and obligation.

> Now then, why do you try to test God by putting on the necks of Gentiles a yoke that neither we nor our ancestors have been able to bear? (Acts 15:10 NIV)

Camp 2 consists of those whose relationship to Jesus is understood to be a supplement to their already busy lives. Believing in Jesus makes them feel a little happier and helps them deal with sad days. But Jesus isn't really central to their lives. These people may not realize it, but they are in bondage to their own desires.

> So, because you are lukewarm—neither hot nor cold—I am about to spit you out of my mouth. (Revelation 3:16 NIV)

It's rare to find a Christian today who doesn't fit into these two camps. Yet they do exist. And my hope is that with the release of this book, their tribe will increase.

The tribe I'm describing—this third camp—is made up of those whose relationship to Jesus Christ is not motivated by guilt, condemnation, shame, religious duty, the fear of hell, or the hope of heaven. *Rather, it's motivated by the compelling sight of the glorious Person of Christ and the irresistible power of His kingdom.*

Regrettably, this motivation has been lost to us today.

We are all products of the kind of gospel we hear and believe. So the quality of the convert is the result of the quality of the gospel preached.

Thankfully, the gospel of the kingdom—and all that goes with it—is being recovered and reclaimed among a small group of people all over the world today.

Rising up from the soil, God is raising up a people who are neither rule-oriented nor halfhearted. They are neither self-righteous nor lukewarm. They are neither legalistic nor libertine.

Instead, these are those who are responding to the explosive power of the kingdom message as it was proclaimed in the early days of the primitive church.

This hearty band constitutes an insurgence to the present order of things.

I wrote this book for one reason: so that the insurgence will grow and spread in our time and beyond.

Recovering a High-Octane Gospel

• • •

With rare exception, the gospel that was preached in the first century doesn't exist today. I realize that's a searing statement, but I plan to establish the point throughout this book with the hopes of reclaiming that gospel.

The gospel that John the Baptist, Jesus, Paul, Peter, and the rest of the apostles unleashed on the world was so titanic, so overwhelming, so radical, and so utterly uncompromising that it made the strongest of men quake.

The early apostles ripped the earth apart by the seams bare-handed, by the power of the gospel they preached and lived. They were firebrands, rare breeds, unlike anything that most of us have ever encountered. They left all to follow Jesus Christ and live for His kingdom. Their devotion was resolute, total, and utter.

Their gospel overturned the status quo, regardless of the country in which it was proclaimed. It was so revolutionary and subversive that it got those who dared preach it into boiling water.

It got John the Baptist beheaded.[*] It got Jesus crucified. It got Peter imprisoned. It got Paul killed. It incited riots. It provoked misunderstanding. It caused division, strife, and conflict, even among friends and family. The claims of Jesus Christ regarding His kingdom are so absolutely total that they threaten our closest relationships.[†]

---

[*] Herod Antipas was the ruler of Galilee and was regarded to be "the king of the Jews." John the Baptist preached the gospel of the kingdom and repentance. John denounced Herod's immoral marriage, which led to his imprisonment and eventually his death (Luke 3:1–20; Matthew 14:1–12). However, I agree with N. T. Wright, who points out that John believed that Herod's immorality demonstrated that he couldn't be the true king of the Jews, and his immorality disqualified him from that position. John believed that his cousin, Jesus of Nazareth, was the coming king, not Herod. So in the end, John was beheaded because of the gospel of the kingdom. N. T. Wright, *Simply Jesus* (New York: Harper One, 2011), 80–81.

[†] See my online article "The Radical Cost of the Kingdom" at InsurgenceBook.com.

This gospel brought persecution, hatred, and disruption wherever it was announced. This is true today, even in countries like the United States of America, where there is freedom of speech.

This gospel was so powerful that Paul of Tarsus could walk into a Gentile city empty-handed, and pagan Gentiles would turn away from their idols and immorality to give their complete allegiance to Jesus of Nazareth as this world's true Lord.

Paul could leave that city after being there for only a few months, abandon it for a year, and return to find those same ex-pagan Gentiles still following Jesus Christ!

Because of the revolutionary message of the gospel, it was a terrifying thing to be a Christian in the first century. You were an insurgent to the present order. A revolutionary. Someone viewed as dangerous.

The gospel of the kingdom is a gospel of spiritual violence. It shakes nations to their foundations and provokes either obedience or rejection. It's so powerful it will upset every generation that hears it, altering the lives of those who submit to its claims.

This is true even in societies like the United States of America where "freedom of speech" is the norm. The gospel of the kingdom, when preached without compromise and in its original purity, sounds treasonous.

Those who obey this gospel stand unmovable on this earth. You can throw anything at them, and it won't shake them from their devotion to the true King, the Lord Jesus Christ. The gospel of the kingdom calls the world to account, and the world is forced to reckon with those who proclaim it. Including the world of religion.

Again, the gospel I'm describing hardly exists today. And this is why we are losing masses of young people to Western consumerism, to gangs, and to terrorist groups. The latter preach a counterfeit gospel and a counterfeit insurgence. It's also why modern-day Christianity is so weak and ineffective.

It is high time for the gospel of the kingdom—the true gospel and the true insurgence—to be recovered today.

I'm writing this book, therefore, to stir your heart and set it aflame with a redisovery of the glorious gospel of God's kingdom.[1]

From Christian to Radical Jihadist

. . .

Jeff grew up in a Christian home in the West. He attended church regularly and even got involved in a Christian youth group. During his teens, Jeff experienced what most teenagers do: a crisis of identity, purpose, and meaning.

In his search, he encountered a recruiter for a terrorist organization that utilizes barbaric forms of violence to further their agenda. At first blush, Jeff was repulsed by the violence that marks this group. But as he continued to read their material, he was arrested by their allegiance, energy, comradery, and excitement.

He found the organization's vision for a worldwide utopia to be both beautiful and compelling. And he began to view the extremist group as a path to adventure. Everyone in the organization portrayed themselves to be "God's warriors," engaged in an important mission on the earth.

After being captivated by the jihadists' literature he was reading, Jeff made his way to Syria to meet the recruiter and the organization.

Jeff spent several months in Syria. At some point during his visit, Jeff gave his full allegiance to the militant jihadist organization. And he received training by its leaders for jihad ("holy war").

Jeff's devotion to the organization was so strong that he admitted he would be willing to execute people for his religion. He no longer identified himself by his country. The terrorist organization became his new identity.

You might ask how this could happen. How could a Western Christian join a terrorist organization known for its horrific violence against others?

Very simple. Jeff discovered a level of devotion, brotherhood, and sense of belonging to an important mission in the radical terrorist organization that was profoundly lacking in his Christian experience.

In terms of their devotion to their faith, Jeff's Christian friends were marginal at best. The radical jihadists were sold out, all in, fully committed, even to the point of giving their lives to the cause. They gave Jeff a profound sense of brotherhood, community, and having each other's backs.

By contrast, Jeff's Christian friends hardly knew one another, lacking deep relationships. They didn't feel that they were taking part in a great project, something cataclysmic, world-changing, and worth dying for. They were more excited about football, their careers, and their material possessions than they were about Jesus Christ.

Beyond going to church today and going to heaven later, Jeff's Christian experience lacked a compelling vision that gave him the reason to wake up every morning. Jeff found this strong sense of world-changing mission, purpose, and challenge in the radical terrorist group.

Here's the irony. If Jeff had lived in the first century, he would have found everything he witnessed in this radical terrorist organization in the early Christian community, minus the ruthless tactics, unbridled brutality, unspeakable horror, and barbarism.

Sadly, multitudes of Christians like Jeff have never heard the explosive, disruptive, earth-shaking gospel of the kingdom. Nor have they ever seen anyone live it out.

And that gospel and that kingdom are both true and real.

Sure, many people in the West haven't given their allegiance to a radical terrorist group. But they've given it to many other things that have nothing to do with Jesus Christ or His kingdom.

This glaring problem is precisely what motivated me to write this book, which I trust provides the remedy.*

---

* Unfortunately, Jeff is not alone among those who grew up in Christian homes only to join terrorist groups like ISIS later. For another example, see "ISIS and the Lonely Young American," by Rukmini Callimachi in the *New York Times*, June 27, 2015. According to that article, through January 2015, at least 100 Americans, among almost 4,000 Westerners, traveled to join jihadists in Syria and Iraq.

Two Enemies of the Gospel

• • •

"History," Martin Luther said, "is like a drunk man on a horse. No sooner does he fall off on the left side, does he mount again and fall off on the right."

The same can be said about the gospel that many (if not most) Christians hear today.

During Paul's day, there were two different gospels that competed with his own. One was the gospel of legalism, which is rule-oriented. The other was the gospel of libertinism, which is self-oriented.

The New Testament letters, especially Paul's, take dead aim at both of these. Yet these two gospels are alive and well in our day.

I believe they are the result of presenting a tamed, diluted, shrunken, reduced form of the true and only gospel found in the New Testament.

Let's explore both of those gospels now.

Four Shades of Legalism

Legalism is the human attempt to gain God's favor by keeping rules, regulations, laws, and expectations.

Legalism is innate to fallen humanity. And it has affected virtually every Christian on the planet.

Because so much fog clouds the issue of legalism, I would like to do some fog-clearing and introduce you to the four different shades of legalism being preached today.

Shade 1 declares that you must believe in Jesus and obey God's Law (the Law of Moses) to be saved.

Shade 2 declares that you must believe in Jesus to *be* saved, but you must obey God's Law to *stay* saved. So believing *gets* you in, but obeying *keeps* you in.

Shade 3 declares that you must believe in Jesus to be saved, but you must obey God's Law to gain His favor and make Him happy.

Shade 4 says that you must believe in Jesus to be saved, but you must fulfill certain expectations to make God happy and earn His favor. These expectations are not explicitly found in the Bible.

Each shade of legalism seeks to win God's favor by human effort.

The Bait-and-Switch Gospel

. . .

Most contemporary Christians have been given a bait-and-switch gospel. Here's the bait:

> Come just as you are. God accepts you. God loves you. It doesn't matter what you've done. Jesus wants to receive you because He loves you without condition.

So you take the bait and trust in Jesus. You're saved. Isn't it wonderful? Now you start going to church, reading Christian books, watching Christian television, and listening to Christian podcasts and radio.

And it dawns on you that the message has switched. The message now becomes,

> God's holy, you're not, try harder.

And you're put under the bondage of some preacher's personal convictions laid upon you and everyone else.

As a result, you live in a state of guilt, constantly feeling that you're not doing enough nor measuring up. You're not praying enough, nor reading your Bible enough, nor making enough disciples, and on it goes.

This is how legalism works. It produces the guilt that Jesus Christ gave His life to remove.

The Gospel of Legalism

Legalism is bootstrap, white-knuckle, performance-based Christianity.

Legalists are people who believe that salvation is by grace alone, but sanctification (holiness) comes by one's own efforts to be a "good Christian."

Legalists tend to push their own personal standards onto everyone else. They are also quick to judge people's motives, thinking the worst of their intentions. Legalists confuse obedience with trying to serve God in one's own strength.

They demand that other people do things that they themselves could never carry out. They also regard the sins of others as more grievous than their own.

> But let none of you suffer as a murderer, or as a thief, or as an evildoer, or as a busybody in other men's matters. (1 Peter 4:15 KJV)

Legalists are blind to their own self-righteousness. They pride themselves on being "clean" on the outside, without realizing that they are defiled on the inside.

For all of these reasons, legalists unwittingly bring a lot of pain and heartache into the lives of others. Yet sadly, they seem to be out of touch with this fact.

Forgive the personal reference, but when I was in my teens, I came to the Lord through a legalistic denomination. I was fed a steady diet of guilt, condemnation, and judgmentalism. And I was surrounded by other legalists who reinforced the message. Like most legalists, I was a legalist without realizing it.

But God was merciful.

The Gospel of Libertinism

In reaction to legalism and the devastation it brings, some have accepted the gospel of libertinism.

Libertinism is often called "easy believism" because it equates mental assent with biblical faith. A head nod to a statement of belief is not what the Bible means by the words "faith" and "believe."

The gospel of libertinism teaches that because we are under grace, anything goes.

Libertines live the way they want, having skirted the lordship of Christ. They are inclined to justify carnality by pulling the "grace card," the "I'm free in Christ" card, and the "don't judge me" card.

For the libertine, grace becomes a license to live in the flesh and silence their conscience.

Some libertines have rationalized that they can continue to practice a particular transgression because (they think) God doesn't really care, regardless of the carnage it brings.

A mark of sin is that it produces unnecessary pain to oneself and others. Sin and love are the exact opposites. Love is benefiting others at the expense of yourself. Sin is benefiting yourself at the expense of others. Sin is selfishness; love is selflessness.

Some libertines have gone so far in their deception that they have reinvented Jesus in their own image to justify their rebellion against God and clothed it with spiritual talk. Others have gone further off the beam and have become practical atheists.

In short, the libertine lives as if there is no God. The legalist lives as though she or he is God to everyone else.

Both attitudes are incompatible with the life of Christ and the kingdom of God. They are equally allergic to the insurgence.

Complicating Factors

What complicates the situation further is that the legalist doesn't know that he or she is a legalist and tends to view all non-legalists as libertines. By contrast, the libertine doesn't know that she or he is a libertine and tends to view all non-libertines as legalists.

Without the Holy Spirit's illumination, this deception is difficult, if not impossible, to break.

Legalism leads to the self-righteousness of the flesh. Libertinism leads to the defiling acts of the flesh. But the source of both is our flesh—the fallen nature. And both lead to bondage.

As J. I. Packer once put it,

> There is no wisdom in jumping out of the frying pan into the fire, and if in our flight from legalism we fell into lawless license, our last state might well be worse than our first.[2]

The truth is, we have all sinned and come short of the glory of God. And we all need is Jesus Christ to forgive, deliver, and keep us each day from both the defiling acts of the flesh on the one hand and the self-righteousness of the flesh on the other.

The Third Gospel

. . .

The third gospel is the gospel that Jesus, Paul, and the other apostles preached.

That gospel is not good advice, good philosophy, good ethics, good religion, good morality, or good views.

That gospel is good *news*.

In the first century, the words "gospel" and "evangelize" referred to heralding the good news that a new emperor had been installed in the Roman Empire. Heralds would go out to proclaim the good news, informing people that a new era of peace, salvation, and blessing had begun. They then exhorted people to get down on their knees to worship the new emperor.

The apostles used this same language to describe the preaching of the gospel of Jesus Christ.

The gospel that the apostles preached was the announcement—the heralding—that Jesus of Nazareth had become this world's true Emperor (Lord), launching a new era of peace, salvation, and blessing, and because of it, everything has changed.

This was the explosive gospel of the kingdom.

The Same Message, Different Names

• • •

In the New Testament, the gospel goes by the following names:

The gospel of the kingdom.

The gospel of the kingdom of God.

The gospel of the grace of God.

The gospel of the Lord Jesus Christ.

The gospel of our Lord Jesus.

The gospel of Jesus Christ.

The gospel of Jesus Christ, the Son of God.

The gospel of His Son.

The gospel of Christ.

The gospel of the glory of Christ.

The gospel of peace.

The gospel of life.

The gospel of your salvation.

The gospel of God.

The glorious gospel of the blessed God.

The glorious gospel of Christ.

The everlasting gospel.

All of these terms refer to the one and only gospel described in the New Testament. Paul called it "my gospel" and "our gospel."

Tragically, over the last century, some Bible commentators have come up with novel inventions in which they have sliced and diced the New Testament up into different gospels for different people. But these inventions are erroneous and cannot be sustained upon close scrutiny.

The gospel of the kingdom is the good news about the universal kingship of Jesus of Nazareth in the earth. And it is a gospel of grace, salvation, and life.

Gospel Confusion

• • •

Years ago I made an eye-opening discovery. The kind of convert made is the result of the kind of gospel preached and received.

Since the mid-1900s, some commentators have divorced the gospel of the kingdom from the gospel of grace.* They've taught that the gospel of grace is mandatory for salvation, while the gospel of the kingdom is optional for discipleship.

Others have said that the gospel of the kingdom applies only to the nation of Israel, while the gospel of grace applies to everyone else.

Similarly, some have argued that the gospel that Paul preached was different from the gospel that Jesus preached.

All of these views are built on a proof-texting approach to Scripture—an approach that can be used to "prove" any doctrine, no matter how unbiblical.

However, if you read the entire story of Scripture as a free-flowing, unbroken narrative, you'll discover that the gospel of the kingdom, the gospel of grace, the gospel of Christ, the gospel of salvation, and so on are all different names for the same message.

And it is that bottled-up gospel that I will seek to unleash throughout the rest of this book.

* I'm speaking of the commentaries written by dispensationalists. The idea that the gospel of the kingdom was for the Jews and the gospel of grace is for the Gentiles began in the mid-nineteenth century with the Plymouth Brethren—the inventors of dispensationalism. Their doctrine was popularized by C. I. Scofield, who published his famous Scofield Study Bible in 1909. Scofield's Bible was used at Moody Bible Institute, and it spread throughout evangelical schools all across America. Although many evangelical scholars have refuted it throughout the years, the doctrine is still with us today.

Lordship and Liberty

. . .

One of the things I've learned in my spiritual journey is that the closer someone gets to Jesus Christ, the less judgmental, self-righteous, harsh toward others, and selfish he or she will be.

And the closer one gets to Christ, the more they will desire to know and live for God's ultimate purpose.

The lordship of Jesus Christ and the liberty of Christ are two sides of the same reality.

The gospel of the kingdom liberates us from the defiling acts of the flesh on the one hand and sets us free from the self-righteousness of the flesh on the other.

TAKING ACTION »

Reading a book without taking action is like flying a plane without landing. So before moving on to the next part of this book, I encourage you to take some time to implement what you've learned so far.

1. Ask yourself these questions. Your candid answers will prepare the soil of your heart for the next part of the book.

Do you recognize any legalistic tendencies in your heart? Some of the indicators are as follows:

- You feel that you're not doing enough to make God happy.
- Deep inside, you doubt God's love and His complete acceptance of you as His child.
- You are quick to think the worst of other people and impute bad motives to their hearts.
- You tend to maximize the sins of others as being worse than your own.
- You feel at liberty to interrogate people—even those you don't know very well—for alleged sins, when you yourself would hate for someone to interrogate you the same way.
- You have a tendency to put your own personal convictions and standards on other believers, judging them according to the dictates of your own conscience (see Romans 14 for this problem).

Do you recognize any libertine tendencies in your heart? Some of the indicators are as follows:

- It doesn't bother you when you violate one of the Lord's clear commandments in Scripture.
- There is little difference between you and those who don't know Christ in the way you talk, the language you use, the kinds of jokes you tell or laugh at, and the hobbies and forms of entertainment you enjoy.

- You feel that because you're under grace, you can do anything you want and there will be no spiritual consequences.
- You don't believe that God disciplines His children.
- You have no sense or understanding of what's worldly.

2. Ask the Lord to shine His light into your heart, revealing where you stand with Him with respect to legalism and libertinism. More light will be shed on this topic as you read further.

Part II
UNVEILING THE KING'S BEAUTY

Preachers often say, "Follow Jesus. Give Him your whole life. Forsake everything, and yield yourself totally to Him." But this exhortation is virtually impossible to follow unless we first have eyes to see our Lord's beauty. When we see Christ as He really is, giving Him our lives is a natural response. Let's explore that idea now.

Ruled by Glory

• • •

In describing how God rules His kingdom, the psalmist asked, "Who is this King of glory? The LORD of hosts, he is the King of glory" (Psalm 24:10 KJV).

God the Father is spoken of as the God of glory (Acts 7:2 NIV). He's also called the Father of glory (Ephesians 1:15–17 KJV). Jesus is called the Lord of glory (1 Corinthians 2:6–8), and the Holy Spirit is called the Spirit of glory (1 Peter 4:14).

So the triune God, the eternal Godhead, is characterized by glory.

God's glory is the visible expression of His character. It includes His beauty, His splendor, and His love.

Glory is the result of grace. Grace is giving to us what we don't deserve. In God's grace, we see His glory. God's life is glory; His nature is grace.

Earthly kingdoms are ruled by force. Fear is the tool that is used to keep its subjects in line. Satan's kingdom is ruled by tyranny, fear, control, deception, and an appeal to self-preservation.

By contrast, the kingdom of heaven is ruled neither by fear nor force. Instead, God's kingdom is governed by two things: God's glory and absolute freedom.

Consider God's rule before creation. The heavenly hosts were subject to God by the sight of His peerless glory. And they were utterly free to follow Him or not follow Him. Some chose not to follow Him. (I'll discuss this in more detail later.)

But what has kept the faithful heavenly host submitted to God's authority since the beginning of time? It's the resplendent beauty of God the King. The angels, who bear the burning bliss of God's holy light, are intoxicated with the beauty of the Almighty. They continuously marvel at His majesty, splendor, and radiance. They are captivated and captured by His glory.[*]

---

[*] I'm using the term "angels" to refer to all the heavenly host, including seraphim, cherubim, the living creatures, the divine council, etc. All throughout the Bible, we find angelic beings worshiping God. Some examples are Isaiah 6:2–3; Nehemiah 9:6; Hebrews 1:6; Revelation 4:8–11; 5:8–14; 7:11–12; 11:12.

Interestingly, when the kingdom of heaven broke into the earth with the coming of Jesus, this dynamic did not change.

Jesus Christ, the true King, rules by His glory. And He still gives human beings the freedom to submit to Him or reject Him.

Solomon's kingdom helps us here. The kingdom of David was primarily a shadow of Jesus in His earthly life. David fought the enemies of Israel and established his kingdom through bloodshed, which depicted the cross of Christ.

But Solomon's kingdom knew no war. His was a peaceful kingdom. And its glory knew no peer. Under Solomon's reign, Israel was brought to the zenith of its power and splendor.

Solomon ruled his kingdom by his glory. People were captured by his incomparable worth. When the queen of Sheba visited Solomon and beheld his kingdom, her response was, "The half has never been told" (2 Chronicles 9:6). The gold alone in Solomon's kingdom was mind boggling. (Throughout the Bible, gold represents divinity.)

The Scripture says that the queen was so overwhelmed by the glory of Solomon's kingdom that it literally took her breath away ("There was no more breath in her," 1 Kings 10:5 ESV).

Jesus even spoke about the glory of Solomon's sumptuous royal attire (Matthew 6:29).

Well, a greater than Solomon has come (Matthew 12:42). And the glory of Jesus Christ is the reality of what Solomon's unspeakable glory foreshadowed.

What captured the twelve disciples to forsake everything and follow Jesus? Simple. They saw His glory and were captured by it.

> And the Word became flesh, and dwelt among us, and we beheld His glory, the glory as of the only begotten of the Father, full of grace and truth. (John 1:14 NKJV)

How will you and I reach the standard of God's kingdom? We will never reach it by being motivated by anything except a sighting of the King's glory. We are standing in the lineage of the heavenly host who have been captured by the glory of God in heaven and have come under His sway.

We are standing in the lineage of the people of Israel who were captured by the glory of Solomon and came under his sway. And we are standing in the lineage of the Twelve who were captured by the glory of Christ and forsook everything to follow Him.

It is the sight of His glory that causes you and me to abandon all else. It is the experience of His grace that causes us to forsake everything for the Lord.

Just as God the Father rules the kingdom of heaven in the heavenly realm by His glory, Jesus Christ rules the kingdom of God on earth by His glory.

> For the LORD Almighty will reign
> on Mount Zion and in Jerusalem,
> and before its elders—with great glory. (Isaiah 24:23 NIV)

So open your eyes and see His glory. Open your heart and receive His grace. Then show His glory and grace to others, especially your brothers and sisters in the Lord.

The New Testament tells us that Jesus is the radiance of God's glory (Hebrews 1:3; 2 Corinthians 4:6). And it is by seeing the glory of Christ that God establishes His kingdom in our hearts.

> And we all, with unveiled face, beholding the glory of the Lord, are being transformed into the same image from one degree of glory to another. For this comes from the Lord who is the Spirit. (2 Corinthians 3:18 ESV)

This is how the insurgence thrives.

In the following pages, I intend to show you the glory of your Lord and remind you of His grace. So that together, we will behold His irresistible beauty, remarkable splendor, and unfathomable love.

> Yours, LORD, is the greatness and the power
> and the glory and the majesty and the splendor,
> for everything in heaven and earth is yours.
> Yours, LORD, is the kingdom;
> you are exalted as head over all. (1 Chronicles 29:11 NIV)

A Fresh Look at Divine Love

. . .

There's a great emphasis today on serving Jesus and working for His kingdom. But if a person doesn't know the secret of serving God in the energy of the Holy Spirit, they will eventually burn out.

When serving the Lord trumps knowing and loving the Lord, something is desperately wrong.

This is one of the reasons why modern Christianity is so shallow. Countless young believers are trying to give away tickets to a place they've never been.

Let me ask a piercing question. What does it take to truly love someone to the point of abandoning your life to them?

What's required to surrender everything you have to another person? If you've come to deeply love someone, how did it happen?

Did someone command you, saying, "You *must* love this person or else!"? Were you responding out of fear? Guilt? Shame? Duty? Or were your eyes opened to behold how beautiful that individual was?

Indeed, that's how it happened, was it not?

You were compelled. Driven. Impelled. Obsessed even.

At some point, there was an unveiling. A revelation. An eye-opening glimpse.

You recognized the person's beauty—inward and outward—and you were captivated by it. And it wrecked you for anyone else.

Well, that's precisely how the gospel of the kingdom and the Christian life were meant to function.

How is love born in our hearts for Jesus Christ our Lord and King? We can't snap our fingers and expect to instantly love Him.

Rather, there must be an unveiling of His beauty.

That's what happened to the first followers of Jesus. They beheld the splendor of His majesty, and they were fascinated by it. And it eventually transformed them.[*]

---

[*] It's significant to note that Jesus chose His twelve disciples quite a while after they spent time in His presence and watched Him display His glory. See Robert Mounce's

We have seen his glory, the glory of the one and only Son, who came from the Father, full of grace and truth. (John 1:14 NIV)

But we all, with unveiled face, beholding as in a mirror the glory of the Lord, are being transformed into the same image from glory to glory, just as by the Spirit of the Lord. (2 Corinthians 3:18 NKJV)

The absence of this unveiling is precisely why devotion to Jesus Christ is profoundly lacking in the hearts of so many Christians today. It's also why the insurgence hasn't had a greater impact. That is, up until now (we hope).

---

landmark book, *Jesus, In His Own Words* (Nashville: B&H Publishing Group, 2010) for the chronology.

The Stunning Beauty of Christ

• • •

Indeed, the Lord's beauty is incomprehensible. I've never been scuba diving, but I've watched a great deal of footage displaying the incredible beauty that lies under the ocean.

These too are glimpses of the Lord's beauty, causing us to stand awestruck. They are pointers to the multifaceted glory of Jesus Christ.

If you and I are going to give our entire lives to the King, which is what He demands, then we must be convinced that Jesus is a good and benevolent King, worthy of our complete devotion.

> In that day the Branch of the LORD will be beautiful and glorious, and the fruit of the land will be the pride and glory of the survivors in Israel. (Isaiah 4:2 NIV)
>
> Your eyes will see the king in all his splendor. (Isaiah 33:17 NLT)

Without this ingredient, our submission to Christ will be partial and halfhearted. It will also be driven by a motive other than love for Him.

In the Song of Solomon, the words of the maiden about her monarch give us a window into the love that's awakened and stirred when we behold the glory of our true King, the Lord Jesus.

> I'm my beloved's, and his desire is for me. (Song of Solomon 7:10 KJV)

Mind-Boggling Love

Behind the wisdom of God, behind the creation of God, and behind the universe there was a heart. A heart beating with love.

> But God, who is rich in mercy, because of His great love with which He loved us. (Ephesians 2:4–5 NKJV)

> [You, Father,] have loved them even as you have loved me. (John 17:23 NIV)

Before you and I came on the scene, God was love. And when God's love reached us fallen mortals, it became grace. We experience God's love as the grace of Jesus Christ (John 1:14, 17).

The untold secret of the Christian life is that before we can fully surrender our lives to the lordship of Christ, we must first be assured that He genuinely loves us.

> We love Him because He first loved us. (1 John 4:19 NKJV)

If you've trusted in Jesus, you are now in Christ, the object of the Father's love. You are God's beloved child, and He cannot but love you.

> To the praise of the glory of his grace, wherein he hath made us accepted in the beloved. (Ephesians 1:6 KJV)

As you read on, I'm convinced that you will feel more secure in God's love. But in addition, His love will draw out of you a full and complete allegiance to Jesus and His marvelous kingdom. An allegiance not born out of guilt, shame, condemnation, religious duty, obligation, or fear. But one drawn from the compelling sight of the King's beauty (2 Corinthians 5:14).

Ruined

· · ·

One day the Lord revealed Himself to the prophet Isaiah as the One who is high and exalted, sitting on His throne, full of glory.

Isaiah was struck deaf and dumb by the splendor of the Lord's majesty. His reaction to the matchless vision is noteworthy. He said, "Woe is me, for I am undone!" (Isaiah 6:5 NKJV). Some translations say, "I am ruined!"

This is humiliation.

A heavenly creature then touched Isaiah's mouth, cleansing it and removing all of Isaiah's guilt.

This is consecration.

The Lord then asked, "Who shall I send?" And Isaiah responded, "Send me."

This is mission.

The scene in Isaiah 6 is one of exalted heavenly creatures gazing upon the enthroned God, covering their faces because they are so overwhelmed by the sight of divine beauty.

Astonishingly, the Gospel of John tells us that Isaiah was beholding the Lord Jesus in His glory, even before He took on human flesh and became a man (John 12:38–41).

In the life of a believer, a fresh apprehension of the Lord's beauty produces a renewed humility that leads to a renewed consecration and a renewed mission.

> I pray that the eyes of your heart may be enlightened in order that you may know the hope to which he has called you, the riches of his glorious inheritance in his holy people. (Ephesians 1:18 NIV)

Alive to Beauty

· · ·

Martin Luther is credited with saying,

> God writes the Gospel not in the Bible alone, but also on trees, and in the
> flowers and clouds and stars.

Properly conceived, the Christian life is one of beholding, enjoying, and reflecting the beauty of Christ.

To be born from above, then, is to become alive to beauty.

It's essential that we become fascinated, gripped, and captivated by the Lord. If not, we will struggle with boredom, and our hearts will be vulnerable to pursue other things.

The tokens of beauty that God has painted in His creation are designed to lead us to worship the source of all beauty itself—Christ. The beauty of God is designed to lead us to wholehearted abandonment, which is the essence of worship.

As we've already established, all real beauty is found in God Himself. Unlike the beauty we find in the created order, the loveliness of Christ can never be exhausted or worn out.

Jonathan Edwards spoke of "the divine beauty of Christ" which "bows the wills, and draws the hearts of men."[1]

The next time you behold an object of exquisite beauty, remember that you are perceiving a pale reflection of the beauty of Christ.

A person's glowing face displays the beauty within them. In the same way, when we behold the dazzling beauty of creation, we're seeing the outward face of the inner beauty of Christ. We are perceiving something of the elegance, artistry, and resplendent beauty of God.

To put it another way, if Jesus hasn't fully captivated your heart yet, it simply means that you've not caught a glimpse of His infinite beauty. According to Paul, it is His unfathomable love, rich kindness, and tolerant patience that leads us to repent and follow Him.

Or do you think lightly of the riches of His kindness and tolerance and patience, not knowing that the kindness of God leads you to repentance? (Romans 2:4 NASB)

This is where the gospel of the kingdom begins.

Attracted to Beautiful

• • •

Jesus Christ is the essence of true beauty. When God created the earth, He created it by, in, and through His Son, the Lord Jesus (Colossians 1:16; Hebrews 1:2–3). For this reason, the universe is brimming with beauty and elegance.

For this reason, everything beautiful in creation is both a token and a pale reflection of the beauty of Christ. Consequently, the beauty we find on earth is fleeting.

Look at a beautiful painting long enough, and you'll eventually grow tired of it. Listen to a gorgeous piece of music enough times, and you'll grow weary of it. Gaze at a good-looking person long enough, and their beauty will start to fade in your eyes.

When you and I are attracted to something or someone, we are exhilarated by that object or person because it emits something of the beauty of Christ. But His beauty is unique in that it is both permanent and inexhaustible, while all created beauty eventually loses its appeal.

The reason there is so much beauty in creation is because it flows from our beautiful Creator. The beauty we find in the sky, sea, and earth is God's self-portrait, showing us what the living God is like. They all give us a glimpse of the glorious face of God.

The human soul longs for the Beauty behind the created beauty. The beauty we consume with our physical senses is both a gift and a compass leading us to the source of all beauty. The wonder we experience in created beauty is meant to lead us to worship the Creator of beauty. In this regard, physical beauty is but a shadow of the real.

Whether it be a majestic mountain, a resplendent night sky, a breathtaking ocean, a stunning flower, a lovely plant, a gorgeous sunset, a radiant sunrise, an elegant animal, a marvelous fragrance, a perfect gourmet meal, an attractive human being, an exquisite piece of music or art, we are seeing, hearing, smelling, tasting a dim reflection of the source of all beauty—Jesus Christ. Of course, the beauty of Jesus was not found in

His physical appearance (Isaiah 53:2). If He were strikingly handsome, Judas would not have had to point Him out by a kiss. No, the beauty of Jesus is found in His irresistible charisma, His uncommon conduct, His unspeakable love, His quiet strength, His awe-inspiring wisdom, and His infinite compassion.

The beautiful things that surround us everywhere in the created order are tokens of God's glory and good pleasure. They are put before our adoring eyes to remind us to worship the One who molded and shaped them.*

Herein lies the source of idolatry. Idolatry occurs when we lose touch with the fact that all created beauty is a reflection of God's beauty. When we are not aware of this revolutionary truth, we end up worshiping the created thing instead of the Creator. And as we shall later see, idolatry stands at the heart of all sin (Romans 1:25). It's a major obstacle to the insurgence.

---

* Someone may object, saying, "How does a beautiful woman reflect Jesus, who is a man?" The answer: a woman reflects the bride of Christ. And the bride reflects and displays the beauty of Christ, the Bridegroom, for she is a part of Him. Paul said, "The woman is the glory of the man" (1 Corinthians 11:7 NIV).

Real Worship

The word "worship" carries the ideas of extravagant love, utter devotion, and total submission.

Why does God desire worship? Is it because He's a narcissist? Not at all. *We become like what we worship.* Those who worship and trust in idols become like them (Psalm 135:18 NLT), and those who behold the Lord in worship become like Him (2 Corinthians 3:18). Conformity to God's Son, after all, is God's original purpose for humans (Romans 8:28–29).

The radiant beauty we find in creation is designed to lead us to wonder at and worship the source of all beauty, Christ. It's meant to awaken our souls to the true beauty, who is God Himself. Jesus is a beautiful Savior, and the Holy Spirit wants to continually fascinate us with the beauty of the King.

Here are some biblical texts toward that end:

> One thing I ask from the Lord,
>   this only do I seek:
> that I may dwell in the house of the Lord
>   all the days of my life,
> to gaze on the beauty of the Lord
>   and to seek him in his temple. (Psalm 27:4 NIV)

Give unto the Lord the glory due unto his name; worship the Lord in the beauty of holiness. (Psalm 29:2 KJV)

> Splendor and majesty are before him;
>   strength and glory are in his sanctuary. (Psalm 96:6 NIV)

O worship the Lord in the beauty of holiness. (Psalm 96:9 KJV)

> From Mount Zion, the perfection of beauty,
>   God shines in glorious radiance. (Psalm 50:2 NLT)

> The heavens proclaim the glory of God.
>   The skies display his craftsmanship.

Day after day they continue to speak;
night after night they make him known. (Psalm 19:1–2 NLT)

The antidote to spiritual boredom—which plagues many Christians, including leaders—is to receive a fresh awakening of the beauty of Christ. In the following pages, I expect God to open your eyes to behold the stunning beauty of the King.

Recasting the Gospel Stories

• • •

There's a great deal that goes on behind the scenes whenever we read our New Testaments. Consequently, a working knowledge of first-century history can shed tremendous light on the Gospel stories.

Such knowledge allows us to see the beautiful parts of those stories that we would otherwise miss.

In the next seven chapters, I will make you a character in some of the Gospel stories so you can view them from a fresh perspective. I'm also going to weave into them bits of first-century Jewish history, which will help bring them to life and unveil their beauty.

P. T. Forsyth was right when he said,

> Do not tell people how they ought to feel towards Christ. That is useless. It
> is just what they ought that they cannot do. Preach a Christ that will make
> them feel as they ought.[2]

That is my intention. I want to show you His glory and remind you of His grace.

An Epic Oversight

It's your wedding day and you are the excited bridegroom. You are fully responsible for supplying both the food and the wine (as is the case with every bridegroom in the first century).

The event is moving along wonderfully until the wine runs out. This oversight is your fault. You failed to properly calculate how much wine was needed.

Some of your guests begin looking for the wine, but there is none in sight. The fact that the wine had run out is a social disgrace. You are humiliated, nervous, and dreading the reaction from your guests.

Thankfully, Jesus of Nazareth is present. And He has compassion on you and your lovely bride. So in order to spare you from major embarrassment on the greatest day of your life, Jesus does the impossible.

He transforms the water held in six stone jars into wine. But it's not your typical wine. Jesus creates *fine wine*, better than the original batch you secured. Not only that, but the stone jars of new wine are the equivalent of 180 gallons (approximately 900 bottles of wine)!

What's going on here? The Lord Jesus Christ has removed your shame. He's eliminated your disgrace. He's covered your oversight. *And He did it extravagantly.*

So despite your failure, Jesus ended up making you look like a hero. Your guests rave about how incredible the new wine is. And they attribute it to you.

Now that's some incredible Lord, is He not?

I can love a Lord like that.

Can't you?

A Piercing Rejection

• • •

You've been paralyzed from the waist down. Because you are sick, your family has rejected you. (Like most Jews of your day, they've concluded that God is judging you. So they keep you at arm's length.)

The healing prophet named Jesus of Nazareth has moved His ministry headquarters to Capernaum, where you live. He is renting a house, and many have come to see and hear Him.

You have four friends who love you. Because they want to see you healed, they carry you to see Jesus. When they arrive at His home, they cannot get in the door because it's too crowded. So they climb on the roof and break it apart, and then lower you down.

Having descended into His living room from the roof, you find yourself at His feet. As you look up at Jesus with both trepidation and hope, you see Him marveling at you, and He is amazed by the faith of your friends.

He lovingly looks into your eyes and says to you, "Son."

Son! That's a word you've not heard in years. Not since your parents abandoned you.

Tears well up in your eyes. Jesus then says, "Your sins have been forgiven." He then heals you and sends you on your way—walking!

Now that's some amazing Savior, is He not?

I can love a Savior like that.

Can't you?

A Sin-Torn Life

* * *

You are a woman. Abused, forgotten, and disgraced by life.

You've been divorced numerous times, and you've lost one husband to death. You've given up on love, so you're now living with a man out of marriage.

One day you come to the well where you draw water. You've grown tired of the gossip, the whisperings, and the sneers, so you visit the well in the afternoon when no other women are present.

On this particular day, however, you see a man sitting by the well. He looks exhausted.

You spot Him out of the corner of your eye and you ignore Him. The man then does the unthinkable. *He talks to you in public.* You are astounded because Jewish men never speak to women in public, especially Samaritan women!

Not only does this man talk to you, but He supernaturally knows about your life, including your present sin. Yet He doesn't condemn you for it.

This man, whom you regard to be a prophet, goes on to share with you some of the greatest truths a mortal can ever know. He then follows you back to your town and breaks Jewish custom by using your utensils and eating with your fellow Samaritan neighbors, things Jews are forbidden to do.

For the first time in your life, you've met a man who truly loves and cares for you. Hope is born in your heart. You're smiling again. Something has changed deep inside of you.

Now that's some remarkable Christ, is He not?

I can love a Christ like that.

Can't you?

An Unrivaled Failure

* * *

You are one of the Lord's closest disciples. For more than three years, you have lived with Him. But unfortunately, you continually fail Him.

One time He walked on water, and He called you over. But you sunk because you lacked faith. Another time He called you an adversary because you spoke things that were contrary to His Father's will (despite your good intentions).

When Jesus was transfigured before your eyes, you blurted out your desire to build three monuments. And God the Father interrupted you out of heaven.

One time you boldly claimed that you would never forsake Jesus, even if all the other disciples did. Yet during Jesus' darkest hour, you did the unimaginable. You denied and disowned your Lord. On three separate occasions to boot.

Now Jesus is crucified, and you are devastated. The weight of guilt and condemnation is too much for you to bear. The agony of your denial of the man to whom you owe your whole life keeps replaying in your mind. It is keeping you up at night with the sting of regret. You are finding it impossible to shake the self-hatred that has gripped your soul.

Yet despite your constant failings, including your horrendous disowning of the Lord, something remarkable happens after Jesus rises from the dead. An angel tells Mary to tell His disciples—*and you*—that Jesus has risen.

Yes, God singles you out to hear the good news of your Lord's resurrection! You're not only amazed, but you are humbled, bowing down in tears.

When you see Him, now risen, you can only weep. And He never once mentions your denial, which occurred just days before.

Instead, Jesus commissions *you*—not any of the other disciples—to feed His sheep. And weeks later, He hands you the keys of God's kingdom, and you have the high privilege of opening its doors to both Jews and Gentiles.

For generations to come, people will say of you, "The man who failed his Lord repeatedly, and even disowned Him, was made chief of the apostles!"

Now that's some glorious Messiah, is He not?

I can love a Messiah like that.

Can't you?

An Unmitigated Shame

．　．　．

You have just been caught in the act of adultery. You're dragged like a rag doll before a blood-thirsty mob of judgmental men.

They throw you at the feet of Jesus. You have your head down, publicly shamed and mortified. You dare to lift your head slightly and squint. But all you can see through your tears are the sandals of the men who have stones in their hands. You quickly close your eyes again, trembling in fear.

Jesus is sitting before them. He opens His mouth and utters one piercing challenge: "Let the one who is without sin cast the first stone."

Silence follows. Suddenly, you hear the sound of rocks dropping one by one. You muster the courage to open your eyes again and you begin to see the sandals that surround you disappear one pair at a time.

Eventually, every sandal is gone, and you are alone with Jesus.

He then says to you, "Neither do I condemn you; go and sin no more."

Now that's some remarkable God, is He not?

I can love a God like that.

Can't you?

A Hopeless Cause

. . .

You've suffered with a relentless illness for twelve long years. The illness has destroyed your life. Because of it, you have been quarantined.

For twelve years you've experienced no human affection from any mortal. Not from friends or family. You are rendered "unclean." Unworthy to even be hugged.

But worse, the disease you carry in your body is incurable. You've spent your entire life savings on doctors, and not one of them has helped you.

You've lost hope.

One day, you hear that a young prophet has come to your town. And He is known for miraculously healing people, even the most impossible cases.

You run out to the streets to find this prophet. You cannot see Him, but you behold a large crowd. Someone says to you, "Jesus of Nazareth is in the crowd!"

Risking everything, your desperation propels you to rub shoulders with the people in the crowd, knowing full well that you are making them all ceremonially unclean.

But given the reports you've heard about this miracle-working prophet, you are convinced that if you can simply touch His garment, you will be cured.

Stealthily, you press through the crowd, and fall to the ground. From that low position, you reach for the garment of Jesus of Nazareth. Instantly, He stops cold and asks the crowd, "Who touched me?"

You are horrified. Here you are, an unclean woman touching a holy man and thus rendering Him unclean also. But He keeps asking. And the pressure mounts.

Finally, you confess that it was you who touched the holy prophet. To your surprise, Jesus doesn't rebuke you. Nor does the crowd. Instead, He publicly commends your faith and even calls you "Daughter," a word that's not been spoken to you since your illness. The crowd rejoices and applauds.

After twelve horrendous years, you can once again know the touch of another human. Jesus has restored your life and removed your shame and pain. He touched you and made you whole, even while you were unclean.

Now that's some extraordinary Healer, is He not?

I can love a Healer like that.

Can't you?

A Painful Exclusion

• • •

You were in need of money, so you did something that would forever put you in disfavor with your family and friends. You colluded with Rome and became a tax collector.

Your own countrymen see you as a traitor. And rightly so. The Romans have oppressed and mistreated the Jewish people for a long time. And instead of standing with your own people, you've sided with the oppressors for a financial kickback.

You are now hated by your own brethren. You are barred from eating another meal in a Jewish home. You are banned from attending the synagogue. You are no longer welcomed by your own kin.

Then Jesus of Nazareth shows up in your town. You're fascinated by the stories you've heard about this uncommon prophet.

Being a man of small stature, you cannot see Jesus amid the crowds as He walks through your village. So you climb a tree to view Him.

Jesus spots you watching Him. He then does something shocking. *He invites Himself to your home to have dinner with you.*

You're stunned. You've been rejected by every Jew who knows you. They have all given up on you. But Jesus, this holy prophet, wants to sup with you in your own house. He extends to you the right hand of friendship and fellowship when no one else will.

The unfailing grace of God touches your life through the surprising invitation, and your life changes. You vow on the spot to repent and return what you've stolen from others with interest added. And you decide to give half your possessions to the poor.

Now that's some wonderful Redeemer, is He not?

I can love a Redeemer like that.

Can't you?

Beyond Human Imagination

• • •

In each Gospel story I've told, we get a window into what God is like. Why? Because Jesus is the human face of God.

Yet beyond all that Jesus did while He was on this earth in putting the glory of God on display, He did something else. Something incredible.

Jesus of Nazareth suffered the most gruesome death a mortal could ever know. Here's what Jesus, your Lord and Savior, did on the cross:

> He took the entire world system that is in rebellion to God (Colossians 2:20; Galatians 6:14).*
>
> He took the entire old creation which is fallen and corrupt (Colossians 1:20; 2 Corinthians 5:17).
>
> He took the Law of Moses and its condemnation (Ephesians 2:15–16; Galatians 3:10–13; Romans 7:1ff.).
>
> He took our flesh—our old fallen Adamic nature (Romans 6:6; 8:3).
>
> He took the very power of Satan himself (Colossians 2:15; Hebrews 2:14; 1 John 3:8).
>
> He took every sin that you and I would ever commit (Colossians 2:13; Hebrews 9:28; 1 Peter 2:24; 1 John 3:5).

And He crucified them all!

But not only that, He—Jesus Christ—became sin itself, condemning and defeating it in His own flesh (2 Corinthians 5:21; John 3:14; Romans 8:3).

In addition, He justified and redeemed you—making you right with God—forgiving you of all your sins (Romans 5:9; Ephesians 1:7; Colossians 1:14).

As a result, you now stand holy, without blame, and free from accusation in His sight (Colossians 1:22).

---

* I discuss the world system in detail later in the book.

Defeating God's Greatest Enemy

. . .

As wonderful as all that is, Jesus did something else on the cross. He squared off with God's greatest enemy, death.

Three days after death won, God the Father drew together all the powers of heaven and earth and sent them straight to a sealed tomb.

And the body of Jesus of Nazareth came to life. And death died!

And Jesus became a "life-giving Spirit" as Paul calls Him in 1 Corinthians 15. Following His resurrection, He took a deep breath in the center of God in the heavenly realm and breathed His own life into His disciples.

And the only begotten Son became the firstborn among many brethren—and they became the sons and daughters of God.

The grave turned into a garden, and the tree of life was back on the earth again in the Person of Christ.

A New Creation

The death and resurrection of Jesus launched an insurgence in the world. When Jesus died, death had the last word and Caesar was still king. But in His resurrection, Jesus Christ broke loose from the power of death and lived beyond its reach, proving that an insurgence had begun.

From the womb of death, Jesus gave birth to a new creation, a new humanity.

And in that new humanity, there is no Jew or Gentile. There is no male or female. There is no slave or free. There is no rich or poor.

All earthly barriers have been erased. All racial, social, and sexual divisions have been removed.

Behold, this is a new humanity, a new race, a new creation, a new kingdom from another realm. And Jesus Christ is its head. This *ekklesia* is the new creation born in the midst of the old (Galatians 3:28; 6:15; 2 Corinthians 5:17; Colossians 3:11).

What an incredible Lord.

The Third Race

· · ·

While the physical body of Jesus was Jewish, He was the first of the new creation.

In the first century, Jewish culture represented moral scruples, self-righteousness, and the ranking of sins. Gentile culture represented immorality, uncleanness, and loose living.

For this reason, in his letters Paul often combated the self-righteousness that marked Jewish culture as well as the immorality that marked Gentile culture.

Paul did this because some of the new converts were either devolving into a Jewish cultural mindset and lifestyle (e.g., Galatians) or into a Gentile one (e.g., 1 Corinthians).

In other words, Paul was constantly battling both legalism (associated with Judaism) and libertinism (associated with Gentile life).

Throughout his letters, Paul kept reminding the members of the ekklesia that because they are in Christ, citizens of God's kingdom, they are now part of a new creation, a new humanity, a new race.

In 1 Corinthians 10:32, Paul mentions three races of people: the Jews, the Gentiles, and the ekklesia of God. For this reason, the Christians in the second and third centuries called themselves "the new race" and "the third race."

Jesus was calling for an insurgence unlike any other before or since. In Christ, God was launching a new world, a new empire, a new order.

And through His death, Jesus put a torch to the entire world system.

We'll explore the dramatic implications of this later.

The Mystery of the Ages

• • •

In his later years, Paul penned words in Ephesians and Colossians that are simply beyond us. They are too high for mortal women and men to conceive.

Ephesians and Colossians are the twin towers of Scripture. They stand up as towering pyramids. Their depths cannot be fathomed; their riches cannot be plumbed.

As you read through each letter, they keep ascending. And no matter how far you go on with the Lord, they will still be ahead of you. They will always be greater than the person who reads them.

That said, both letters contain a high and sublime truth.

Namely, that the mystery hidden within God for ages is that this incomparable Christ whom I've been describing to you . . .

This amazing Jesus who existed before time and eternity,

This Jesus who took on flesh and showed us what God is like,

This Jesus who died on a cross and put to death all negative things,

This Jesus who rose again on the third day, victorious over the grave,

This Jesus who is seated at the right hand of power, exalted far above all principalities and powers,

This Jesus who is the head of a new creation, a new humanity, a new race called "the ekklesia,"

This Jesus,

This glorious, matchless, incomparable, incredible, radiant, peerless Lord . . .

Lives In You!

The mystery that has been kept hidden for ages and generations, but is now disclosed to the Lord's people. To them God has chosen to make known among the Gentiles the glorious riches of this mystery, which is Christ in you, the hope of glory. (Colossians 1:26–27 NIV)

And you have been given the privilege, the honor, and the high calling to live by His life.

I have been crucified with Christ and I no longer live, but Christ lives in me. (Galatians 2:20 NIV)

Christ, who is your life. . . . (Colossians 3:4 NIV)

For to me, to live is Christ. (Philippians 1:21 NIV)

Who Loves You the Most?

. . .

Think of the person who loves you the most right now.

For some of you, it will be your mother. For others, it will be your father. For still others, it will be your spouse, or a sibling, or a best friend.

Now consider this. The love that this person has for you wanes in comparison to the love that God has for you.

Think about it. The love that this mere mortal has for you is a pale yet tangible reflection of the love that God has for you.

> If you, then, though you are evil, know how to give good gifts to your children, how much more will your Father in heaven give good gifts to those who ask him! (Matthew 7:11 NIV)

In fact, the Father loves you just as much as He loves His Son. Jesus said so Himself.

> Then the world will know that you [Father] sent me and have loved them [my disciples] even as you have loved me. (John 17:23 NIV)

What is more, no one can separate you from God's love. Not even yourself.

> Who shall separate us from the love of Christ? Shall tribulation, or distress, or persecution, or famine, or nakedness, or danger, or sword? As it is written,
>
> > "For your sake we are being killed all the day long;
> > we are regarded as sheep to be slaughtered."
>
> No, in all these things we are more than conquerors through him who loved us. For I am sure that neither death nor life, nor angels nor rulers, nor things present nor things to come, nor powers, nor height nor depth, nor anything else in all creation, will be able to separate us from the love of God in Christ Jesus our Lord. (Romans 8:35–39 ESV)

That's quite a thought, is it not?

The Missing Ingredient

The problem with so much of today's preaching and teaching is that the stress is on obeying Jesus, submitting to Jesus, and "being radical" for Jesus without first unveiling how glorious, wonderful, and beautiful He is.

You see, you and I cannot properly obey Jesus if we aren't first laid to the ground by an earth-shaking sighting of His radiant glory, stunning beauty, and incomprehensible love.

Without this, we will try to obey out of duty, guilt, condemnation, fear, shame, or some earthly ambition (like impressing others or gaining recognition).

In other words, we'll be operating out of legalism.

The result is that we will eventually burn out from serving "the god" of serving God.

Either that or our hearts will turn colder and more legalistic, spewing out judgments and venom on those who genuinely love the Lord but don't follow our religious playbook.

We'll turn into modern-day Pharisees, religious hypocrites who are clean on the outside but corrupt on the inside.

> They [the Pharisees] tie up heavy, cumbersome loads and put them on other people's shoulders, but they themselves are not willing to lift a finger to move them. (Matthew 23:4 NIV)

When Jesus preached the gospel of the kingdom, He did so to a people who saw Him in the flesh. They beheld His glory. They witnessed His compassion, His infinite wisdom, mercy, and love.

Later, Paul and the other apostles so vividly portrayed Christ in their preaching that it was as if Jesus had been crucified right before their eyes. Consider Paul's statement to the Galatian believers who lived hundreds of miles away from Jerusalem and never witnessed the crucifixion of Jesus.

You foolish Galatians! Who has bewitched you? Before your very eyes Jesus Christ was clearly portrayed as crucified. (Galatians 3:1 NIV)

The apostolic message of Century One was so powerful that it brought Christ and His love to life before its hearers.

An unveiling of Christ to our hearts, then, is the necessary prerequisite to a genuine surrender to the Lord Jesus. It's the starting point of the insurgence.

The Untold Secret to Loving Christ

. . .

In the previous chapters, I've given you a description of the character of Jesus. The good news is that He—this same Christ—is the One who has been made ruler of the world, including being the ruler of your life.

And the safest and happiest place you and I can ever be is under His absolute rule.

These timeless lyrics sum it up well:

> What has stripped the seeming beauty
> From the idols of the earth?
> Not a sense of right or duty,
> But the sight of peerless worth.
>
> The look that melted Peter,
> The face that Stephen saw,
> The heart that wept with Mary,
> Can alone from idols draw.[3]

The unconditional, unfathomable, incomprehensible love of Christ makes demands. And one of those demands has to do with the gospel of the kingdom.

But remember: any demand that the Lord puts on us is motivated by love. And it also provides the power required to fulfill it. Therefore, all of the Lord's commands aren't really demands.

They are promises.

Captured for Christ

. . .

I'll end this part of the book with the words of T. Austin-Sparks regarding the book of Philippians. He can say it much better than I can.

When Christ really captivates, everything happens and anything can happen. That is how it was with Paul and with these people. Christ had just captivated them. They had no other thought in life than Christ. They may have had their businesses, their trades, their professions, their different walks of life and occupations in the world, but they had one all-dominating thought, concern and interest—Christ. . . .

There is no other word for it. He just captivated them. And I see, dear friends, that that—simple as it may sound—explains everything. It explains Paul . . . it explains these believers, it explains their mutual love. It solved all their problems, cleared up all their difficulties. Oh, this is what we need! If only you and I were like this, if we really after all were captivated by Christ! . . . After all, nine-tenths of all our troubles can be traced to the fact that we have other personal interests influencing us, governing us and controlling us—other aspects of life than Christ.

If only it could be true that Christ had captured and captivated and mastered us, and become—yes, I will use the word—an obsession, a glorious obsession! When it is like that, we are filled with joy. There are no regrets at having to "give up" things. We are filled with joy, filled with victory.

There is no spirit of defeatism at all. It is the joy of a great triumph. It is the triumph of Christ over the life . . . but, oh, we need the captivating to wipe out our selves—our reputations, everything that is associated with us and our own glory—that the One who captivates may be the only One in view, the only One with a reputation, and we at His feet. This is the gospel, the good news—that when Christ really captivates, the kind of thing that is in this letter happens, it really happens. Shall we ask the Lord for that life captivation of His beloved Son?[4]

TAKING ACTION »

Before moving on to the next part of this book, take some time to implement what you've learned so far. I recommend you do three simple things:

1. Carve sixty minutes out of your schedule to be undistracted. During that undivided time, listen to my conference message "Rethinking Discipleship" at InsurgenceBook.com.

2. After you've heard the message, spend the next twenty minutes contemplating the love that Jesus Christ has for you. Consider the Gospel stories I've told. Consider the magnitude of what Jesus did for you on the cross. Consider the examples of human beings in your life who love you, knowing that the Lord loves you even more.

3. As you contemplate the love of Christ for you, open your mouth and tell Him, "Lord, You love me." Then with the same love with which the Lord loves you, return that love back to Him, saying, "I love You, Lord."

Contemplating the Lord's love for you and speaking it to Him ("Lord, You love me"), then returning that love back to Him ("I love You, Lord") can become a regular practice in your life. One that can be quite transformational.*

---

* I call this practice "Loving and Listening" and I explain it in detail in my course "Living by the Indwelling Life of Christ." If interested, you can check out the course at InsurgenceBook.com.

Part III
THE GOSPEL OF THE KINGDOM

The gospel of the kingdom has been lost to us. We rarely hear it preached today. And if we happen to hear a version of it, it's usually mixed with legalism and legalistic attitudes. So in the end, the message gets emptied of its revolutionary power. By God's mercy and grace, I hope to present the gospel of the kingdom now.

Diluted Gospels

For the most part, the gospel we have today has been reduced to a fire-insurance policy—a "get-out-of-hell-free" card. The name of the game is to get to heaven when you die. And "the gospel" is presented as the trump card that wins that game.

In reaction to this version of the gospel, a growing number of Christians understand the gospel in purely social terms. For this crowd, the gospel is designed to make the world a better place through social activism and reform. The name of the game is "fixing a broken world."

In this section of the book, I argue that both versions of the gospel (the "fire-insurance" view and the "fixing the world" view) have diluted and distorted the gospel of Jesus Christ—otherwise known as "the gospel of the kingdom."

Radicalized

. . .

As I write this book, the term *radicalized* is in common use today. And it has extremely negative connotations. Radicalization is the process by which a person converts to a "radical" or extremist terrorist group.

The story of Jeff that I told in Part I is an example of what it means to be radicalized.

A person becomes radicalized when they sever all present allegiances and give their full devotion to a terrorist organization that's built on an uncommon ideology.

In the first century, when the gospel of the kingdom was preached and accepted, people gave their full allegiance to Jesus of Nazareth as this world's true Lord.

Those who believed the gospel severed their allegiances to all other systems and empires, bending their knee to the new King, Jesus.

> May I never boast except in the cross of our Lord Jesus Christ, through which the world has been crucified to me, and I to the world. (Galatians 6:14 NIV)

The irony here is that adherents to religious terrorist groups have more in common with the first-century Christians than do most contemporary believers. (Obviously, there are many differences between these radical groups and the early Christians, but I'm speaking strictly in terms of the absolute devotion they have to their faith.)

When a person converts to groups like ISIS and Al-Qaeda, we say they are *radicalized.* But as you will shortly see, the gospel of Jesus Christ that was preached and received in Century One—*the gospel of the kingdom*— was just as radical, total, and utter.

It called for extreme devotion and absolute allegiance. Not to a false gospel or cause, but to this world's true Lord.

The allegiance that the early Christians had to Jesus was so extreme that to receive the gospel in the first century was to be "radicalized."

Put another way, the early Christians were seen as insurgents.

They switched all their allegiances to Jesus Christ. As a result, the early Christians were viewed as outcasts who were extremely dangerous (just like terrorists are today). They were regarded as subversive to the existing empire.

Unfortunately, modern Christianity is so far removed from what it was in the first century that the association of radicalization with Jesus may be offensive to some and perplexing to others.[*]

But this was the gospel that Jesus, Paul, and all the other apostles preached. And wherever it was preached, transformation took place. It transformed individuals, communities, and cultures. It turned a hateful religious bigot into an apostle. Saul of Tarsus became Paul, the sent one, and embodied the transforming, reconciling power of the gospel in his own life.

This is the gospel that must be reclaimed today if we will see the Lord's kingdom advance in any significant way.

[*] See my online article "The Radical Cost of the Kingdom" at InsurgenceBook.com for just how extreme the demands of the kingdom of God really are.

What's Past Is Prologue

. . .

William Shakespeare is credited with the phrase "What's past is prologue," meaning that what comes beforehand is the beginning (or prologue) of what comes next.

The Old Testament story is the prologue of the insurgence. So before we can rightly understand the gospel of the kingdom, we must take a quick trip back to the Hebrew Scriptures. I will tell the story as if it were happening in real time.

The story begins before time. God creates the heavenly realm and populates it with angels and other celestial (heavenly) beings. The angels live in God's presence, and they minister to Him.*

God rules the heavens. He is the King of that realm. Hence, it is called "the kingdom of heaven."

One of the celestial beings revolts. As a result, he is exiled from the heavenly realm, put outside of God's presence.

The celestial being is known as Lucifer.† He rebels against God and becomes what the Bible calls "the devil" (which means slanderer, false accuser, or liar) and "Satan" (which means adversary or opponent).

The devil is also referred to as Beelzebub, Belial, the evil one, the tempter, the thief, the enemy, the father of lies, murderer, deceiver, the prince of demons, the god of this world, the prince of this world, and the prince of the power of the air. He's also described as a roaring lion and an angel of light.

I agree with those scholars who believe that Satan (the devil) is the same entity as Lucifer who was once a celestial creature of high status.‡

---

* Luke 1:19 NKJV; Matthew 18:10 NLT; and Revelation 8:2 HCSB are three texts that reveal that angels stand in God's presence.

† The name "Lucifer" appears in the Latin Vulgate of Isaiah 14:12. Other versions translate the Hebrew word as "morning star." It's significant to observe that God commanded Adam to *guard* the Garden of Eden. This indicates that there was an impending threat from which to protect the garden. That threat was already on the earth. It was the serpent. Lucifer's fall, therefore, occurred before or at the same time the first humans were created.

‡ These scholars base their interpretation on texts like Ezekiel 28; Isaiah 14; and 1 Timothy 3:6 (on the prideful conceit of Satan). Also, Revelation 12:9; 20:2; and 2 Corinthians

Point: when you leave God's presence, you leave God's rule.

God then creates the earth and crowns it with the pinnacle of creation—human beings. Humans live in God's presence and minister to Him in a garden called Eden. Eden is to be the beachhead from which humanity is to rule the earth with God's authority.*

Tragically, the first humans follow the devil in rebelling against their Creator. As a result of their disobedience, Adam and Eve are exiled from the garden. They are put outside of God's presence.

> And they heard the sound of the LORD God walking in the garden in the cool of the day, and the man and his wife hid themselves from the presence of the LORD God among the trees of the garden. . . . *therefore the LORD God sent him out from the garden of Eden to work the ground from which he was taken. He drove out the man.* (Genesis 3:8, 23–24 ESV)

The devil now begins ruling the earth, instead of humans (I'll explain more about this later.) God seeks to restore the earth back to human beings and chooses a man named Abraham to relaunch His original intention. God gives Abraham's descendants—the nation of Israel—a land called Canaan.

Canaan is to be the new Eden, the place where heaven and earth meet. Canaan is also to be the place where God will rule the earth through human beings, the place where the kingdom of heaven will touch the planet.

It's no accident, therefore, that Scripture connects Canaan (and Zion, which is in Canaan) with Eden (Genesis 13:10; Isaiah 51:3; Ezekiel 36:35; Joel 2:3). In fact, some scholars argue that Eden was located in what later became the land of Canaan.† To continue the story, the land of Canaan

---

3:3–14 identify the serpent to be Satan and/or the devil. Note that Old Testament prophetic literature often contains dual meanings, one contemporary and another past or futuristic. Isaiah 7:14 and Hosea 11:1 are examples. In the same vein, Isaiah and Ezekiel appear to be speaking about the king of Babylon and the king of Tyre (respectively) as well as Satan's fall. For a compelling sketch of this perspective presented with academic integrity, see Michael Heiser, *The Unseen Realm* (Bellingham, WA: Lexham Press, 2015), 83–91; Greg Boyd, *God at War* (Downers Grove, IL: InterVarsity Press, 1997), 154–67; C. Fred Dickason, *Angels Elect & Evil* (Chicago: Moody Press, 1995), 135–45.

* I give a detailed sketch on the meaning of Eden in my audio message "Vantage Point: The Story We Haven't Heard—Part I" at InsurgenceBook.com.

† John Sailhamer connects Adam in the land of Eden with Israel in the promised land, physically as well as theologically. Sailhamer writes, "The garden of Eden extended from the 'river that flows through all the land of Cush' to the 'River Euphrates.' Since in Genesis the land of Cush is linked to Egypt (Genesis 10:6), the second river, the Gihon (Genesis

and the Garden of Eden symbolize God's presence and life. Exile from each symbolizes death and separation from God.

God's will is for the kingdom of heaven to descend to Canaan. Through Canaan, God will reclaim the whole earth. Interestingly, when the kingdom of heaven comes to earth, it is called "the kingdom of God."

In short, Israel was to show the world what it looks like when God is in charge.

Regrettably, Israel follows the way of the fallen celestial beings and the first humans. They too rebel against God. As a result, Israel is exiled from the land of Canaan. They are put out of God's presence, just like the angels and the first humans were, and God no longer lays claim to the earth.

Strikingly, throughout the Old Testament, whenever Israel is in the land of Canaan, God is called "the God of heaven and earth." But when Israel is exiled from the land, He is just called "the God of heaven."[*]

There's a powerful point here. If a person wasn't in the land of Israel, they were under the dominion of false gods.[†] In the mind of God, the land of Canaan was sacred ground. It represented the whole world, just as the garden of Eden represented the whole world.

When God has His people in the land, under His kingship and in His presence, He lays claim to the whole world. Canaan (the land of Israel)

2:13), was apparently understood by the author as 'the river of Egypt.' . . . When we move to Genesis 15, we find that the land promised to Abraham—the promised land—is marked off by these same two rivers, the Euphrates and the River of Egypt (Genesis 15:18). Note that the area marked off by these two rivers in Genesis 15 is essentially the same region covered by the garden of Eden in Genesis 2. When the general boundaries are compared, it becomes clear that the writer of the Pentateuch intends us to identify the two locations with each other. God's promise of the land to the patriarchs is thus textually linked to His original 'blessing' of all humanity in the garden of Eden." John Sailhamer, *Genesis Unbound* (Sisters, OR: Multnomah Books, 1996), 50–51, 72. In addition, Ezekiel 28:13 calls Eden "the garden of God" and the "holy mount" (v. 14)—a likely reference to Mount Moriah, which is in Canaan and the site of the Jewish temple. See also Paul Kissling, *The College Press NIV Commentary, Genesis*, vol. 1 (Joplin, MO: College Press Publishing, 2004), 162–63.

[*] Genesis 14:1–19; Joshua 3:11–13; Ezra 1:2; 7:12, 21, 23; Nehemiah 1:4–5; 2:4; Daniel 2:18, 28; Matthew 11:25. Also, in my book *From Eternity to Here* (Colorado Springs: David C. Cook, 2009), chap. 17, I explain how the story told in Genesis 1 and 2 is replayed throughout the story of Israel and culminated in Revelation.

[†] This is confirmed by David when he associates being outside of Israel with the worship of false gods (1 Samuel 26:19). It's also confirmed when Namaan, a military leader in Syria, visits Israel, is healed, and then wishes to take soil from Israel back to his land (2 Kings 5). In the ancient world, the land of Israel was viewed as sacred and under the dominion of the true God.

becomes the new beachhead from which God will restore the entire world under His dominion.

> For he [Jesus] must remain in heaven until the time for the final restoration of all things, as God promised long ago through his holy prophets. (Acts 3:21 NLT)

This is why all throughout the Old Testament, a battle rages over the land. It's a turf war that has massive spiritual parallels.

So the story of Israel repeats the story of Adam and Eve, which repeats the story of Lucifer's fall. But there is more.

Israel's Calling

. . .

We have learned that God chose Israel to be His people and recover His original intention for humans. Israel was called to be different from the other nations. She was to live by a different dream, a different vision, and a different story from those that the pagan nations lived by.

Israel was to be a sign to the pagan nations of what the world looks like when God is King. By looking at Israel—when she was faithfully submitting to her rightful King—the world saw what it meant for God to run the show.

Israel was called to be a light to the world (Isaiah 49:6). And God promised that through Israel, all the nations of the earth would be blessed (Genesis 12:1–3; 22:18; Luke 24:46–47; Isaiah 2:2–4).

Some of the ways in which Israel served as a light to her pagan neighbors, as well as a blessing to them, are as follows:

- The Israelites didn't charge interest when they lent money (Deuteronomy 23:19).
- When the Israelites harvested their crops, they left the corners and the gleanings for the poor and the strangers who weren't Israelites (Leviticus 19; 23).
- The Israelites were given the law of the tithe, which was to bless those without property, the widows, the orphans, and the strangers who weren't Israelites (Deuteronomy 14; 26:12; Numbers 18).
- Every fifty years, liberty was proclaimed throughout the whole land. It was the Year of Jubilee. All debts were forgiven. Those who had been sold as slaves were set free. All land was returned to those who had lost it. The Jubilee year was a huge statement against oppression. It was a picture of what a restored creation would look like. Injustices were all sorted out. It leveled the playing field; everyone was given a fresh start. Jubilee was a witness to God's justice in the earth.

The Gospel of the Kingdom

All of these practices were woven into the fabric of Israel's way of life. Israel's testimony was, "We hold this land in trust for our God who will one day restore the whole earth. We are a sign of that restoration here and now."

By looking at Israel, the world saw what it meant for God to be King of the earth.

The people of Israel were called Hebrews. They had a distinct culture, value system, and way of life. It's no accident that the word Hebrew probably meant "a people who have crossed over."[1]

91

A Royal Cliff-Hanger

• • •

The entire Old Testament narrative promised the fulfillment of God's eternal purpose, which is the kingdom of heaven coming to earth (or to put it another way, the kingdom of God "on earth as it is in heaven").

Through Israel, God would reclaim the nations of the world (more on this later).

By the mouth of the prophets of Israel, God's people looked forward to seeing the following come to pass:

- Israel's long exile out of the land of Canaan will one day end.
- Israel's sins will be forgiven (exile is the punishment for sin; the end of exile is the forgiveness of sins).
- Israel will experience a new Exodus in which God will deliver her from pagan domination.
- God will return to Zion (another name for Jerusalem) and dwell in His holy temple again.
- God will reign over the whole world.
- God will send His Servant to liberate His people.
- God will create a new covenant wherein He will put His Spirit inside His people. That new covenant will eventually lead to a new heaven and a new earth.*
- God will restore His image and His authority to human beings.
- The Davidic kingdom, which was promised to never end, will appear on the earth again.
- The eyes of the blind will be opened, the ears of the deaf will be unstopped, the lame will leap, and the tongues of the mute will sing.

* God will not abandon His creation. Scripture never teaches that He will destroy the earth or heaven. It does teach that He will restore and renew them, refining both the earthly and heavenly elements with fire—2 Peter 3:7–12.

- A voice crying out in the wilderness will show up, clearing the way for the Lord's arrival.

- The Messiah, God's Anointed One, will come at last, bringing peace, justice, and salvation.

- The Anointed One will be called "God's Son," and His kingdom will be glorious and have no end.

- God will reclaim and bless all the nations of the earth through Israel, Abraham's seed.

- Daniel's "Seventy Weeks" will finally come to pass. There will be an end of sin, wickedness will be atoned for, and everlasting righteousness will begin.[*]

All of these themes are woven into the heart of the Old Testament.[†] Yet no one expected how they would be fulfilled.

The Old Testament story ends like a cliff-hanger. There's no climax nor ending to the narrative. And that's precisely where the Gospels begin.

---

[*] For an explanation of how Jesus fulfilled this particular prophecy, see my online article "Daniel's Seventy Weeks" at InsurgenceBook.com.

[†] See Psalms 2; 22; 72; 89; Isaiah 2; 9; 11; 35; 40; 42–66; 89; 2 Samuel 7; Daniel 7; 9; Ezekiel 34; 36–37; 43; Jeremiah 31; Zechariah 8–9; Malachi 3. Also see F. F. Bruce, *The Time Is Fulfilled* (Grand Rapids: Eerdmans, 1978) and *The New Testament Development of Old Testament Themes* (Grand Rapids: Eerdmans, 1969); and Leonard Sweet and Frank Viola, *Jesus: A Theography* (Nashville: Thomas Nelson, 2012).

Introducing a Strange Prophet

· · ·

The insurgence began with a strange prophet named John. He was known as "the Baptizer." It was in John's ministry that all the cliff-hanging prophecies contained in the Old Testament started to come rushing together to form their climax.

John was the voice crying in the wilderness, to make clear the Lord's arrival (John 1:23).

If you examine John the Baptist's message carefully, it was beyond radical.

Because we don't live in the first century, it's difficult for us to grasp the dramatic element of his message. So let's contemporize it in order to feel its impact.

If John the Baptist were here today, he would have said something like this:

> The United States of America [*or* insert your own country] is not being ruled by God. You belong to the United States of America and have given your allegiance to it.
>
> Organized religion is not being ruled by God.
> Your political system is not being ruled by God.
> Your educational system is not being ruled by God.
> Your entertainment system is not being ruled by God.
> Your economic system is not being ruled by God.
> These systems are all part of this world.
>
> But God is laying His axe to the root of these systems, and He's going to begin swinging hard very soon. And when He does, they will eventually come crashing down. But I have good news. God is about to inaugurate a new nation on this earth. This new nation will not belong to the present world and its systems.
>
> This new nation will not be part of your national system; it will not be part of your religious system; it will not be part of your political system; it will not be part of your educational system; it will not be part of your entertainment system or your economic system.

This new nation will come from the heavenly realm, and very soon it's going to touch this earth. And it will have a king. And that new nation, once it gets here, will never end. And eventually, it will topple all other kingdoms and nations.

One more thing: the king of that new nation will be the Son of Almighty God.

And then he would have added something like this:

To be part of this new nation, all of your loyalties to the present systems of this world must be severed. So untangle your heart from them and leave them behind.

Pull out of the present empire, pull out of the religious system, pull out of the political system, and pull out of every other damnable system of this world, all of which have enslaved you, because the new empire is about to descend on this planet.

Break your attachment to earthly things. Be generous and fair in your dealings with others.

The new King is going to bring judgment, righting the wrongs of the world and separating the wheat from the chaff. He is going to bring forth a great purging.

So get down here in this water, confess your sins and they will be forgiven, as the prophets promised. Turn away from your old way of life, sever your ties with this present world, and be baptized—denoting your death to the old system and your aliveness to the coming nation.

When He comes, the new Emperor will immerse you with the Spirit of the living God. And God Himself will dwell inside of you! Therefore, this new empire will not operate by human wisdom or human power. It will operate by God's own Spirit.

Stay here in the desert with me until the new empire arrives. If you cannot stay in the desert, go about your business, but keep yourself unattached and wait for the promised King to come and establish His new nation.

But I issue a warning: The kingdom of heaven is about to descend on the earth. Rethink. Reconsider. Recant. Get out of the kingdom of darkness because it's coming down. The kingdom of heaven is about to invade the planet and declare war on all other kingdoms and rivals in this world. Leave them behind while there is still time.

John the Baptist was preaching an insurgence.

The Insurgence Begins

. . .

John the Baptist was the first to preach the gospel of the kingdom. While the Old Testament prophets foretold of its coming, John was the first to announce that it was about to break forth in the earth.

John preached his gospel boldly and without fear or compromise. For that reason, when a man or a woman received John's message, they were renouncing everything in their lives.

Many who listened to John were astonished at what he had to say. In fact, his very attire was a metaphor for his revolutionary message. He was a walking, breathing sign of the insurgence. His outward appearance matched his message. John showed outwardly what God was looking for inwardly.

He wore a coat made of camel's hair, which is a ceremonially unclean animal. In this way, he was defying religious tradition.

He ate locusts and wild honey, showing that he had broken with materialism, greed, and worldly pleasure.

He never cut his hair or beard (imagine his hair extending down to his waist and his beard reaching his chest).* This showed that he defied human custom.

He lived in the wilderness, showing that he had no attachments to this present world.

John was a walking insurgence. He was outrageous, scandalous, and disruptive. He pulled out of the world system entirely, including the religious system.

Some of the Lord's early followers were disciples of John the Baptist. Peter and Andrew were among them.

Before they ever met Jesus, these men pulled out of the worldly systems of their day.

* John appears to have taken the Nazirite vow mentioned in Numbers 6. Compare with Luke 1:13–17. John also wore a leather belt. The description of John in the Gospels reminds us of Eljiah the prophet (Matthew 3:4; 2 Kings 1:8).

Consequently, when Jesus said that the new wine could not be contained in old wineskins, He was referring to the fact that His disciples had become new, empty wineskins under John's influence. And because they were empty vessels, Jesus could pour His new wine into them (Matthew 9:14–17).

John's disciples stopped giving their pledge to the flags of this world. They believed that the whole system was coming down and God was about to plant something new in its place.

John's message was total, utter, and absolute. And it demanded complete devotion and total allegiance.

The message of John, and later Jesus and Paul, was a call to join the insurgence. One that contained no violence, no armed conflict, and no rebellious overthrow.

Rather, the insurgence that John announced was built on a subversive message that people believed, lived out, and heralded to others.

It constituted a nonviolent revolution, a quiet revolt against the present order.

John's revolutionary message prepared the arrival of the Son of God, the new King and His new nation, which was about to enter history. John's ministry was to serve as the curtain-raiser for the Son of God.[*]

This was the beginning of the insurgence.

[*] I explain John's ministry in much more detail in my book with Leonard Sweet, *Jesus: A Theography*, 109–16.

A New Nation

. . .

The name of the new nation that John the Baptist announced is called "the kingdom of God." In the Gospel of Matthew, it's called "the kingdom of heaven."*

The "kingdom of heaven" focuses on the origin of the nation, which is the heavenly realm. The "kingdom of God" focuses on the person who runs the kingdom, which is God Himself.

Both terms refer to the same thing.

The kingdom of God is the rule of heaven come to earth.

* Matthew is the only New Testament writer who uses the phrase "kingdom of heaven," and he uses it approximately thirty-two times in his Gospel.

The Time Has Come!

. . .

With the Old Testament story as a backdrop, Jesus of Nazareth opened His ministry with an earth-shaking bang, saying,

> The time is fulfilled, and the kingdom of God is at hand; repent and believe in the gospel. (Mark 1:15 ESV)

The NIV translates the opening words of this text as "The time has come!" Jesus of Nazareth entered the drama of human history. He came to fulfill all the old covenant prophecies, but in a surprisingly shocking way.

In Jesus, the new age of the kingdom had burst into the present evil age. Jesus inaugurated the age to come in His life and ministry. And in His ascension, the promised new age broke loose into the earth. Consequently, the new age began even as the old age continues.

Jesus was the Passover Lamb constituting the new Exodus. By His death, Jesus ended the exile of God's people and brought in the forgiveness of sins. He came to earth as God in the flesh—for when God sent His Son, He was sending His own Self. The God of Israel was present in and as Jesus Christ. And Jesus Himself was God's temple on earth.

Jesus was also the new Adam, defeating the tempter in the wilderness in contrast to the way the first humans were defeated by the serpent in the garden. Jesus, the second Adam, succeeded where the first Adam failed.

Jesus was also the new Jacob. He is the ladder connecting heaven and earth, upon which angels ascend and descend. Just like Jacob, Jesus meets a woman at a well at noon. This woman symbolizes the bride of Christ.*

Jesus was also the new Israel, coming out of Egypt (just as Israel had), living in the wilderness for forty days (corresponding to Israel's forty years in the wilderness), and choosing twelve disciples to launch His mission (corresponding to the twelve tribes of Israel).

---

* The biblical parallels between John 4 and Genesis 29 are remarkable. I expound the connections in my book *The Day I Met Jesus* with Mary DeMuth (Grand Rapids: Baker Books, 2015), 106–7.

Jesus was also the new Moses, the builder of God's house, crossing seas, feeding multitudes in the wilderness, and delivering the Lord's people from exile.

Significantly, Jesus' wilderness temptation replayed Israel's temptation in the wilderness. In fact, when Jesus quoted Scripture to Satan, he was directly quoting what Moses said to Israel during their wilderness testing.[2]

Jesus was also the embodiment of the Garden of Eden and the land of Canaan, for in Himself, God's space (heaven) and man's space (earth) were fused together.

Jesus Christ fulfilled the Old Testament story and brought it to its climax.* And with His resurrection, He began the insurgence that was foretold in ages past.

In sum, Jesus incarnates the three major elements of Israel's life. He embodies the Law, He embodies the temple, and He embodies the Sabbath.

Like Israel, the ekklesia is here today to manifest the kingdom of God on earth so that Jesus can indeed be "the God of heaven and earth" again in concrete, visible ways.

And when Jesus returns to earth again, He will bring forth the fullness of His kingdom—the promised "restoration of all things" (Acts 3:21 NLT). This includes the restoration of Israel and the reclaiming of the nations that rebelled against God.

That restoration and reclaiming has now begun in and through us, God's kingdom people.

Consequently, those who are part of the insurgence know Christ as the climax of Israel's story and the beginning of a new revolution—a revolution to restore God's eternal purpose in the earth.

* For scriptural support on how the Old Testament story replays itself in the story of Jesus, see Sweet and Viola, *Jesus: A Theography*; and Frank Viola, *From Eternity to Here* (Colorado Springs: David C. Cook, 2009) as well as the audio messages "Vantage Point: The Story We Haven't Heard—Parts I and II" at InsurgenceBook.com.

The King Declares His Kingdom

• • •

Jewish kings were first anointed before they spoke or acted as royalty. When John baptized Jesus in the Jordan, Jesus was publicly portrayed as God's royal Son. God the Father anointed Jesus with the Holy Spirit to begin His kingly reign.

> After being baptized, Jesus came up immediately from the water; and behold, the heavens were opened, and he saw the Spirit of God descending as a dove and lighting on Him, and behold, a voice out of the heavens said, "This is My beloved Son, in whom I am well-pleased." (Matthew 3:16–17 NASB)

When Mark records the baptism of Jesus, he says that Jesus saw the heavens "splitting apart" (Mark 1:10 NLT). The Greek term for this word is the same used in Exodus 14:21 in the Greek Old Testament.[*] Exodus 14:21 is speaking about the "splitting apart" ("dividing") of the Red Sea at Israel's exodus.[3]

Mark is signaling to his readers that Jesus is inaugurating the new Exodus and the end of exile. But that's not all. When the Father calls Jesus His "beloved Son," readers are to think of David. David's name means "beloved" in Hebrew. David, God's beloved king and "firstborn," was destined to rule the nations (Psalm 89:20–29). Mark is signaling that Jesus is the new David, the rightful ruler of the world.

> And Jesus went throughout all the cities and villages, teaching in their synagogues and proclaiming the gospel of the kingdom. (Matthew 9:35 ESV)

When Jesus began preaching the gospel of the kingdom, His message was essentially the same as John the Baptist's. Only He added three words to it:

[*] The Greek word is in the verb form in Exodus 14:21, Septuagint (the Greek Old Testament). The Septuagint is the Bible that Jesus and the apostles used.

Come follow Me.*

In other words, "Get in My presence."

Jesus came to this earth as a revolutionary. He came to launch the insurgence. He came to overthrow the kingdom of darkness and set up His own kingdom in its place.

In Jesus, the time had come for God to inaugurate an indestructible kingdom that would take over all other kingdoms.

Jesus repeated His kingdom message over and over again all throughout Judea, Galilee, and even Samaria. It sounded something like this:

> This entire world and all its systems are in the hands of the devil. And you have been serving them in one form or another. But I have good news. The kingdom of God is breaking into this world. My Father's kingdom is a new nation that will eventually take over the entire world. So leave everything behind, forsake all you have, and follow Me, the new King, and you will be part of the new nation that I'm establishing. My Father rules the heavenly realm. But in Me, the God of Israel and the Creator of the world is going to rule planet Earth. He will start running the show in Me and through Me just as the Hebrew Scriptures foretold. Leave everything and follow Me today.

He then went on to say something like this:

> Everything is now changing. You've heard it said that you must do this and not do that, but I say to you something even more extreme. I am the new Moses, and I am also the new Law (Torah). The radical revolutionary empire of God is here. It's time to change your thinking and your life. Follow Me into a new way of living and being. I am the son of Man, the new Adam, appointed to do what Adam failed to do—bear My Father's image and have dominion over the earth. I am a son of Abraham, the man through whom God promised to bless and inherit the whole world. But that's not all. I'm also the son of David, the rightful heir to God's throne on earth. I am also the Son of God, the rightful heir to God's throne in heaven. Therefore, I will rule both heaven and earth. As the prophets foretold, I have come to end the exile and rule every inch of this planet. Today, I am calling a people

* Both John and Jesus preached, "Repent for the kingdom of God is at hand." They also both preached that every tree that doesn't bear good fruit would be thrown into the fire (compare Matthew 3:10 with 7:19).

to follow Me, and they will be My kingdom on this planet. My kingdom is like a mustard seed. It will be planted in the ground, hidden and unseen, but it will grow until it eventually covers the entire world. My Father's original intent of expanding Eden throughout the whole earth will finally come to pass. All the nations of the world will be reclaimed by Me and for Me. They are my inheritance.

A Cutting Message

• • •

The gospel of the kingdom that both John the Baptist and Jesus preached contains a cutting message. Wherever it is rightly preached and heard, it cuts all ties with the present world.

Once you hear it, you cannot sit on the fence. You either receive it, casting all your hopes, dreams, and ambitions at the feet of Jesus and walk away from the world system. Or you ignore it and go on with life as usual.

In Matthew, Mark, and Luke, the central message of Jesus was the kingdom of God. In John, the central message of Jesus was life. Both terms describe the same thing. *Eternal life, the life of God, is the life of the kingdom.*

Jesus began His ministry proclaiming the kingdom of God (Mark 1:15). And He ended it by speaking about the kingdom during the forty days that followed His resurrection (Acts 1:3).

Paul of Tarsus began preaching the kingdom in the opening of his ministry (Acts 14:22; 20:25). And he ended his ministry by unleashing the kingdom message at Caesar's back door in Rome (Acts 28:16, 30–31).

Interestingly, the Bible never defines the kingdom of God. It only illustrates it.

Repeatedly, Jesus said, "The kingdom of God is like . . ."

However, if we put all the references of the kingdom of God together, we get a clear look at what it is.[*]

---

[*] To read every reference to the kingdom in the New Testament, see my online article "The Kingdom in the New Testament (Every Reference)" at InsurgenceBook.com.

What Is the Kingdom?

· · ·

There are basically three views of the kingdom of God among Christians today.

One view says that the kingdom equals heaven. According to this view, Christians are waiting to escape this dirty little planet called Earth to be in a better place. Advocates of this view believe this "better place" is the kingdom of God or "heaven." All who believe in Jesus will enter the kingdom when they die.

Another view says that the kingdom equals God's miraculous power to cast out demons, heal the sick, and raise the dead. Those who advocate this view talk a great deal about "doing the work of the kingdom," which for them means displaying the supernatural power of God here and now on the planet.

Still another view says that the kingdom equals the alleviation of poverty and the implementation of social justice. Advocates of this view talk about "building the kingdom" or "doing kingdom work." By those terms they mean striving for peace and justice in order to make the world a better place.

All of these views are held in tension with one another. And one can find various verses in the Bible to support each. But they all fall short of the scriptural understanding of the kingdom of God.

Manifesting God's Rule

. . .

If we don't count its repeated occurrences, the kingdom of God is uniquely mentioned eighty-five times in Matthew, Mark, and Luke and three times in John.

Taken together, I believe the best description of the kingdom is as follows:

The manifestation of God's ruling presence.

To break that sentence down, the kingdom contains three key elements:

1. The King (which focuses on the word "presence").
2. God's reign (which focuses on the words "God's ruling").
3. The people ruled (which focuses on the word "manifestation").

Alva McClain put it this way:

A general survey of the Biblical material indicates that the concept of a "kingdom" envisages a total situation containing at least three essential elements: first, a *ruler* with adequate authority and power; second, a *realm* of subjects to be ruled; and third, the actual exercise of the function of *rulership*.[4]

In sum, the kingdom of God includes the King (*the ruler*), God's reign (*rulership*), and the people ruled (*realm*). Again, the kingdom is the manifestation of God's ruling presence. And His ruling presence is manifested in and through Jesus and in and through God's people.

A Kingdom of Priests

. . .

Old Testament Israel failed in her mission. She lived to retain God's blessings only for herself rather than to be a blessing to the world. She also ran after other gods. Therefore, she lost her place of representing the kingdom of God.

Tragically, Israel became a reflection of all the other nations. Her light had gone out. In fact, because of Israel's sins, the pagan nations blasphemed God (Romans 2:24).

But where Israel failed, the ekklesia was called to succeed.

When the ekklesia—the people of God under Christ's lordship—is living as she should, wherever she is found, the world understands what it means for God to be King.

For this reason, Scripture reveals that the ekklesia is called to be the fulfillment of ancient Israel, a kingdom of priests, a holy nation. Compare these texts in the Old and New Testaments:

To Israel in the Old Testament,

You will be for me a kingdom of priests and a holy nation. These are the words you are to speak to the Israelites. (Exodus 19:6 NIV)

To the ekklesia in the New Testament,

But you are a chosen people, a royal priesthood, a holy nation, God's special possession, that you may declare the praises of him who called you out of darkness into his wonderful light. (1 Peter 2:9 NIV)

He has made us a Kingdom of priests for God his Father. All glory and power to him forever and ever! Amen. (Revelation 1:6 NLT)

You have made them to be a kingdom and priests to serve our God, and they will reign on the earth. (Revelation 5:10 NIV; see also Revelation 20:6)

Image and Authority

. . .

God's original intent for human beings was to bear His image and exercise His authority in the earth (Genesis 1:26–28). The first humans lived in God's presence. They were also invited to partake of the tree of life, which contained God's life.

But the Lord's holy intention was lost when humans fell.

God, however, rebooted His purpose with Abraham. As we've seen, Abraham's descendants, the nation of Israel, were called to be "a kingdom of priests."

Priests were those who stood in God's presence and ministered to Him.

This point is significant because before creation, the heavenly host of angels and celestial beings lived in God's presence and ministered to Him. And so did the first humans when they were created in the garden.

Take note: there's a close connection between living in the conscious presence of God and being in His kingdom.

The Lord planted the nation of Israel in an elevated spot on the earth (Jerusalem) so that all the other nations could look up and see what the kingdom of God was all about and how it operated.

Before creation, the kingdom (God's rule) was comprised of angelic beings who stood in God's presence. When some of the heavenly host left God's presence, they left the kingdom.

When Israel failed in her calling to be a kingdom of priests, she too left God's presence—just like the angels and Adam had done previously. And so the kingdom was lost to Abraham's children.

The Davidic Kingdom Returns

• • •

The kingdom of Israel was at its greatest peak when David was on the throne. In the book of Acts, David is quoted as saying that he always lived in God's presence (Acts 2:25).[*] Remarkably, David was both a king and a priest.[†]

God promised that David would have a descendant who would rule the entire world and whose kingdom would never be toppled. This new King would also come from the house of Jesse, from the village of Bethlehem, and from the tribe of Judah.

The only way to gain a throne is to be born into royalty. So in order to sit on the throne of David, a person had to be kin to David. And in order to sit on the throne of God, a person had to be kin to God.

Now consider what the angel Gabriel said about Jesus:

> He will be great and will be called the Son of the Most High; and the Lord God will give Him the throne of His father David; and He will reign over the house of Jacob forever, and His kingdom will have no end. (Luke 1:32–33 NASB)

In this text, Jesus is called the Son of the Most High God *and* the son of David. So Jesus alone stands in the lineage of two thrones—as the Son of God, heir to the kingdom of heaven, *and* as a son of David, heir to the kingdom of David.[‡]

Jesus of Nazareth, then, has the right to the throne of God in heaven and to the throne of David on earth.

---

[*] Acts 2:25 quotes a psalm written by David which is also a Messianic prophecy communicating that Jesus always lived in the presence of God the Father.

[†] Though David wasn't an official priest, he wore the linen ephod, he made sacrifices, and he ate the showbread—functions that only priests could lawfully carry out.

[‡] Throughout the Gospels, Jesus is called "the son of David"—a Messianic title (Matthew 9:27; 12:23; 15:22; 20:30–31; 21:9, 15; 22:42; John 7:42). Luke calls David the father of Jesus (1:32). Jesus also identifies Himself as "the root and offspring of David" (Revelation 22:16). In John 7:42, Jesus is said to come from "the seed of David." Luke 2:4 states that Jesus was born in the city of David (Bethlehem), "of the house and lineage of David" (NKJV). All of these references point to the kingship of Jesus of Nazareth.

Just as the prophets foretold, God would return to Zion in the person of the Davidic king. And He would rule not only Israel but the entire world.

At His ascension, Jesus was crowned King of both heaven and earth, for He is the son of David *and* the Son of God (Acts 2:31–36). The ascension of Jesus symbolized His enthronement, and it's where He began His worldwide reign.

I think that's marvelous. How about you?

The Presence of the Future

• • •

The kingdom of God is embodied in Jesus Christ, the King. And wherever Jesus was in the first century, there too was His kingdom. Wherever Jesus is active today and His lordship is submitted to, there is His kingdom.

In the Gospels, Jesus would sometimes make Himself the equivalent of the kingdom. For instance, sometimes Jesus would say "for My sake" and other times He would say "for the sake of the kingdom" (Matthew 19:29; Luke 18:29). In addition, the Gospels make clear that to be a disciple of Jesus is to be a disciple of the kingdom (Matthew 13:52; Luke 14:27).

This is why the early church fathers called Jesus the *autobasileia,* which means the "self-kingdom" or "kingdom in person."* Jesus not only proclaimed the kingdom, He embodied and demonstrated it.

So the kingdom entered space and time in the person of Christ. Consequently, you can't separate the kingdom from the King. It is for this reason that the kingdom of God is also called "the kingdom of Christ" (Ephesians 5:5 NIV; Revelation 11:15 NKJV) and "the kingdom of the Son of His love" (Colossians 1:13 NKJV).

To put it another way, Jesus was bringing the future into the present in His ministry.

---

* Origen and Tertullian are known to have been the first to use the term *autobasileia* to refer to Jesus. See C. E. B. Cranfield, *The Gospel According to St. Mark* (Cambridge: Cambridge University Press, 1966), 66, citing Tertullian, *ad Marcion* 4.33 and Origen, *Commentary on Matthew*, Matthew 18:23.

The Fusion of Heaven and Earth

. . .

God's ultimate will from the beginning, harkening back to Genesis, was the fusion of heaven and earth (Genesis 1–2).* These two realms were brought together in Jesus and thrust into visible reality through His earthly ministry. When Jesus returns to earth at His second coming, heaven and earth will be fully fused again (Revelation 21–22).†

In Jesus Christ, the rule of God is revealed.

But if I drive out demons by the finger of God, then the kingdom of God has come upon you. (Luke 11:20 NIV)

Then he got up and rebuked the winds and the waves, and it was completely calm. The men were amazed and asked, "What kind of man is this? Even the winds and the waves obey him!" (Matthew 8:26–27 NIV)

In Jesus Christ, the presence of God is displayed.

Anyone who has seen me has seen the Father. (John 14:9 NIV)

I am in the Father and the Father is in me. (John 14:11 NIV)

I and the Father are one. (John 10:30 NIV)

Jesus, then, is both the expression of God's image and the exercise of God's authority. He fulfills God's eternal purpose stated in Genesis 1:26–28, and He shows us what the kingdom of God looks like.

The kingdom of God, then, is another name for God's eternal purpose. And it is the heartbeat of the insurgence.

* When the New Testament writers speak about the Lord's second coming, they often use the word "appear" to describe it (Colossians 3:4; Hebrews 9:28; 1 Peter 5:4; 1 John 2:28: 3:2). The implication is that Jesus is now in a different realm where He is present, yet invisible. When He returns, the curtain will be lifted, and He will appear visibly to every human eye (Revelation 1:7).

† See Frank Viola, *From Eternity to Here*, chap. 13, for a biblical explanation of how the garden of Eden was the overlap of man's space and God's space. It was the intersection between God and humans.

Right in Your Midst

. . .

Many years ago I went on a trip with an old ex-pastor and an acquaintance who happened to be a professional debater with a reputation of being devious. My acquaintance also happened to have attended Bible school (something I chose not to do).

All three of us were having lunch together and the old ex-pastor asked us, "In Luke 17:21, Jesus said that the kingdom of God is 'within you' in the King James Version. Do you think He meant 'within you' or 'among you'?"

I answered, "I don't think He meant 'within you' because Jesus was speaking to the Pharisees. And that would mean that Jesus was saying the kingdom was dwelling in the Pharisees, which cannot be the case."

My acquaintance responded and said he disagreed. He boasted that he had written a paper for his Bible class on that passage, and the professor gave him an A on it.

Attempting to impress the old ex-pastor, my acquaintance tried to convince me of his viewpoint. Here's how he proceeded.

He asked me, "Do you know the Greek word used in that passage?"

I answered, "I do not."

He said, "The word is *entos*. Did you know that Luke 17:21 is not the only time the New Testament uses it, and it doesn't mean 'among'?"

He then concluded, "It means 'within you.'"

The old ex-pastor was impressed. And my acquaintance sported a smirk on his face as if he'd won some battle.

But then I asked him, "You do realize that in order to properly understand a Greek word, one must also interpret it by the context in which it's used. So tell me, since the Pharisees were hostile to Jesus Christ and His kingdom, how could Jesus say the kingdom of God resided within them, since a person cannot even *see* the kingdom unless they are born from above?"

He responded, "I don't know."

I then asked him to send me a copy of his A-graded paper when he got home (which he never did).

I don't interpret Luke 17:21 to mean the kingdom of God is "within" or "among" you. A better interpretation of that text is that the kingdom of God is "in the midst of" you. And that's precisely what *entos humōn* means—"in the midst of you."

Most first-rate New Testament scholars interpret the text this way.* A few interpret it to mean "within your reach" or "within your grasp," which gives the same basic meaning. Jesus Christ was standing in the midst of the Pharisees, so the kingdom was available to them, within their reach.

But "within you" simply doesn't fit the context nor the rest of the New Testament.

Jesus was in effect saying to the Pharisees, "You no longer have to wait for the kingdom of God to come. The kingdom is standing right here in your midst! I'm within your reach! I am the incarnation of God's kingdom."

Luke 17:21 is one of many texts that show us that the kingdom of God is embodied in Christ. Wherever Jesus is acting in the capacity of His lordship, there too is the kingdom.

---

* George Eldon Ladd, *A Theology of the New Testament* (Grand Rapids: Eerdmans, 1993). Ladd wrote, "While Mark 10:15 makes it clear that the Kingdom is to be received in the inner person, it is unlikely that Jesus would have said to the Pharisees, 'the Kingdom of God is within you.' The translation 'in your midst,' in Jesus' person, best fits the total context of his teaching" (65). See also the ESV, NASB, NIV, RSV, BSB, BLB, The Net Bible, and *The Anchor Yale Bible Dictionary* (New York: Doubleday, 1992), vol. 4, 59. According to *A Greek-English Lexicon of the New Testament and Other Early Christian Literature* (*BDAG*), 3rd ed., 2000, the semantic range of *entos* includes, "in," "within," "in the midst," and "among" (340–41). The Pharisees were expecting the kingdom to come with apocalyptic signs; they were using natural perception. But Jesus was saying, enigmatically, that the kingdom was already in their midst. (Luke 17:20–21). Because the Pharisees weren't born from above, they couldn't "see" the kingdom, even though it was standing in their midst (John 3:3). Jesus was pointing to the presence of the kingdom in this text, not its inwardness. The New Testament refers to people entering the kingdom, not the kingdom entering people. Scot McKnight is dead-on when he wrote, "Once, on being asked by the Pharisees when the kingdom of God would come, Jesus replied, 'The coming of the kingdom of God is not something that can be observed, nor will people say, 'Here it is,' or 'There it is,' because the kingdom of God is in your midst.' Here the temptation is to *reduce kingdom to an inner reality*, and this focuses 'in you' as an inner, spiritual reality. The expression more properly means 'in your midst' (as in, I Jesus am here in your midst), but the reduction is often found." Scot McKnight, "A Robust Kingdom," Jesus Creed Blog, February 23, 2015. Other scholars who believe Luke 17:21 should be translated "in the midst of you" are Craig Keener, Ben Witherington, Darrell Bock, Robert H. Stein, J. C. Ryle, Kenneth Wuest, and Marvin Vincent. Following C. H. Dodd, N. T. Wright supports the translation "within your grasp," which carries the same idea. Tom Wright, *Luke for Everyone* (London: Westminster John Knox Press, 2004), 207.

Consequently, the kingdom of God is not an internal, private thing. It's a public, social reality that shapes our entire lives, both inside and out. It is the manifestation of God's ruling presence. The Christ who lives inside you wishes to be manifested with the other citizens of His kingdom.

A People Ruled

. . .

A kingdom cannot exist without a people who are ruled by a king. Consequently, not only does the kingdom of God refer to the King (Jesus) and God's rule in and through Him, but it also includes the people who submit to His kingship.

> You have made them to be a kingdom and priests to serve our God,
> and they will reign on the earth. (Revelation 5:10 NIV)

After Jesus rose again from the dead, the kingdom of God got a new name. That new name is *ekklesia*. Ekklesia is the Greek word that's most often translated "church" in our New Testament.

I hesitate to use the word "church" because it conjures up all sorts of images that are unbiblical.

The ekklesia doesn't refer to a building or a certain denomination. Nor does it refer to all the Christians in the whole world who are disconnected from one another. In addition, the ekklesia doesn't refer to a two-hour service that's held every Sunday morning or Wednesday night. Nor does it refer to a worldwide organization.

In the first century, the ekklesia of God referred to a local community of people who put themselves under the lordship of Jesus Christ, who met together regularly, and who were learning to live by the life of their King and express that life in visible ways. *

The ekklesia was the very body of Jesus Christ in a particular city.

It didn't matter where they gathered, or how often they met, or what they called themselves. Their outstanding characteristic was that they were the people in the city who gave their full allegiance to Jesus of Nazareth. And they demonstrated that allegiance by their shared life together.

---

* In Frank Viola, *Reimagining Church* (Colorado Springs: David C. Cook, 2008), I explore what the ekklesia is in great detail. You can find this book at InsurgenceBook.com.

So if you wanted to find the kingdom of God in your city in Century One, you'd have to find the people who had given their allegiance to Christ. And those people met together, often. That's why they were called the ekklesia in the city (the ekklesia in Corinth, the ekklesia in Jerusalem, the ekklesia in Thessalonica, etc.). The word *ekklesia* means a meeting, a gathering, an assembly.

The Divine Paradox

Today, the ekklesia is made up of those in every city who acknowledge that Jesus of Nazareth is Lord of the world. The ekklesia, then, is the repository of the sovereign reign of God as well as the embodiment of that reign.

Those who are part of the ekklesia are learning to live by a life not human.

> For by these [promises] He has granted to us His precious and magnificent promises, so that by them you may become partakers of the divine nature, having escaped the corruption that is in the world by lust. (1 Peter 1:4 NASB)

As they lay down their lives, the members of the ekklesia live by the life of Christ through the Holy Spirit. And by this life, they experience the divine paradox: "When I am weak, then I am strong" (2 Corinthians 12:10) and "My power is made perfect in weakness" (2 Corinthians 9).

The reason why so many believers today have separated the "church" from the "kingdom" is because they've envisioned the church in strictly modern terms. They see church as an event (a worship service) and the kingdom as an activity (working for justice).

But this is not the biblical view.

The ekklesia is the community of the King, the embodiment of the kingdom of God.

Just as Jesus embodied the kingdom in His physical body while He was on earth, He continues to embody His kingdom through His spiritual body—the ekklesia—today. That is, when the ekklesia is functioning as God intended.

Putting a Myth to Bed

• • •

Just as you cannot separate the King from His kingdom, you cannot separate the kingdom from the kingdom society—the ekklesia, the people who are ruled by the King.

A widely held claim asserts something like this: "Jesus only mentioned the ekklesia [church] a few times, but He mentioned the kingdom over 100 times. So the kingdom is more important than the ekklesia."

Well, Jesus didn't mention the kingdom over 100 times—there are 88 distinguishable references to the kingdom in the four Gospels. Nevertheless, this statement is false and misleading in another respect. And I've fully discounted it elsewhere.

To summarize the argument, Jesus did use the word "kingdom" more than He used the word "ekklesia" in the Gospels. But so what? Jesus made abundant references to the ekklesia in the Gospels, He just didn't use the word "ekklesia" every time He referred to it.[*]

For example, whenever you see that little band of twelve men and five to eight women following Jesus closely and faithfully in the Gospels, you are seeing the embryonic expression of the ekklesia. That little band of women and men was the community of the King, the new society that Jesus was creating.

And every time you see Jesus use the word "you" when speaking to His disciples, He is almost always speaking to and about the ekklesia, the community of the King.

Consequently, you cannot separate the ekklesia from the kingdom of God any more than you can separate the body from the head. The two are inseparably connected.

So let's finally, once and for all, put this myth to bed, shall we?

[*] See Frank Viola, *Jesus Now* (Colorado Springs: David C. Cook, 2014), chap. 7. You can find the book at InsurgenceBook.com.

Distinct But Not Separate

· · ·

To separate the ekklesia from the kingdom is like separating light from visibility. It cannot be done. The kingdom and the ekklesia are distinct, but they are not separate.

Whenever Jesus is enthroned by a group of people today, that's where the kingdom of God is. Wherever a group of people submit to the kingship of Christ, the kingdom of God is in their midst and they experience righteousness, peace, and joy in the Holy Spirit.

> For the kingdom of God is not a matter of eating and drinking, but of righteousness, peace and joy in the Holy Spirit. (Romans 14:17 NIV)

Jesus Christ is righteousness, peace, and joy incarnate (1 Corinthians 1:30; Ephesians 2:14). And He is in the Spirit (1 Corinthians 15:45; 2 Corinthians 3:17).

So again, Christ is the kingdom of God embodied. And He is embodied in the ekklesia—the people of the insurgence.*

---

* The ekklesia and the kingdom are and aren't used interchangeably in the New Testament. For instance, the head and body are interchangeable sometimes, while other times they are not. We can say Christ has a body on the one hand. And on the other, we can say that Christ is the body (see 1 Corinthians 12:12; Acts 9:4). Consequently, we can say that a genuine ekklesia manifests the kingdom in one respect. And in another respect, we can say the ekklesia is the kingdom (e.g., He "made us a kingdom" in Revelation 1:6 ESV. A kingdom includes the people who are ruled). Some ekklesias in the first century manifested the kingdom better than others. For instance, Corinth didn't do so well here while Thessalonica and Ephesus did better.

Already But Not Yet

Regarding the question of when the kingdom will arrive, there are two major views among Christians.

There are those who believe that *the kingdom is not yet*. These are often escapists who are waiting for "the sweet by-and-by" when Jesus will return and set up His kingdom on earth.

In the meantime (they say), we are to consign ourselves to the fact that the world is going to get worse. There's nothing we can do about it except to wait for our "exit strategy" when Jesus returns.

Then there are those who believe that *the kingdom is already*. These Christians believe that the kingdom is right here, right now. We don't have to wait for anything. Instead, we must engage in works of social justice and peace to "build" the kingdom that's already present.

Both views contain elements of truth, but neither is complete. Pushing the kingdom off into the future severs the nerve of God's eternal purpose. At the same time, making the kingdom something that we "build" through social activism empties it of its spiritual reality and power.

When we read all the references to the kingdom of God in Scripture, something remarkable emerges in bold relief.

The kingdom of God is already but not yet.

In other words, the kingdom is here (already), but it hasn't arrived in its fullness (yet). The kingdom is present, yet it's future. The kingdom is today, yet it's tomorrow.

The kingdom is here now in the people of God and manifested whenever they are bearing the image of Christ and exercising His authority. But one day it will descend on this earth in its full power and glory.

The Two Ages

. . .

When Jesus ascended into heaven, God the Father "seated him at his right hand in the heavenly realms, far above all rule and authority, power and dominion, and every name that is invoked, not only in the present age but also in the one to come" (Ephesians 1:20–21).

Notice the terms "the present age" and "the one to come."

With respect to "the age to come," Jesus will return to earth and the kingdom will come in its fullness. The result: "The earth will be filled with the knowledge of the glory of the LORD as the waters cover the sea" (Habakkuk 2:14), and He shall "have dominion also from sea to sea, and from the River to the ends of the earth" (Psalm 72:8 NKJV).

At that time, every knee shall bow to Christ, and every tongue shall confess that Jesus is Lord of the world (Romans 14:11; Philippians 2:10–11). There will be no more war, death, suffering, or tears. Jesus will set all things right and judge every person.

> I solemnly charge you in the presence of God and of Christ Jesus, who is to judge the living and the dead, and by His appearing and His kingdom. (2 Timothy 4:1 NASB)

According to Jesus and Paul, the kingdom is the future-in-the-present.[*] So we now live in the parenthesis between the accomplished redemption and the awaited consummation.

We are called to enter the kingdom, enjoy it, proclaim it, embody it, and demonstrate it in the present age. And if we are faithful, we will inherit the kingdom in the age to come.[†]

---

[*] See my online article "The Kingdom Present and Future" at InsurgenceBook.com for a list of biblical references showing that the kingdom of God is both present and future.

[†] See my online article "Action Terms for the Kingdom in the Gospels" at InsurgenceBook.com. Each term fits neatly into these five aspects.

Yet those who enter the kingdom of God today are promised the exceeding riches of God's grace in this age as well as in the coming age (Mark 10:30; Luke 18:30; 20:34–36; Ephesians 2:7; 1 Timothy 6:19).

As we learn to live by the life of the King with our sisters and brothers in Christ, we are living the presence of the future, tasting "the powers of the age to come" (Hebrews 6:5 NKJV).

I don't know about you, but I find this amazing. And it's a key characteristic of the insurgence.

Not From This World

· · ·

In Jesus Christ, God's future has broken into time. When Jesus faced Pilate before He went to the cross, we see the collision of the kingdom of God and the kingdom of this world. In His response to the worldly ruler, Jesus said,

> My kingdom is not of this world. (John 18:36 ESV)

According to the original Greek, Jesus said, "My kingdom is not *from*—or out of—this world." Jesus was saying that the origin of His kingdom—its source—was not the world system. Christ's empire was from another world, the heavenlies.

At the same time, the kingdom of God is *for* this world. Recall the Lord's Prayer that He taught His disciples to offer up to God, "Your kingdom come, your will be done, *on earth as it is in heaven.*"

So the kingdom is not *from* this world, but it is *for* this world. Yet it doesn't operate like the political kingdoms of this world.

> Jesus, knowing that they intended to come and make him king by force, withdrew again to a mountain by himself. (John 6:15 NIV)

While the kingdom is heaven-born, it is earthbound (Matthew 6:10). When you read the end of the story, the kingdom of God—represented by the holy city of the new Jerusalem—will descend out of heaven and make its home on earth (Revelation 21:2).

This has always been God's intention—the joining together of heaven and earth. Or to put it another way, the return to Eden.

The Signs of the Kingdom

• • •

Throughout His ministry, Jesus performed many awe-inspiring signs that revealed what the kingdom of God looks like when it breaks into the earth.

To reframe it into a question, What does it look like when God is running the world? What does it look like when the kingdom of God is manifested?

Or to bring it closer to home, what would your city look like if Jesus Christ was in complete charge of it?

The answer:

You would see peace and reconciliation between fallen humans.

You would see the end of racism, sexism, ageism, and crime.

You would see people forgiving one another.

You would see justice done for all.

You would see love, compassion, and mercy shown.

You would see freedom from oppression and deliverance from bondage.

You would see the naked clothed.

You would see the poor fed.

You would see the sick cared for and healed.

You would see deliverance from Satan's power and allegiance to Jesus Christ displayed.

You would see the power of God overcoming the power of His enemy.

The miracles that Jesus performed were signposts of the future kingdom breaking into the present age. They were electrifying signs that God's future was arriving in the present.

Through each sign and wonder, Jesus was showing us what the new nation—the kingdom community—looks like.

When God runs the show, human suffering is alleviated. There is peace, justice, healing, forgiveness, compassion, reconciliation, and love.

These are the fruits of the insurgence.

Are You the One?

. . .

When John the Baptist was put in prison, He asked Jesus through messengers, "Are you the one who is to come, or shall we look for another?" (Luke 7:20 ESV).

Here is the answer that Jesus gave to John through these messengers:

> Go back and report to John what you have seen and heard: The blind receive sight, the lame walk, those who have leprosy are cleansed, the deaf hear, the dead are raised, and the good news is proclaimed to the poor. (Luke 7:22 NIV)

Jesus gave John the signposts of the promised Messiah (King) and His kingdom.

Consider again all that Jesus did while He was on earth.

> How God anointed Jesus of Nazareth with the Holy Spirit and power, and how he went around doing good and healing all who were under the power of the devil, because God was with him. (Acts 10:38 NIV)

In that same line, note His words at the beginning of His ministry.

> "The Spirit of the Lord is on me,
>   because he has anointed me
>   to proclaim good news to the poor.
> He has sent me to proclaim freedom for the prisoners
>   and recovery of sight for the blind,
> to set the oppressed free,
>   to proclaim the year of the Lord's favor" . . .

Today this scripture is fulfilled in your hearing. (Luke 4:18–19, 21 NIV)

The phrase in Luke 4, "to proclaim the year of the Lord's favor," is a reference to the Year of Jubilee, which I will explain later.

But to put it in a sentence, when the kingdom comes, God's will is done on earth as it is in heaven.

The Kingdom Society

During the ministry of Jesus, heaven was invading planet Earth. Consequently, if you were living in first-century Palestine and you wanted to see God's kingdom, you had to find Jesus.

But after the Lord Jesus ascended into heaven and poured out His Spirit, the kingdom of God broke into the earth again. And the kingdom came in and through the ekklesia, the people of God.

The ekklesia is the very body of Christ—His presence on the earth. The ekklesia is the only nation to which you ought to give your full allegiance. The new nation of the ekklesia has a King, so there are no elections. All He demands of you is your absolute, total, and complete surrender.

This is the meaning of the words "repent" and "believe," the avenues through which one enters the kingdom (Mark 1:15).

Repent means to rethink and sever your ties with your old life and allegiances.

Believe means to entrust yourself to the new Lord of this world, Jesus of Nazareth.

When you repent from your old way of thinking and living, and you entrust yourself to Jesus as Lord and Savior, you are "born from above." That is, you are born from the heavenly realm, born into the kingdom, and made part of the ekklesia—the kingdom society—the vanguard of the insurgence.

Ruler of Both Realms

• • •

It was by the death of Jesus—Israel's Messiah and the world's true Lord—that He absorbed the punishment for both Israel's sins and the sins of the whole world (Isaiah 52–53).

It was by His death that Jesus ended the exile of His people, which traces back to the fallen celestial being, to Adam, and to Israel.

It was by His death that the forgiveness of sins was secured (Ephesians 1:7).

It was by His death that a new Exodus was made for the people of God, wherein they have been delivered from the enslaving powers of the present evil age (Galatians 1:4).

It was by His death that Jesus Christ stripped the evil principalities and powers of their dominion and dethroned them all (Colossians 2:15). Jesus grabbed the scepter from the hand of Satan, the usurper, and cast out the prince of this world (John 12:31).

Christ rose again victorious over death, and God the Father gave Him all authority over heaven and earth (Matthew 28:18). Exalted at the right hand of God, Jesus has been made both Lord and Messiah (Acts 2:33–36). And He is seated far above all rule and authority (Ephesians 1:21; 1 Peter 3:22).

It was by His death and resurrection that Jesus was able to impart the divine life into human beings, which was God's original purpose in the garden.

Consequently, the gospel of the kingdom is not about *making* Jesus Lord of your life.

Since His ascension, Jesus of Nazareth has already been established as Lord of the world.

He has been crowned ruler of heaven and earth. All authority in both realms is now in His hands. Therefore, Jesus Christ *is* Lord, including *your* Lord. He is the Messiah (Christ), including *your* Messiah.

The people of the earth may not recognize this fact yet, but every mortal will eventually bow to Jesus as Lord one day.

Therefore God exalted him to the highest place
and gave him the name that is above every name,
that at the name of Jesus every knee should bow,
in heaven and on earth and under the earth,
and every tongue acknowledge that Jesus Christ is Lord,
to the glory of God the Father. (Philippians 2:9–11 NIV)

So the issue isn't one of making Jesus Lord. He already is Lord. The issue is about *submitting* to His lordship—for it's far better to bow the knee now than later.

Yet given what a merciful, loving, and compassionate Lord He is, that's the only reasonable thing for us to do.

To the King of the ages, immortal, invisible, the only God, be honor and glory forever and ever. Amen. (1 Timothy 1:17 ESV)

The Gospel of Paul

· · ·

Some have taught that Jesus preached the kingdom, but Paul preached grace. This is an idea that Scripture cannot bear.

Paul and Jesus both preached the kingdom of God, and they both preached grace (John 1:17; Acts 20:24).

Consider the following texts where we clearly see Paul preaching the kingdom:

> Paul entered the synagogue and spoke boldly there for three months, arguing persuasively about the kingdom of God. (Acts 19:8 NIV)

> Now I know that none of you among whom I have gone about preaching the kingdom will ever see me again. (Acts 20:25 NIV)

> They arranged to meet Paul on a certain day, and came in even larger numbers to the place where he was staying. He witnessed to them from morning till evening, explaining about the kingdom of God, and from the Law of Moses and from the Prophets he tried to persuade them about Jesus. (Acts 28:23 NIV)

> He [Paul] proclaimed the kingdom of God and taught about the Lord Jesus Christ—with all boldness and without hindrance! (Acts 28:31 NIV)

Paul's gospel of the kingdom was the same as what John the Baptist and Jesus preached. It just included the death and resurrection of Jesus, the events through which Jesus became Lord of the world. It also strongly emphasized the grace of God in salvation.

Philip, the evangelist (as well as all the other apostles) preached the gospel of the kingdom also.

> But when they believed Philip as he preached the gospel of the kingdom of God and the name of Jesus Christ, they were baptized, both men and women. (Acts 8:12 BSB)

Jesus Is Lord

. . .

When a person said "Jesus is Lord" in the first century, they were saying that Caesar is not lord. They were also saying that Kratos (the god of power) is not lord, Plutus (the god of wealth) is not lord, and Aphrodite (the god of lust) is not lord. (By the way, the near equivalent of these three gods are Eros, Mammon, and Mars.)

Unfortunately, in our day, "Jesus is Lord" does not mean that Kratos, Plutus, or Aphrodite are not. It's common for many Christians to have Jesus as their Lord on Sunday morning, Plutus as their lord at work, Kratos as their lord at home, and Aphrodite as their lord late at night on the internet.

Paul's message that Jesus is Lord was an in-your-face challenge to Caesar and every other pagan god.

Today, the announcement that Jesus is Lord challenges all earthly powers as well as the invisible "principalities and powers" of the hostile spiritual world that stand behind them. The gospel of the kingdom also brings opposition from those forces which worship the pagan gods of power, greed, and lust.

Indeed, the gospel of the kingship of Jesus summons every person to repent of giving their allegiance to false gods and entities, and to give their only allegiance to Jesus of Nazareth instead.

The blessing of salvation and the blessing of the kingdom is a matter of grace through faith. For this reason, the gospel of the kingdom and the gospel of grace are two sides of the same message.

For the law was given through Moses; grace and truth came through Jesus Christ. (John 1:17 NIV)

Our God Reigns

• • •

In Isaiah 52, we have an amazing prophecy. It reads:

> How beautiful on the mountains
>   are the feet of those who bring good news,
> who proclaim peace,
>   who bring good tidings,
>   who proclaim salvation,
> who say to Zion,
>   "Your God reigns!"
> Listen! Your watchmen lift up their voices;
>   together they shout for joy.
> When the LORD returns to Zion,
>   they will see it with their own eyes.
> Burst into songs of joy together,
>   you ruins of Jerusalem,
> for the LORD has comforted his people,
>   he has redeemed Jerusalem.
> The LORD will lay bare his holy arm
>   in the sight of all the nations,
> and all the ends of the earth will see
>   the salvation of our God.
>
> Depart, depart, go out from there!
>   Touch no unclean thing!
> Come out from it and be pure,
>   you who carry the articles of the LORD's house.
> But you will not leave in haste
>   or go in flight;
> for the LORD will go before you,
>   the God of Israel will be your rear guard. (Isaiah 52:7–12 NIV)

Here's the backdrop to Isaiah's prophetic word.

Jerusalem has been destroyed by Babylon—one of the world's greatest superpowers. The people of God have been removed from their land, exiled to Babylon. Only a few Jews remain in the holy city. And those few are wondering, "Has God abandoned us?"

Suddenly, the watchmen spot a runner far off in the distance. The messenger is running on the mountains toward the city, carrying a beautiful message. He is shouting and proclaiming peace, good news, and salvation.

The messenger announces that despite Jerusalem's destruction, Israel's God still reigns as King. And God Himself will one day return to the city of Jerusalem, take up His throne in Zion, and bring salvation and peace to the whole world. The watchmen shout for joy because of the good news that God still reigns.

Because God will bring salvation, the Lord says to depart from the ways of the world and touch not the unclean thing.

With the ministry of Jesus Christ, the reality of the new King had arrived. And both the King and the messenger of "good news" was Jesus Himself.

The long-awaited kingdom of God was being ushered in with Jesus of Nazareth.

Isaiah foretold of the insurgence.

The Gospel Remixed

The first-century apostles lived when the "cult of Caesar" was the dominating religion of the Roman Empire. The "pledge of allegiance" in the Empire was "Caesar is Lord."

The message of the kingdom preached by Paul and the other apostles was deeply subversive. It was a countercultural, counter-imperial announcement.

The word "gospel" as it is used in the New Testament contains two elements.

First, it was the fulfillment of Isaiah 40–55 and Ezekiel 43, which promised that God would one day return to Zion, deliver His people, and judge the world. Peace, salvation, and justice to the whole earth would be the outcome.

Second, as we've already seen, the gospel referred to the announcement that a new Roman emperor had taken the throne.

Therefore, when Paul and the other apostles used the term "gospel," they were referring to the good news that Jesus of Nazareth, crucified and risen, was Israel's true Messiah and the world's true Lord.

Israel's King, now embodied in Jesus, was always destined to be the King of the world (Psalm 72:8; Isaiah 11:10). Strikingly, God came to be the true Lord and King in the person of a craftsman from Nazareth.

To say "Jesus is Lord" in the first century, then, was to declare one's allegiance to a different kingdom and a different empire. For this reason, the early Christians were persecuted. They lacked patriotism and loyalty to Rome, refusing to pledge their allegiance to Caesar. They pledged their allegiance to Jesus Christ alone, not to any nation, empire, political ideology, or party.

The gospel of the kingdom was a direct summons to abandon every other allegiance and offer total loyalty to Jesus. For this reason, all who surrender to the kingship of Christ today are part of the divine insurgence that was launched in Century One.

Good News, Bad News

• • •

The gospel of the kingdom carries its own power. In fact, Paul said that the gospel is the very power of God.

> For I am not ashamed of the gospel, for it is the power of God for salvation to everyone who believes, to the Jew first and also to the Greek. (Romans 1:16 ESV)

Whenever a Roman emperor died, there was unrest and uncertainty in the land. People asked, "Will there be food? Will there be war? What will happen to us?"

The gospel of the kingdom was the joyful announcement that Jesus, the crucified and risen Nazarene, is the new Lord, and He will put an end to poverty, injustice, slavery, and human suffering.

This was good news to the poor. It was good news to the oppressed. It was good news to sinners who were ready to repent. Why? Because the gospel offered them forgiveness, hope, deliverance, and salvation. It also promised a new form of economics in the community of the King, where all would have enough and there would be no lack.*

But it was bad news to all earthly powers and those who exploited others, prospering on the backs of the less fortunate, because the powers of this earth had to move aside to make way for the lordship of Jesus. The Lord Jesus was starting to bring forth the ultimate status reversal, which will be consummated in the future (Luke 1:53; 6:20–26; Revelation 18).

---

* In our current addictive-compulsive society, capital has replaced community in the realm of economics. This trend can be traced to Egypt where wealth and power were identified by surplus accumulation. Israel, on the other hand, was called to circulate her wealth by redistributing it to the tribes and caring for the poor, rather than centralizing it through private accumulation. God's ancient people practiced the Sabbath, which was a check against self-limitation, production, and consumption. It was also a way for the people to recharge, renew, and remember that all sustenance and provision was a gift from God. Israel was called to share her "stuff" with others, rather than to be possessed by her possesions. "If anyone is poor among your fellow Israelites in any of the towns of the land the LORD your God is giving you, do not be hardhearted or tightfisted toward them" (Deuteronomy 15:7 NIV).

For these reasons, Jesus fulfilled the Old Testament Scriptures promising that the poor would have the gospel preached to them (Luke 4:18; 7:22). It also explains why God especially loves the poor and has made them rich in faith when it comes to His kingdom (Luke 6:20; 16:22; James 2:2–6).

Point: The gospel of the kingdom was and still is an insurgence against the present order of things.

Israel's way of life was to be an affront to the dominant imperial economy, which was marked by predatory greed. Jesus spoke against this predatory instinct in Luke 12 and other texts. Taking his cue from Jesus, Paul called greed "idolatry" (Colossians 3:5; Ephesians 5:5). The ekklesia is called to live out the story that God gave to Israel about economics. She is to share her capital with the other members of the community rather than privately accumulating it. This is clear from texts like Mark 10:29–30; Acts 2; 4; 2 Corinthians 8; 9; and Romans 15. I will address this subject in more detail later in the book.

Inevitable Opposition

* * *

The gospel of the kingdom is scandalous. And so it brings great opposition.

It got John the Baptist beheaded.

It got Jesus crucified.

It got Peter, Paul, and most of the others apostles imprisoned and killed.

It caused Herod to tremble in fear and kill a cluster of male children in Israel simply because he heard that the Magi were looking for the One who would be the next king—"the king of the Jews" (Matthew 2).

When Paul preached the gospel of the kingdom, riots broke out everywhere. Paul was stoned, beaten, imprisoned, and eventually martyred. Why? Because he had the unmitigated gall to declare that there was another ruler on earth besides Caesar.

Around AD 51, Paul stood in the marketplace in the Greek city of Thessalonica and announced something that sounded like this:

> There is now a new Lord of the world. He was born Jewish, but He is from the heavens. Twenty years ago, the Jews had Him crucified by the hand of the Romans. But God raised Him from the dead, exalted Him to the heavenly throne, and He is now the ruler and King of both the heavens and the earth. Repent—cut all your ties to the present world order—and entrust your life to the new King, whose name is Jesus of Nazareth. He is the One who will bring peace, justice, and righteousness into the world. Give Him your believing allegiance, and He will forgive your sins and deliver you from this present evil age. You will also receive eternal life now and in the age to come.

Paul told the Thessalonians that outrageous story. *And amazingly, many believed it.* A number of Thessalonians trusted Jesus of Nazareth as Lord and gave Him their wholehearted, believing allegiance. And an ekklesia—a kingdom society—was born in Thessalonica.

Yes, the gospel that Paul and the other apostles preached sharply challenged Caesar and his kingdom. Their message was radical, subversive, and treasonous—fomenting a revolution. Note these words in the book of Acts:

These men who have upset the world have come here also; and Jason has welcomed them, and they all act contrary to the decrees of Caesar, saying that there is another king, Jesus. (17:6–7 NASB)

When the kingdom of God is announced, things happen. The heavenly realm is moved. Fallen men and women repent. Hell is awakened and incited. Those who herald the gospel are criticized, attacked, and persecuted.

The kingdom of God calls all the kingdoms of this world to account. It confronts the temporary powers of this world system. Hence the backlash.

To put a finer point on it, Paul and the other apostles were ambassadors of the insurgence.

A Clash of Kingdoms

. . .

The four Gospels tell the story of how God became king of the earth in and through Jesus of Nazareth. The story of the Gospels is the saga of the clash of the kingdoms of this world with the kingdom of God.

The Gospels open with Herod hunting down the new King, Jesus, born in the city of David. And they end with Jesus announcing His kingdom to Pilate, then sending out His disciples as ambassadors to proclaim the arrival of the new kingdom.

The book of Acts also contains that same clash of kingdoms. Acts opens with Jesus teaching about the kingdom. And it closes with Paul preaching the gospel of the kingdom in the city of Rome, right at Caesar's doorstep.

Acts 1–12 is the story of the kingdom being proclaimed to the Jewish people. Acts 13–28 is the story of the kingdom being proclaimed to the Gentile world.

From beginning to end, Acts shows us the announcement that Jesus is Lord and King of the world by His disciples, who herald it from Jerusalem all the way to Rome. In that regard, the book of Acts is all about the launching of God's rule on the earth as it is in heaven, in and through Jesus. And this launch is challenged at every point.

However, the book ends with Paul proclaiming the kingdom in Rome "with all boldness and without hindrance!" (Acts 28:31 NIV).

Again, in the Roman world, the word *gospel* was an edict of good news issued by a political leader. It was the nonnegotiable declaration of a political sovereign that was heralded throughout the Roman world. It was the political announcement that Caesar is lord, and it demanded a loyalty oath to Caesar.

When the Christians emerged and announced that Jesus is Lord, their announcement wasn't a spiritual or theological affirmation. It was a political declaration of treason and sedition against Rome. That's why the early Christians were persecuted.

The early Christians weren't competing with the Roman gods. The Jewish people had already disavowed the pagan gods, and they didn't pose an immediate threat to the empire. No, the Christians were breaking the loyalty oath of the empire by proclaiming that Jesus of Nazareth, not Caesar, is Lord and King.

In the same way, whenever and wherever the gospel of the kingdom is received today, it breaks the loyalty oath to the world system, including the political, national, entertainment, educational, and even religious systems.

The kingdom of God constitutes no small revolution. It's a revolt against all that dehumanizes God's good creation, against everything that distracts and detracts from the beauty and majesty of Christ. It's not a revolution of physical violence or political power. It's a spiritual insurgence.

> Jesus answered, "My kingdom is not of this world. If My kingdom were of this world, then My servants would be fighting so that I would not be handed over to the Jews; but as it is, My kingdom is not of this realm." (John 18:36 NASB)

As I argued in *Pagan Christianity* with George Barna, Jesus Christ was a revolutionary. Here's a short excerpt:

> Jesus was never a rabble-rouser nor a ranting rebel (Matthew 12:19–20). Yet He constantly defied the traditions of the scribes and Pharisees. And He did not do so by accident, but with great deliberation. The Pharisees were those who, for the sake of the "truth" as they saw it, tried to extinguish the truth they could not see. This explains why there was always a blizzard of controversy between the "tradition of the elders" and the acts of Jesus.
>
> Someone once said that "a rebel attempts to change the past; a revolutionary attempts to change the future." Jesus Christ brought drastic change to the world. Change to man's view of God. Change to God's view of man. Change to men's view of women. Our Lord came to bring radical change to the old order of things, replacing it with a new order. He came to bring forth a new covenant—a new Kingdom—a new birth—a new race—a new species—a new culture—and a new civilization.[5]

During His short ministry, Jesus revolted against every aspect of the world system.* He challenged the Jewish and Roman hierarchies and those in power, while identifying with those at the bottom of the social order.

For these reasons, Jesus died the death of an insurgent.†

The same characteristics also mark the Lord's loyal followers—the people of the insurgence.

* Greg Boyd has written an entire book on how Jesus revolted against the present order of things. See Greg Boyd, *The Myth of a Christian Religion* (Grand Rapids: Zondervan, 2009).

† Barabbas and the two men crucified with Jesus were called *lēstēs*, which means those who agitate with a political motive (Mark 15:27 NLT; John 18:40, NLT). "Revolutionary" or "insurrectionist" is a better translation of *lēstēs* than "robber" or "bandit." Those three men were political insurrectionists, insurgents, revolutionaries, guilty of sedition. And Jesus was considered to be of the same stripe.

Exceeding Worth

. . .

The late Jim Elliot said, "He is no fool who gives what he cannot keep to gain what he cannot lose."

That statement is a concise summary of the gospel of the kingdom.

The apostles of Jesus forsook everything when they responded to the gospel. And what did they gain from it? Three years of living in the conscious presence of Jesus Christ, the greatest honor a mortal could ever know.

They lost all to gain Christ. And they continued to live in the Lord's presence after His resurrection (Acts 4:13). In gaining Christ, they gained everything that truly matters: righteousness, joy, peace, an extended family, eternal life, and all the resources of heaven.

These words from Paul of Tarsus sum up his gospel, the gospel of the kingdom:

> But whatever gain I had, I counted as loss for the sake of Christ. Indeed, I count everything as loss because of the surpassing worth of knowing Christ Jesus my Lord. For his sake I have suffered the loss of all things and count them as rubbish, in order that I may gain Christ. (Philippians 3:7–8 ESV)

Except for his blinding vision of Christ on the road to Damascus, Paul never saw the face of Jesus. Not physically, anyway. But in this text Paul says that he forfeited everything "because of the surpassing worth of knowing Christ Jesus my Lord."

Notice he didn't say "the surpassing worth of going to heaven," or "the surpassing worth of making the world a better place," or "the surpassing worth of helping the poor and standing for social justice," or even "the surpassing worth of serving God."

No, the exceeding worth is knowing Jesus Christ! And that's where the gospel of the kingdom leads. To truly know the Lord Jesus Christ, to live in His presence, and to please His heart. The gospel of the kingdom

The Gospel of the Kingdom

is relational at its core. The Lord's desire is not that we work *for* Him. Rather, He wants us to live *with* Him.

By leaving all, you and I receive the peace and joy of being in God's kingdom and having access to the inexhaustible riches of Christ. Your security and prestige are no longer in money, material possessions, and worldly position. They are in Christ and His kingdom. To gain Christ, the greatest honor in history, is worth more than everything made up of atoms.

Paul continues saying,

> That I may know him and the power of his resurrection, and may share his sufferings, becoming like him in his death. . . . But one thing I do: forgetting what lies behind and straining forward to what lies ahead, I press on toward the goal for the prize of the upward call of God in Christ Jesus. . . . Brothers, join in imitating me, and keep your eyes on those who walk according to the example you have in us. (Philippians 3:10, 13–14, 17 ESV)

Those who are part of the insurgence follow Paul's example and make their "one thing" the high calling of knowing Jesus Christ. He is their passion and obsession in life.*

---

* Today, the Christian world suffers acutely from the plague of JDD (Jesus Deficit Disorder). For details on this disorder and its cure, see Leonard Sweet and Frank Viola, *Jesus Manifesto* (Nashville: Thomas Nelson, 2010) at InsurgenceBook.com.

143

Sheer Grace

. . .

Indeed, the gospel of the kingdom is the royal announcement that Jesus of Nazareth is the Messiah of Israel, as the Old Testament Scriptures foretold. And He is now enthroned as the true Lord of the world. A descendant of David is seated at the right hand of God in heavenly realms, and He is seated there as Lord forever.

When the gospel of the kingdom is preached today, the Holy Spirit calls people to repent and trust in Jesus as the risen Lord and Savior of heaven and earth.

But that call is given by sheer grace. And those who respond to it do so by sheer grace.

Consequently, the gospel of the kingdom is a gospel of grace. And grace is the lifeblood of the insurgence.

Meet Katie

• • •

Here is the testimony of a woman named Katie who was liberated after she heard the gospel of the kingdom.

My husband and I were attending a particular church and we started listening to the pastor, who taught that in order to be "radical" for Jesus, we had to start giving away our valuable items to the poor. Like many others in the congregation, we began with sheer excitement. We thought, "Now we were really following Jesus." But we couldn't sustain it. We all burned ourselves out.

Every week, we watched our friends in the church strive harder to obey the teaching by their own efforts. We grew tired of feeling guilty all the time, of not doing enough, of not measuring up, so we eventually left the church.

The teaching sounded biblical at first. But in our attempts to implement the vision, we realized that the focus was never Jesus Christ. It was about trying to be "obedient," and in a subtle way, it was really about earning our way to be more favored by Jesus.

In the end, we were exhausted and discouraged. I didn't want to attend any church anymore. Whenever I heard the word "obedience," I felt tired and even bitter.

I then heard someone preach the gospel of the kingdom. But he preached it with grace and no hint of legalism. It was then that I realized that I'm not capable of living for Jesus on my own. And the answer is not about feeling guilty or trying harder.

I was freed by the message. I gave up trying to live the Christian life, and started to learn how to let Jesus live it in and through me. My Christian walk was no longer about me or my obedience. It was now all about Christ. Those weren't just words anymore, they became reality. Grace, which I heard a lot about previously, became sweet music to me. I felt like I knew what grace was for the first time. It was Christ.

And you know what, my husband and I have never had more passion for the Lord since then. Any obedience that comes from us is His Spirit working in and through us. We are free, but more radical for the Lord than we ever have been before.

Meet Tom

. . .

Tom grew up in a fundamentalist Christian home that was marked by legalism and religious duty. Tom's devotion to the Lord was mostly outward, and he was plagued by a continual sense of condemnation, feeling that he was never doing enough for God.

During his college years, however, Tom was exposed to a progressive form of Christianity that didn't put much emphasis on personal holiness or evangelism. Instead, it was focused entirely on social justice.

Tom was drawn to this new version of Christianity and immersed himself into various causes that sought justice and world peace. At first, Tom was enthusiastic with his new brand of Christian emphasis. But after working effortlessly for justice for years, he became disillusioned with the pursuit.

He saw little fruit from his labors, concluding that the fight for justice wasn't all it was cracked up to be. In addition, he noticed that most of his activist friends would mention Jesus, but they had little to do with Him. They didn't appear to have a relationship with the resurrected Christ. The only time they mentioned Jesus was when citing one of His teachings about the poor or the rich.

While Tom still knew that his early Christian upbringing wasn't right for him, he came to realize that his lifestyle was no different from people who lived in and for the world. He also became burned out from his tireless efforts at working for justice and world peace, feeling that none of it made an ounce of difference.

His conscience was also troubled by the fact that he allowed himself to fall prey to various addictions of the flesh, things he had stayed clear from during his earlier days as a fundamentalist.

While living with this inner turmoil, Tom attended a gathering held on a college campus and heard someone preach the gospel of the kingdom. Suddenly, a shift happened in his mind and heart.

When it was all over, Tom gave himself fully to Jesus Christ, not to a cause or a new theology. In addition, Tom's surrender to Christ was not out of guilt, religious duty, fear, condemnation, or shame.

Instead, he was captivated by the stunning beauty of the King as it was presented through the gospel of the kingdom.

As a result, Tom was liberated from the two versions of the gospel that he had been exposed to in his past—the fundamentalist version and the progressive version. Tom had been "radicalized" for the kingdom of God and began a new journey with other believers on knowing Christ and expressing His life with them.

TAKING ACTION »

In light of what I've written in this part of the book, I recommend that you do these three things:

1. If today you believe that Jesus truly is Lord of the world, how does that belief change the way you've been living for the last year? Write your answer out as a list. Be as detailed as you can.

2. If Jesus was the actual, literal, and practical Lord of your city—meaning, He was running the show and calling the shots—how would your city be different than it is today? Be as detailed as you can.

3. Before you go to the next part of the book, ask the Lord to open your eyes to see the implications of His lordship in your life anew and afresh.

Part IV
ENTERING AND ENJOYING THE KINGDOM

We will now explore the practical application of the gospel of the kingdom—namely, how does a person enter the kingdom of God and enjoy the spiritual riches that lie within it?

The Great Panacea

Many Christians today know Jesus as their Savior. Some even possess the joy of salvation, especially after they first trusted Christ. But many—if not most—are living defeated, frustrated lives.

This is because they have never fully submitted themselves to Jesus as Lord. When the lordship of Christ is established in a life, it brings with it both power and liberty.

In this connection, if the gospel of the kingdom was preached and received by even a quarter of those who identify themselves as Christians today, it would solve countless problems.

It would take the Christian life out of the realm of being just another segment of acceptable Western or Eastern social life. And it would make it what it truly is—a foreign element to this planet. An enemy to all that is not of Christ on the globe.

Surpassing Devotion

Consider this passionate confession by a young adherent to communism expressing his radical allegiance to the Communist Party:*

> We Communists have a high casualty rate. We're the ones who get slandered and ridiculed and fired from our jobs and in every other way made as uncomfortable as possible. A certain percentage of us get killed or imprisoned. We live in virtual poverty. We turn back to the Party every penny we make above what is absolutely necessary to keep us alive. We Communists don't have time or the money for many movies or concerts or T-bone steaks or decent homes and new cars. We've been described as fanatics. We are fanatics! Our lives are dominated by one great overshadowing factor, the struggle for World Communism. We Communists have a philosophy of life which no amount of money could buy. We have a cause to fight for, a definite purpose in life. We subordinate our petty, personal selves into a great movement of humanity. And if our personal lives seem hard or our egos appear to suffer through subordination to the Party, then we are adequately compensated by the fact that each of us in his small way is contributing to something new and true and better for mankind. The Communist cause is my life, my business, my religion, my hobby, my sweetheart, my wife and mistress, my bread and meat. I work at it in the daytime and dream of it at night. Its hold on me grows, not lessens, as time goes on. Therefore, I cannot carry on a friendship, a love affair, or even a conversation without relating it to this force which both guides and drives my life. I evaluate people, books, ideas and actions according to how they affect the Communist cause and by their attitude toward it. I've already been in jail because of my ideas, and if necessary, I'm ready to go before a firing squad.[1]

Compare these words to the allegiance that the average Christian gives to Jesus today.

Something is clearly wrong, is it not?

---

* Billy Graham read this letter at the Urbana Conference in 1957. The letter reflects a devotion to a cause that still trumps the devotion that most Christians have for Jesus today, over sixty years later.

Now, if you've been ingrained with legalistic teaching, you're probably thinking, "Frank is trying to guilt me into doing more for God by comparing my devotion to that of Communists and Socialists! I've heard this emotional appeal before. Back to your homes, citizens. Nothing to see here."

Unfortunately, this is how legalistic teaching warps a person. It inoculates them from the sharp edge of the gospel, wrongly equating it with guilt and religious duty.

My point is simple. In the first century, the gospel was something to be obeyed with the whole of one's life. But that obedience was not motivated by guilt or duty but by a powerful and compelling love for Jesus Christ. One that was governed by pure freedom and liberty.

> Through him we received grace and apostleship to call all the Gentiles to the obedience that comes from faith for his name's sake. (Romans 1:5 NIV; see also 2 Thessalonians 1:8 and 1 Peter 4:17, which use the phrase "obey the gospel")

Legalism and legalistic thinking have associated the word "obey" with guilt, duty, and religious obligation. Consequently, a better word for obey is "respond."

In the New Testament, a person responded to the gospel of the kingdom by repenting and entirely entrusting themselves to Jesus as this world's true Lord.

This is still the proper response to the gospel today. And that response is birthed from the soil of childlike faith and humility.

> And he said: "Truly I tell you, unless you change and become like little children, you will never enter the kingdom of heaven." (Matthew 18:3 NIV)

> Blessed are the poor in spirit, for theirs is the kingdom of heaven. (Matthew 5:3 NIV)

> Let the little children come to me, and do not hinder them, for the kingdom of God belongs to such as these. (Mark 10:14 NIV)

On the matter of responding to the Lord, A. W. Tozer said this about the great saints of old who knew God well:

They differed from the average person in that when they felt the inward long-
ing they did something about it. They acquired a lifelong habit of spiritual
response. They were not disobedient to the heavenly vision. As David put
it neatly, "When thou saidst, Seek ye my face; my heart said unto thee, Thy
face, Lord, will I seek" (Ps. 78:8).[2]

What Tozer calls "the lifelong habit of spiritual response" begins with
a believing allegiance to Jesus Christ, and it continues from there.

Seeing the Kingdom

• • •

While the signs and evidences of the kingdom of God are visible, the kingdom itself is spiritual and invisible (Luke 17:20).

But those who have been born from above have been given a new set of senses whereby they can "see" the kingdom.

> Jesus replied to Nicodemus, "I can guarantee this truth: No one can see God's kingdom without being born from above." (John 3:3 GW)

When we receive the Spirit of God, we are born from above. That is, we are born into the heavenly realm. And that birth gives us a new consciousness and a new perception that is not possessed by those who are outside God's kingdom.

The ability to perceive spiritual things is not a special ability given to those who struggle to earn it. It's ours by birth—spiritual birth. It's our birthright.

So if you have been born from above, you have a new set of senses that enable you to detect the unseen things of the kingdom (2 Corinthians 3:18; 4:18; Ephesians 1:17–18; Hebrews 2:9; 12:2).

All who are part of the insurgence possess this capability.

Getting Into the Kingdom

. . .

So how does one enter the kingdom of God?

As I pen these words, I live fairly close to the Magic Kingdom, which is a part of Disney World in Orlando, Florida. It doesn't take long to enter the gate of the Magic Kingdom. You simply give the attendant your ticket, he opens the gate, and you're in. But the Magic Kingdom is a massive place with many attractions to see and experience.

The kingdom of God is similar. We enter the gate of the kingdom by repenting and believing in Jesus.

> The kingdom of God has come near. Repent and believe the good news! (Mark 1:15 NIV)

To *repent* is to experience a mental U-turn. It means turning away from the way we used to think and live. In the case of the kingdom of God, to repent means to disavow the world system which you and I have been serving all our lives.

To *believe* means to trust in Jesus of Nazareth as our Lord (King) and Savior. It means to give Him our trusting allegiance. It doesn't mean to mentally assent to the idea that Jesus is Savior and Lord. It means to entrust one's entire life to Him.

When we repent and believe the gospel, the Spirit of God imparts His life into us—the life of the kingdom—which the Bible terms a "new birth" (John 3:3, 5).

Interestingly, John 3:3 and John 3:7 in Young's Literal Translation is closer to the original. It translates the text "born from above" instead of the more traditional "born again."

Birth is the impartation of life. So the new birth means that we receive the life of God's kingdom into the deepest part of our beings.

However, to enter the kingdom *fully* and enjoy the riches of Christ that are in it, we must go through much tribulation, hardship, and suffering. Note these texts:

. . . strengthening the disciples and encouraging them to remain true to the faith. "We must go through many hardships to enter the kingdom of God," they said. (Acts 14:22 NIV)

Therefore, among God's churches we boast about your perseverance and faith in all the persecutions and trials you are enduring. All this is evidence that God's judgment is right, and as a result you will be counted worthy of the kingdom of God, for which you are suffering. (2 Thessalonians 1:4–5 NIV)

If we endure hardship, we will reign with him. (2 Timothy 2:12 NLT)

Entering the kingdom, therefore, is both an initial crisis event and a continuous progressive event. In this regard, it's just like entering the Magic Kingdom.

There's an initial entry through repentance and faith. Then there is a continuous entering, taking further ground in which we enjoy a greater measure of righteousness, peace, joy, and all the other riches of Christ that are in the Spirit (Romans 14:17).

Revelation 1:9 says,

I, John, your brother and partner in the tribulation and the kingdom and the patient endurance that are in Jesus. (ESV)

F. F. Bruce's thoughts on this text are insightful:

His placing of "the kingdom" between "the tribulation" and "the patient endurance" underlies a recurrent New Testament theme—that the patient endurance of tribulation is the way into the kingdom of God.[3]

The kingdom of God is neither "meat" nor "drink." It is an invisible kingdom, corresponding to the spiritual blessings that we receive in heavenly realms in Christ (Ephesians 1:3).

We enter the kingdom initially by submitting to the absolute lordship of Jesus and partaking of the divine nature (2 Peter 1:4). But the rest of the riches of the kingdom await to be experienced and enjoyed in this life as well as in the life to come.

The Old Testament gives us a vivid picture of this truth.

The Promised Land

As I demonstrated in *From Eternity to Here*, the land of Canaan is a vivid picture of the unsearchable riches of Jesus Christ. But it's also a picture of the kingdom of God.

As Paul declares in his letter to the Ephesians,

> To me, though I am the very least of all the saints, this grace was given, to preach to the Gentiles the unsearchable riches of Christ. (Ephesians 3:8 ESV)

In Hebrews 4, the writer speaks about the promised land of Canaan. And he points out that Joshua couldn't bring all the people of Israel into the land of Canaan—which he calls a land of rest—because some of them hardened their hearts to the Lord's voice and failed to believe His promise.

That generation subsequently died in the wilderness because of their disobedience and unbelief.

The writer of Hebrews goes on to say,

> For whoever has entered God's rest has also rested from his works as God did from his. Let us therefore strive to enter that rest, so that no one may fall by the same sort of disobedience. (4:10–11 ESV)

Notice the paradox. Those who enter the land have "rested" from their own works just as God rested on the Sabbath day following creation. But then the writer exhorts his readers to "strive to enter that rest."

The paradox clears when we understand how Israel took the promised land. They had to fight to enter it. They had to be violent in order to take the fullness of the land. They couldn't get completely in any other way.

The application is certainly not one of becoming physically violent for the cause of the kingdom. Instead, the application is that the kingdom of God is taken by a relentless, aggressive, absolute exercise of unwavering faith. The same kind of "violent" faith that operated when Jacob wrestled with the angel of God, refusing to let him go until Jacob received the divine blessing (Genesis 32:22–31).

I will speak more about this brand of spiritual violence later, but it's an essential element to entering the kingdom fully.

Israel's initial entry into Canaan was relatively easy. The city of Jericho fell fast and Israel quickly stepped right into the land.

> By faith the walls of Jericho fell, after the army had marched around them for seven days. (Hebrews 11:30 NIV)

But conquering the rest of the cities in the land was a progressive challenge.

In the same way, our initial entrance into the kingdom of God is one thing. But taking its ground and enjoying its riches is costly (Acts 14:22; 2 Thessalonians 1:4–5).

A Watery Grave

· · ·

Repentance and faith are not human works. They are attitudes of the heart that God enables through the Holy Spirit. Consequently, the gospel of the kingdom is a gospel of grace, not works.

> Do not be afraid, little flock, for your Father has been pleased to give you the kingdom. (Luke 12:32 NIV)

If you are a follower of Jesus Christ, God's grace enabled you to believe that Jesus is who He said He was. God's grace enabled you to repent and believe the gospel (Acts 11:18; 2 Timothy 2:25). God's grace also enabled you to give your full allegiance to Christ.

When a person accepted the gospel of the kingdom in the first century, they repented from their old allegiances, believed the good news about the universal kingship of Jesus, and were baptized in water in His name.

Baptism meant death to the old world. It also meant resurrection and birth into God's new kingdom. Baptism was the act of switching sides—a renunciation of the world system and the principalities and powers who run it under Satan. (I'll unravel this more later.)

To enter and enjoy the kingdom, you have to start new. This is what baptism is for—it is your new beginning where you put everything else behind you, your loyalty pledge that you have changed kingdoms (1 Peter 3:21 NIV).*

All throughout the book of Acts, the message of the apostles was, "Repent, believe, and be baptized." It wasn't "believe and say the sinner's prayer."†

In this regard, baptism has a very deep meaning that we have lost today. If you were baptized in the first century, you were signing your death warrant.

---

* While water baptism is the loyalty pledge to enter the kingdom, the Lord's Supper is the renewal of that pledge. See Viola, *Reimagining Church*, 73–82.

† For the origin of the "sinner's prayer," which is a postbiblical tradition, see Frank Viola and George Barna, *Pagan Christianity* (Carol Stream, IL: Tyndale, 2008), 190–91.

You were publicly separating yourself from the world system. You were breaking all ties to the old kingdom.

For this reason, the world looked upon a first-century Jesus-follower as someone who had renounced everything for another kingdom. And that kingdom laid claim to the entire planet.

In baptism, you are no longer part of this world's order. You no longer belong to the way the world does things. You announce to the entire universe that you have been made a new creation, that you have become part of a new kingdom, a new nation.

> Therefore if anyone is in Christ, he is a new creature; the old things passed away; behold, new things have come. (2 Corinthians 5:17 NASB)

Water baptism is analogous to crossing the Jordan to enter the promised land (Joshua 3).

That's how powerful water baptism is. It's the initial sign that you've joined the insurgence.*

---

* For further details on what water baptism means according to the New Testament, see my online article "Rethinking Water Baptism" at InsurgenceBook.com.

Death to All Other Allegiances

• • •

If you were living in Century One and you were baptized, this is what you were saying through that dramatic act:

> I am a male. [I am a female.] I'm a citizen of [your country]. I am addicted to this or that. But here I am. I'm about to die. And the person I am now will cease to exist. It is not that I'm going to change and give up my associations. *It's that the man [the woman] that I am is going to die.*

You were also saying,

> I believe that Jesus of Nazareth is the Son of God. I believe He died for my sins and rose again from the dead. I believe He ascended into heaven, and He is now the Lord of the world. So I'm finished with the old world. Take me out to the graveyard and bury me. All of my allegiances will be buried with me, and I will rise out of the water as part of a new creation, a new nation, a new kingdom where Jesus is King.

Once you emerged out of that watery grace, you came up a new creature who didn't belong to the old creation. Out of the water emerged a citizen of the new people of God, a new nation called ekklesia—the physical and visible headquarters of the kingdom of heaven.

Those who repented, believed, and were baptized in the name of Jesus in Century One belonged to a new world with a totally different set of values from the old world. Their life as they knew it had ended, and they were as those who had risen again from the dead to live for the new King of the world.

> Or don't you know that all of us who were baptized into Christ Jesus were baptized into his death? We were therefore buried with him through baptism into death in order that, just as Christ was raised from the dead through the glory of the Father, we too may live a new life. . . . Do not offer any part of yourself to sin as an instrument of wickedness, but rather offer yourselves to

God as those who have been brought from death to life; and offer every part of yourself to him as an instrument of righteousness. (Romans 6:3–4, 13 NIV)

The baptized person may still be involved in the political process, but politics no longer defines him. Nor does race or social status. She may still be involved in the educational system, but she's no longer influenced by it.

The baptized person no longer pays allegiance to any political or educational flag of this world.

This is how the early Christians understood baptism. It was a total and final ending. A burial. Their past was gone, forgiven, and forgotten. And they were now part of a new civilization headed up and led by almighty God Himself.*

* I use the term "civilization" metaphorically. The word "tribe" describes it better. I'll discuss this more later.

Taking Care of Business

. . .

Every seasoned servant of God knows one thing: If you mean business with God, He will mean business with you (James 4:8).

For those who have left the old world behind and stepped into the kingdom of God, there are certain things that should be taken care of at the very outset.

I will give you the general principles on what those things are. However, I refuse to be specific. The reason is simple. When preachers and teachers get specific on what God's people should and shouldn't do, they have moved into legalism.

No mortal has the right to lay down their own personal standards on another individual. That's the job of the Holy Spirit. We can find the general principles concerning the will of God in Scripture. But the application of those principles is the Holy Spirit's role.

When I started preaching the gospel of the kingdom in 1998, I refused to lay down any rules. I didn't give a list of "dos" and "don'ts" or "thou shalts" and "thou shalt nots." That sort of thinking belongs to the old covenant dispensation.

Under the new covenant, we have been given the Spirit of God who teaches us what is according to Christ and what is not. And the leading of the Spirit will always conform to the general principles of Scripture.[*]

> But you have received the Holy Spirit, and he lives within you, so you don't need anyone to teach you what is true. For the Spirit teaches you everything you need to know, and what he teaches is true—it is not a lie. So just as he has taught you, remain in fellowship with Christ. (1 John 2:27 NLT)

---

[*] The Lord Jesus Christ speaks to us today through His Spirit as well as through His written Word. I talk in detail about how to practically recognize and respond to the Lord's voice today in Leonard Sweet and Frank Viola, *Jesus Speaks* (Nashville: Thomas Nelson, 2016), which you can find at InsurgenceBook.com.

Now about your love for one another we do not need to write to you, for you yourselves have been taught by God to love each other. (1 Thessalonians 4:9 NIV)

The promise of the new covenant is that God has put His Spirit in us. So His laws are now in our minds and hearts, and Jesus speaks to us through His Spirit (Hebrews 8:10–12).

This is one of the greatest blessings of the insurgence.

A People for the Lord

• • •

God is after a people whom He can possess completely, a people of the kingdom.

> The field is the world, and the good seed represents the people of the Kingdom. (Matthew 13:38 NLT)

Consider Paul's words in Titus:

> He gave his life to free us from every kind of sin, to cleanse us, and to make us his very own people. (2:14 NLT)

The NASB translates this text as follows:

> . . . to purify for Himself a people for His own possession.

It is my opinion that the Lord has never had a large group of people who were completely His own. And I seriously doubt He ever will.

The Lord is after a people who are solely His. A people marked by undying devotion to Christ and His unshakable kingdom.

Whenever the Lord talked about the kingdom of God in the Gospels, He gave us the highest standard that a human being could imagine.

The insurgence represents the Lord's desire to have a people who will go as far with Christ as Christ Himself will go. A people who will go on with Jesus, be it rain or shine, death or life, ups or downs, joy or sorrow, pleasure or pain, fire or blood, heaven or hell.

The world has enough lukewarm Christians. It has enough halfhearted Christians. It has plenty of Christians who lack devotion to Christ. Therefore, the Lord is after a people who are fully His, who seek to be possessed totally and completely by Him and Him alone.

> I am saying this for your own good, not to restrict you, but that you may live in a right way in undivided devotion to the Lord. (1 Corinthians 7:35 NIV)

Note the words of Paul, "undivided devotion to the Lord."

God is calling you and me to be a people who are undivided in our devotion to Him without a shred of legalism, religious obligation, or duty. A people who have been captured by the sight of His glory. A yielded people who are seeking to reach God's full will.

Such a people are scarce in this world today. But they do exist, and they make up the insurgence.

Do Whatever He Tells You

· · ·

The first generation of Israel didn't enter nor enjoy the promised land because they disobeyed the voice of the Lord. After telling this tragic story about Israel, the writer of Hebrews admonishes us with these sober words:

> Today, if you hear his voice, do not harden your hearts. (4:7 NIV)

Later, Saul (Israel's first king), lost his place in the kingdom due to disobedience (1 Samuel 13–15).

Entering and enjoying the kingdom is a lifelong process that results in inheriting the kingdom in the future. And it's based on hearing the Lord's voice and responding to it.

In the following chapters, I will present to you a strong word on how to make a clean break with your past. In so doing, you will make a clear way for the Lord to bring you into the fullness of His kingdom.

The story of the Old Testament Israel and King Saul teaches us that we can lose the fullness of the kingdom when the word of the Lord is given to us and we continue to disobey it.

At the wedding of Cana, Jesus' mother said to the servants, "Do whatever He tells you" (John 2:5 NIV). If you are a follower of Jesus Christ, you are in the kingdom of God. Therefore, you are under true, genuine authority.

Those who are completely devoted to the Lord will know within their hearts where they need to make adjustments, what to let go, when to make a change, and so forth. Their spiritual instincts will lead them in the Lord's direction. They don't need to be told by a human. Devotion to Christ does away with legalism and legality.

That said, the Lord is looking for a people in every generation whom He can completely possess. A people who wish to be His own—wholly, utterly, totally.

Lord, shake us until there's nothing left but You, the One who can never be shaken.

See that you do not refuse Him who speaks. For if they did not escape who refused Him who spoke on earth, much more shall we not escape if we turn away from Him who speaks from heaven, whose voice then shook the earth; but now He has promised, saying, "Yet once more I shake not only the earth, but also heaven." Now this, "Yet once more," indicates the removal of those things that are being shaken, as of things that are made, that the things which cannot be shaken may remain. (Hebrews 12:25–27 NKJV)

So to quote the mother of Jesus, "Do whatever He tells you."

The Termination of That Which Is Immoral

. . .

There was one thing that Paul struggled with in all the Gentile churches he planted. It was woven into the very culture in which those churches existed.

That one thing was immorality. Paul said that those who *practice* (live a lifestyle of) immorality will not inherit the kingdom of God (1 Corinthians 6:9–10; Galatians 5:21; Ephesians 5:5).

Let me be clear: if you are presently practicing immorality, there is forgiveness and grace to cleanse and cover you. Even better, the same grace that forgives you also empowers you to put an end to this sin.

> For the grace of God has appeared, bringing salvation to all men, instructing us to deny ungodliness and worldly desires and to live sensibly, righteously and godly in the present age. (Titus 2:11–12 NASB)

If you will go on with the Lord in His kingdom and enjoy its riches, it's vital that you deal with immorality before Him. And terminate it by the power of God's Spirit.

The Destruction of That Which Is Idolatrous

• • •

Another problem that Paul dealt with in the Gentile churches he worked with was idolatry.

In the ancient world, an idol was the means by which a deity became present to people. It was thought to be the visible embodiment of a divine being. An idol, therefore, involved false worship and false imagining.

Idolatry in the first century was easy to spot. People worshiped inanimate objects. Idolatry is not so easy to detect today because individuals idolize people, possessions, power, and pleasure.

And we are usually blind to the fact that one of these things holds a more prominent place in our lives than the Lord.

A person falls into idolatry when he or she has lost sight of the beauty, majesty, splendor, and glory of Jesus Christ. Consequently, something else replaces Him in their eyes, something in the created order.

Therefore, my dear friends, flee from idolatry. (1 Corinthians 10:14 NIV)

Dear children, keep yourselves from idols. (1 John 5:21 NIV)

Dear children, keep away from anything that might take God's place in your hearts. (1 John 5:21 NLT)

When I was in my late teens, the Lord put His finger on an idol in my life. I owned a valuable collection that I prized dearly. There was nothing wrong with the collection in and of itself. The problem was that my affections were attached to it, and it competed with my Lord. So it was an idol in my life. Therefore, I rid myself of it. And once I took that step, I felt completely liberated.

Some thirty years later, I replaced the collection with a new one because it no longer had a hold on me.

We should also be aware that we can turn God's blessing into an idol.

In Numbers 21, we have the story of God healing the people of Israel by beholding a bronze serpent that Moses created. God told Israel to look and live (Numbers 21:8). Hundreds of years later, Israel still had the bronze serpent. But they made an idol out of it. *They turned the blessing of God into an object of worship.*

When Hezekiah became king, he smashed the bronze serpent and called it *Nehushtan*, "a piece of bronze." That's what we are called to do with idols. Smash them into powder.

Ask the Lord to point out the idols in your life. If you are willing to part with them, without becoming defensive, He will put His finger on them.

I will speak more about idolatry in a future chapter, but if you will fully enter the Lord's kingdom, it's essential that you destroy any idols in your heart.

The Ending of That Which Is Improper

You may be in an improper romantic relationship, unequally yoked with someone who doesn't follow Jesus (2 Corinthians 6:14).

You may be in an improper friendship with someone who is dragging you back into the world.

You may be in an improper relationship with another believer, living as though you are married while you are not.

The New Testament also mentions that there are improper ways to talk, reflecting the world's values rather than the values of the kingdom (Ephesians 4:29; 5:4; Colossians 3:8).

There are also improper ways to dress, ways that seek to draw others into lust. Unfortunately, conservative as well as liberal Christians have a hard time talking about this subject without sounding silly. Many who are conservative want to constitute a dress code on all women. (Some of them are even more comfortable with a woman in a hijab than a woman in a skirt!)

On the other hand, many who are liberal decry the fact that women are objectified, but say nothing about a fashion industry that encourages women to reveal more and more of their bodies, which encourages objectification.

If your heart is open to the Lord, the Holy Spirit will show you what is improper when it comes to all of these matters. No human should play that role, whether conservative or liberal.

Yet to go forward in God's kingdom, you must end that which is improper in your life.

The Restitution of That Which Is Stolen

If you have stolen an item from someone, returning it to them is making restitution.

If you've borrowed something from someone and never returned it, that in effect is stealing. Sure, it's unintentional, but it's stealing nonetheless because the item belongs to someone else.

Sometimes we can make restitution instantly. Sometimes it may take years to pay something back.

When Zacchaeus met the Lord Jesus, he responded by returning fourfold to everyone he cheated. Zacchaeus made restitution and cleared the record (Luke 19).

If you've taken something from another person and you no longer have it, the Spirit may lead you to write a letter to that person, letting them know that you have given your life to Jesus as Savior and Lord and you are dealing with your past.

I once had an item I borrowed that belonged to someone else. I tried to contact the person to return it but received no response (they were in the middle of a move). So I dropped the item at their front door before they moved. It was a small item that was worth around US $7.00 new. But I didn't want it on my conscience.

My point is that there is always a way to make restitution. On the flip side, I own books that I've lent to people and they have never returned them. Those books constitute stolen property, even though the people may have lost track of them.

I used to lend money to people, fellow Christians even. But I stopped doing that because very few of them ever paid me back. So I started giving people money instead of lending it. In that way, I released them from the need to make restitution to me.

These are just some examples of how making restitution can be practical. I encourage you to let the Lord speak to you in this area.

The Elimination of That Which Is Unclean

• • •

Things which are unclean should be destroyed, and not sold.

What is unclean? Anything that has the touch of sin or the demonic upon it. Or anything that will tempt you to live in an unclean way.

Those things that are part of the occult or that are obscene and perverse are unclean.

It could be certain films, games, magazines, or objects. It could also be certain locations where people serve the gods of power, wealth, and lust.

First-century Ephesus was the headquarters of sorcerers all over the world. The sorcerers sold scrolls that contained magic potions. These sorcerers possessed priceless occult books that explained how to conjure up demons. These books were routinely sold in Ephesus and they were highly valuable.

In Acts 19, Paul came to Ephesus preaching the gospel of the kingdom. Those who believed the gospel burned their valuable occult books. All combined, they burned the equivalent of 50,000 pieces of silver. That is an astronomical figure. It would be over 7 million US dollars in today's money.

Because the books were unclean, they were not sold. They were destroyed.

Again, I refuse to be a legalist and tell you which films, magazines, objects, and locations are unclean. Bring the issue to the Lord, and He will show you. If you have to ask someone, it's probably unclean for you.

The Breaking of That Which Is Addictive

• • •

We live in an addicted culture. And many have addictive personalities. There are addictions to pornography, alcohol, illegal drugs, and prescription drugs. There are also food addictions.

(I'm not using the term "addiction" in its scientific or psychological sense. I'm using it in the popular sense to refer to any habit that seems impossible to break.)

In my experience and observation, unless you break an addiction, you cannot go on with the Lord in the fullness of His kingdom. You will be handicapped.

Addictions are rooted in a misdirected passion and a distorted sense of beauty. And that misdirected passion and distorted sense of beauty hamper our eyes from seeing the true beauty of Christ and smother our hearts from having a true passion for God.

I will say that every person I've known who did not deal with their addiction hit a ceiling in their spiritual walk.

Consequently, to go on with the Lord in His kingdom, the addiction must be broken. The good news is that any addiction can be broken. I'm told that the most addictive substance on the planet is heroin, which is a refined opiate. But even the addiction to heroin can be broken. In one of my available articles, I explain how to break any addiction.*

* See my online article "How to Break an Addiction" at InsurgenceBook.com.

Public Confession

As you deal with these six areas of your life, let me issue a word of warning. It is unwise to make things public that have the element of shame attached to them.

For years, I've watched Christians make public confessions about highly shameful and inappropriate things, and it brought more damage than good. F. F. Bruce has given us wise counsel regarding the public confession of sin. He wrote,

> The confession should be as public as the sin. A sin committed against God alone need be confessed to God alone; a sin committed against an individual should be confessed to that individual; a sin committed against the church should be confessed to the church; and if a sin is committed against the general public, the confession should have the same publicity the sin had. And where sin is of a kind that calls for material or moral restitution, such restitution is a necessary part of the confession.[4]

To summarize Bruce's point, the circle of offense is the circle of confession. Also, if something has shame attached to it, it should be confessed in private rather than in public.*

Sinning privately against your husband, your wife, your child, your parent, your sister, your brother, or your friend should remain between you and the individual you've sinned against. Jesus underlined this principle when He said to correct the person who has sinned against you *in private* (Matthew 18:15).

If, on the other hand, you've sinned publicly and out in the open against another person, then that sin should be confessed publicly to the audience who witnessed it.

---

* This subject is beyond the scope of this book, but some examples of how righteous people dealt with shame are when Joseph wanted to break off his engagement to Mary privately when he thought she was unfaithful. Joseph didn't want her to be publicly shamed. Also, God was displeased with Ham when he uncovered the shame of his father, Noah. In Ephesians 5:12, Paul said that it is shameful to even mention certain matters.

In addition, Jesus taught that if a person sins against another, they should be corrected in private first. Only after multiple attempts to get the sinning party to repent should their sin be made public (Matthew 18:15–17).

Paul echoes the teaching of Jesus when he says that elders who persist in their sin should be rebuked openly after two or three witnesses have established the credibility of the accusation (1 Timothy 5:19–20 ESV). So in extreme cases like this, public confession is appropriate.

These are spiritual principles. The Holy Spirit will guide you into the specific application.

Offering Our Bodies

. . .

Before the Israelites crossed the Jordan, Joshua told them,

> Consecrate yourselves, for tomorrow the LORD will do amazing things among you. (Joshua 3:5 NIV)

The word "consecrate" means to give God what is rightfully His. It means to separate, set apart, or sanctify oneself to the Lord. Put another way, consecration is giving Jesus Christ back His body.

All throughout Romans chapters 1–11, Paul speaks to the church in Rome about the mercies of God. In chapter 12, Paul introduces the subject of the body of Christ. I'm going to paraphrase what he writes in Romans 12:1–2 for emphasis:

> In light of all that God has done for you by His mercy, I now urge you by the mercies of God that you present your bodies a living and holy sacrifice acceptable to God which is your reasonable and rational service of worship. And do not be conformed to this world system. But be transformed by the renewing of your mind, so you might prove what the will of God is in your own life—the good, acceptable and perfect will of God.

There's a lot contained in these words. Let's look deeper at the text now.

The Altar

. . .

The tabernacle of Moses in the Old Testament was a picture of God's house. The first thing that God's people came to when they entered the tabernacle was the altar of burnt offering. The altar was the place of sacrifice and death.

Imagine a bull standing out with the herd in an open meadow. A priest separates the bull from the herd and brings him close to the tabernacle. According to Scripture, the bull has been "consecrated," "sanctified," "set apart," "separated," "made holy."

The bull is then slain on the altar. Once the bull is slain, the priest takes his hands off it, signifying that the bull now belongs to the Lord.

This is the image that Paul is seeking to get across in Romans 12:1–2. To be laid upon the altar means that we have lost control over the ownership of our lives. We are now wholly in the hands of and at the mercy of Another.

Paul is saying to the Christians in Rome, "Let God have your bodies. Let Him do whatever He wills with them. Give yourself unreservedly to the Lord. Look at the altar and climb on it, declaring, 'Lord, whatever You want. I'm yours. I leave the reins in Your hands.'"

Know this: if you take this step and put yourself on the altar, the Lord will take you to your utter end, and even beyond it.

But the Lord leaves the choice with you. You can live your own life and keep the reins in your hands. But entering the fullness of the kingdom won't be an option for you. You will only get so far.

The kingdom of God needs those who have placed themselves utterly in the hands of God. A people who have taken the long trek of the total dealing of God in their lives, having offered their bodies completely to Him.

Your Reasonable Service

. . .

The high calling of God is for you and me to penetrate the altar that Paul speaks about in Romans 12:1–2. In one translation, the text reads this way:

> I beseech you therefore, brethren, by the mercies of God, that you present your bodies a living sacrifice, holy, acceptable to God, which is your reasonable service. And do not be conformed to this world, but be transformed by the renewing of your mind, that you may prove what *is* that good and acceptable and perfect will of God. (NKJV)

Notice the words "reasonable service." Another translation says "spiritual service of worship" (NASB).

According to Paul, offering your body as a living sacrifice to God is your "reasonable service." It's an act of worship. You see, the Lord Jesus Christ purchased your body by His own blood on the cross. He went into the store, found you, took out money, put it on the counter, and said, "Okay, [insert your name] is now mine." This is the meaning of redemption. To redeem means to buy back.

Only Jesus didn't use gold to pay for you. He used His own life.

> Or do you not know that your body is a temple of the Holy Spirit who is in you, whom you have from God, and that you are not your own? For you have been bought with a price: therefore glorify God in your body. (1 Corinthians 6:19–20 NASB)

The pressure on you right now is to rob God of something. The pressure is to steal from God what is rightfully His. And that "something" is yourself.

> And he died for all, that those who live should no longer live for themselves but for him who died for them and was raised again. (2 Corinthians 5:15 NIV)

But the attitude of worship says, "Nothing for myself. Everything for the Lord. I belong to Jesus Christ. He bought me so I'm His. Therefore, I live to do the Lord's will. I'm here for His kingdom. I'm dead to the world and alive to God."

> And do not be conformed to this world, but be transformed by the renewing of your mind. (Romans 12:2 NASB)

The truth is, someone already owns you. It could be your spouse, your children, your parents, your job, your house, your ambitions, your dreams, your hopes, your reputation, and so on.

You are already owned by something or someone.

But Jesus Christ has the right to own you because He purchased you for Himself. However, even though He rightfully owns you, He stands back, not forcing His ownership upon your life.

Jesus brought this home another way when He was asked if it was proper to pay taxes. The Lord's response contains more than meets the eye.

> "Bring Me a denarius [coin] to look at." They brought one. And He said to them, "Whose likeness and inscription is this?" And they said to Him, "Caesar's." And Jesus said to them, "Render to Caesar the things that are Caesar's, and to God the things that are God's." And they were amazed at Him. (Mark 12:15–17 NASB)

According to Jesus, taxes belong to Caesar because Caesar's image appears on the coins. In the same way, we were made in God's image. So His image appears on us. Therefore, we belong to God.

So I would urge you: Give your life to God. Lay yourself on that altar. But don't do it unless it's in your heart to do so. Yet if you decide to do it, do it with an utter completeness, thoroughly and totally.

Our bodies rightfully belong to Jesus. Do you think He purchases you so He can make your life miserable and load you down with guilt and duty?

Not at all. He bought you so you can enjoy true provision, true enjoyment, and true security in Him rather than their imitations in a counterfeit system called "the world," which I will talk about later.

In light of His mercy and all that He has done for you, it is irrational and unreasonable for you to not give your life to Him and become "a living sacrifice." And in so doing, you have the high honor of being an agent of His already-but-not-yet kingdom.

The Eternal Marriage

· · ·

What does it mean to present yourself to the Lord and offer your body as a living sacrifice to Him?

It doesn't mean that you are vowing to be perfect. Because I assure you, that's not possible. You and I will make mistakes. We will fall short. We will fail. Thankfully, the blood of Christ has been shed to forgive and cover us when we do.

We are instead vowing to be married to Christ. And whether our love feels strong or cold, we recognize we belong to Him.

If "marrying" Christ sounds strange to you, listen to Paul:

For a married woman is bound by law to her husband while he lives, but if her husband dies she is released from the law of marriage. . . . Likewise, my brothers, you also have died to the law through the body of Christ, so that you may belong to another, to him who has been raised from the dead, in order that we may bear fruit for God. (Romans 7:2, 4 ESV)

For I am jealous for you with a godly jealousy; for I betrothed you to one husband, so that to Christ I might present you as a pure virgin. (2 Corinthians 11:2 NASB)

This understanding is the essence of the insurgence.

The Denial of the Soul

I agree with those theologians who teach that the word "soul" in the Bible includes our mind, will, and emotions.

Beyond the outward things I just talked about in the foregoing chapters, the Lord calls us to go even deeper and "deny our souls."

> And calling the crowd to him with his disciples, he said to them, "If anyone would come after me, let him deny himself and take up his cross and follow me. For whoever would save his life will lose it, but whoever loses his life for my sake and the gospel's will save it. For what does it profit a man to gain the whole world and forfeit his soul? For what can a man give in return for his soul? (Mark 8:34–37 ESV)

In Luke 9:23–25, Jesus uses the term "self" as a synonym for the soul.

The soul is your self, primarily your natural life. It's your personality. To deny your soul means that your thoughts, your desires, and your will are surrendered to the Lord. It means that you are willing to lose rather than win. It means laying your life down for the Lord and for others (John 15:13).

The words of Jesus about denying yourself, taking up your cross, losing your life, and laying your life down do not just refer to physical death. They refer to the principle of the cross—denying your own desires to do the will of God, right here, right now.

As Jesus-followers, we are called to deny ourselves daily (Luke 9:23).

What the Lord demands in this area is humanly impossible. It also involves a process. So it's a marathon, not a sprint. But as Jesus said, "With God all things are possible." So by the Spirit of God, we can deny ourselves for the sake of His kingdom.

The insurgence is marked by self-denial for the Lord's sake.

The Depths of the Altar

• • •

I want to expand what I've written in the previous chapters about Romans 12:1–2. Let's look at it again from the NLT version of the Bible:

> And so, dear brothers and sisters, I plead with you to give your bodies to God because of all he has done for you. Let them be a living and holy sacrifice—the kind he will find acceptable. This is truly the way to worship him. Don't copy the behavior and customs of this world, but let God transform you into a new person by changing the way you think. Then you will learn to know God's will for you, which is good and pleasing and perfect.

Do you have any idea what it costs for the Lord to gain control of your life? It takes a kind of breaking that one can hardly imagine. The truth is, it's going to cost you everything. For that reason, it cannot be done overnight.

> So therefore, any one of you who does not renounce all that he has cannot be my disciple. (Luke 14:33 ESV)

I've been on this journey for years, and I'm still discovering areas of my life to hand over to the Lord.

Even though consecrating your life will be a process, there must be a radical beginning.

The kingdom of God is not established on a bed of roses. We enter it through suffering and sacrifice.

Once you lay yourself on the altar, you are no longer your own. You are now the Lord's. But let me explain how far this goes. It runs deeper than most of us think.

Many Christians climb on the altar holding a contract. And here's what that contract says: "I give you my life, Lord. But I give it to You so that You can use me."

That's a contract. When the bull lies on the altar, he doesn't have a will of his own. He doesn't stipulate how, or even if, God will use him. What God does with the bull is up to God and God alone.

After the bull is slain, he is burnt as an offering to the Lord. So the bull loses his future. He comes to a complete and total end.

Now let me ask: Are you willing to lose your future and put it entirely in God's hands? He may choose to use you or He may choose to have you live in obscurity for the rest of your life. Are you okay with that?

He may decide that you'll never be recognized as being "a mighty servant of God." He may choose that you'll never receive honor from others for your spiritual service.

Why, then, would you and I put ourselves on the altar of burnt offering? The only reason is to meet the Lord's heart. To be burned and consumed for the Lord's pleasure alone.

> It is a burnt sacrifice, an offering made by fire, a sweet aroma to the LORD. (Leviticus 1:17 NKJV)

The vessel doesn't choose how to be used. That's the Master's choice. Again, the burnt offering is for the Lord. The burning of the ashes is for God's pleasure and satisfaction.

The choice to use you or not is God's. But one thing is clear. If He does choose to use you, He must first work in your life deeply before you can bear lasting fruit.

In other words, our very ambition to serve God must also be slain and burnt to ashes. To put it succinctly, God's choice for us is ashes. And in those ashes the Lord gains a sweet aroma, an offering for His satisfaction.

Note the words of Jesus to the religious leaders of His day:

> How can you believe since you accept glory from one another but do not seek the glory that comes from the only God? (John 5:44 NIV)

Faith is always hampered when we seek glory (honor) from other mortals, rather than from God Himself.

God's kingdom is founded on the altar of sacrifice.

Talent to Ashes

Let me go further on the subject of the altar. Many Christians have the idea that when they come to Christ, they should offer their natural talents to Him. So a great piano player comes into the kingdom, and now she offers her piano talent for God's kingdom, hoping to be a great pianist for the Lord.

A gifted speaker gets saved and now he wishes to offer his oratorical skills to God, hoping to become a great preacher for the kingdom. The speaker even thinks he's doing God a favor by serving Him with his wonderful gifts and talents.

The problem here is that these desires are all driven by human ambition. These individuals have just switched their ambition from the world to God's kingdom. But the root is the same.

It's possible to clothe worldly ambition in the garb of religious sacrifice.

In such cases, denying one's soul means completely surrendering one's musical talent, oratory skills, or any other talent completely to Jesus, laying them down at the foot of His cross and agreeing that if the Lord chooses to never use them again, it's okay with us.

When we offer ourselves to the Lord, our natural talents belong to the Lord. And He can do whatever He wishes with them. This includes having them die and rise again from the dead in a different form, energized by His life and not by our fallen human life. Or He may just choose to have them lie in ashes.

I'm keenly aware that what I'm saying runs contrary to the modern church push for congregants to quickly "identify" and "use" their gifts. But this isn't the mind of God. It's no accident that Paul's discussion of spiritual gifts in Romans 12 follows his exhortation to offer our bodies on the altar of death.

I hope you're beginning to get an impression of how deep our sacrifice to God goes. Surrendering to Christ as King means laying *everything* at His feet, including our ambitions, our talents, our dreams, our reputation, our hopes, and even our gifts. It means accepting an obscure life if that's what God wills for us.

This is the attitude that marks those who go all the way into the kingdom.

An End to Your Future

. . .

Let's get back to the example of the sacrificial bull.

From the bull's viewpoint, he has no future. He is finished. True consecration means that we aren't here for achievement. Our dreams, ambitions, and aspirations—whether worldly or religious—are burnt up in flames.

The Western enterprise is woven into millions of believers today. That enterprise teaches us that "bigger" and "more" is what we should strive for. As a result, countless Christians embrace an ambition to do something great for God. But if you peel back the layers of that onion, self is lurking behind it all.

Indeed, the pleasure of being used, recognized, and seen as valuable to God must be laid upon the altar and burnt to ashes.

The altar also means the willingness to lose our reputations. Most assuredly, if you go all the way with the Lord in His kingdom, you will attract opposition, persecution, slander, and smears.

Let me ask: Are you willing to let your reputation go to the cross? Are you willing to see it go up in ashes?

If your heart is willing, God will meet you. He will bring you through deeper waters to get what He wants.

I'll be candid. You cannot do this on your own. Neither can I. No one can. But by God's grace and mercy, you can get started. And you can yield yourself to Him again and again.

Why? So that Jesus Christ might have a people who have no other ambition than to be utterly His, and His alone.

This is the motivation of the insurgence.

The Charter of the Kingdom

• • •

A charter is an official document that outlines the conditions, rights, and privileges of a sovereign nation. Matthew chapters 5 to 7—the so-called Sermon on the Mount—lays out a charter for God's kingdom.

In the ministry of Jesus, we see the inbreaking of God's future kingdom on earth. The kingdom of God is the new world breaking into the old. And the Sermon on the Mount is a description of what life in that new world looks like.

Beyond everything else, Matthew 5–7 describes the character of Jesus Christ, the King. As we let Christ live His life in and through us, these characteristics will find expression in our lives.

The charter of God's kingdom involves turning the other cheek when attacked, going the extra mile when pressured, loving our enemies when treated unjustly, and forgiving those who don't deserve it.

It means treating others the same way you want to be treated in every situation. It means benefiting others at the expense of ourself.

We as individuals cannot possibly live up to the standards of the kingdom. But a local expression of Christ that's learning to live by His life can.

For this reason, the Sermon on the Mount was given primarily to the Lord's disciples, those who were called to be the collective nucleus of God's sovereign rule (Matthew 5:1–2).

Spiritual Violence

. . .

Just as the Israelites took the land of Canaan by physical violence, we "press into" the kingdom of God today by an act of *spiritual* violence.

And from the days of John the Baptist until now the kingdom of heaven suffers violence, and the violent take it by force. (Matthew 11:12 NKJV)

The law and the prophets were until John. Since that time the kingdom of God has been preached, and everyone is pressing into it. (Luke 16:16 NIV)

Another term for violence is "aggressive desperation."

Only those who are desperate and take violent action toward the things that are preventing them from experiencing the fullness of Christ are those who will enter the fullness of God's kingdom.

The more violent you take the kingdom, the more sure is your citizenship and the more established is your transformation.

By dealing with each area of your life in a ruthless, desperate, relentless manner, you're giving the Lord free course in your life. You're opening the door to experience the fullness of His kingdom.

T. Austin-Sparks put it this way:

The Kingdom means a very great deal more than merely getting into it, far more than being converted. There is a great deal more in the purpose of God for our lives than we have ever imagined, and if we are to enter into that, violence has to characterize us. We must desperately mean business. . . . The only way for us to come into all that the Lord means—not only into what we have seen but into all that He has purposed—is to be desperate, to be men of violence; to be men who say, "By God's grace, nothing and no one, however good, is going to stand in my way; I am going on with God." Have that position with the Lord, and you will find that God meets you on that ground.[5]

The fact is, if we don't thoroughly deal with the things that hold us back, we will get only so far in Christ.

Therefore, since we are surrounded by such a great cloud of witnesses, let us throw off everything that hinders and the sin that so easily entangles. And let us run with perseverance the race marked out for us. (Hebrews 12:1 NIV)

I exhort you, then, to come into the Lord's presence and declare those things in your life that must go. I urge you to deal with the Lord to the fullest limits and hold nothing back. Not just for yourself, but for the kingdom. Why? So that Jesus Christ might have something for Himself that nothing can shake or blow over (Matthew 7:24–27).

All who are part of the insurgence have dealt violently with the Lord so that He might gain further ground in their lives.

Break Up Your Fallow Ground

· · ·

Fallow ground is land that hasn't been tilled or broken up. It is unplowed, hardened soil. Imagine a farmer. He owns 500 acres of land. But he leaves 200 acres unused. That land lies fallow.

There are parts in you that have never been broken up for Jesus Christ. There's land in you that has never been plowed. There's ground in you that has never been cultivated or seeded. There are acres in you that have never been tilled, employed, or exercised for Christ.

Imagine a field. The ground is so hard that even a sharp-ended shovel can't penetrate it. Then imagine a tiller with sharp blades churning up the soil, making it soft, pliable, and ready for seed.

In the same way, it is the Lord's desire to break up the fallow ground of your heart.

> Sow for yourselves righteousness; reap steadfast love; break up your fallow ground, for it is the time to seek the LORD, that he may come and rain righteousness upon you. (Hosea 10:12 ESV)

So I lay down a challenge: Allow the Lord to gain more of you until He has all of you. The vessel must be enlarged to contain the riches of God's kingdom. And this requires that the vessel be broken.

How? I will address that question in the next chapter.

Wrestling With God

· · ·

James gives us the flavor of what it looks like when a person wrestles with God violently, seeking to break up the fallow ground of their hearts.

> Submit yourselves, then, to God. Resist the devil, and he will flee from you. Come near to God and he will come near to you. Wash your hands, you sinners, and purify your hearts, you double-minded. Grieve, mourn and wail. Change your laughter to mourning and your joy to gloom. Humble yourselves before the Lord, and he will lift you up. (James 4:7–10 NIV)

I don't want to use any personal illustrations, so I will use the experiences of friends who have dealt with the Lord in a violent way. (They did this to achieve certain objectives, such as to seek God's presence, to purge themselves from certain besetting sins, to see prayers answered, to move further into God's kingdom, to receive divine guidance, to make a way for the Lord to do His deeper work, and so forth.)

Examples: Praying outside wearing shorts in the rain. Pursuing the Lord while fasting (only drinking water) for days. Praying all night with one's face buried in the floor. Crying out to God with hands wringing. Beating the bed, throwing pillows, raising one's voice, kicking the walls, fasting from television and movies for weeks while seeking the face of God. For married people, fasting from sex for a time to subdue the body and deal with the Lord (1 Corinthians 7:5).

In the same vein, Paul talked about striking a blow to his body to make it his slave.

> No, I strike a blow to my body and make it my slave so that after I have preached to others, I myself will not be disqualified for the prize. (1 Corinthians 9:27 NIV)

These are just some of the things that holy men and women of God have done in their desperate, violent dealings with the Lord.*

---

* I give specific illustrations of how some people in the Gospels violently pressed into the kingdom in my audio message "Pressing Into the Kingdom," which can be found at InsuregenceBook.com.

Keep in mind that when I talk about dealing with the Lord desperately and violently, I'm speaking about something you do privately before God. Paul talked about being "crazy," "out of one's mind," and "beside one's self" *before God*, but in one's "right mind" *before others* (2 Corinthians 5:13 NIV, NLT, ESV).

Desperation is the currency of God's kingdom. The more desperate you are, the more ground you take in the kingdom.

Those who are part of the insurgence understand what it means to press into the kingdom of God by force.

Deal With Yourself, Not Others

· · ·

While I urge you to deal violently with those matters that must be removed from your life, I ask that you not deal violently with another brother or sister in Christ.

As Christians, we must not force others to do anything. So take what I've written for yourself and yourself only.

Also, don't make the mistake of handling any of these matters of your life for outward show. Take care of them wisely and discreetly and in a way that doesn't bring shame.

Without a shred of legalism, go to your Lord and deal with these matters privately. If something has got a stranglehold on you, consider going to one or two others whom you trust. But again, do so in private.

Dealing with these matters is how we make progress in the insurgence.

What Holds Us to the Altar?

· · ·

Once you've laid yourself on the altar of burnt offering, what will hold you there? What will prevent you from climbing off it?

I believe two things will keep you there. These two things are easy to forget, so it's wise to find ways of reminding yourself about them:

1. A deep and firm realization that Jesus Christ owns you. We can easily forget that, so regular reminders are helpful.
2. The love of Christ. The love that compelled you to put yourself on the altar in the first place is the same love that will keep you from climbing down from it.

For Christ's love compels us . . . that those who live should no longer live for themselves but for him who died for them and was raised again. (2 Corinthians 5:14–15 NIV)

Keep yourselves in the love of God. (Jude 21 NASB)

Many years ago, I delivered a series of messages on our glorious liberty in Christ to a young church. In response to those messages, a young woman made this statement in one of our gatherings:

The moment He set me free was the moment He captured me.

That's something worth remembering.

Notice that when speaking of consecrating our lives to the Lord, Paul prefaced his exhortation with "the mercies of God" in Romans 12 and then with "the love of Christ" in 2 Corinthians 5.

It is by the love and mercy of God that we are empowered to give our lives completely to Jesus Christ. God calls you and me out of the world system to be brought into the riches of His kingdom, and that call issues out of love.

He brought us out from there in order to bring us in, to give us the land which He had sworn to our fathers. (Deuteronomy 6:23 NASB)

The need, then, is to continue to be compelled and impelled by the Lord's love.

So make it a regular practice to allow the Lord to touch you with His love. Make it a habit to behold His tender mercies wherein you can say, "I want nothing but the Lord and to know Him."

In this regard, Watchman Nee rightly observed,

> Love, therefore, is the basis of consecration. No one can consecrate himself without sensing the love of the Lord. He has to see the Lord's love before he can ever consecrate his life. It is futile to talk about consecration if the love of the Lord is not seen. Having seen the Lord's love, consecration will be the inevitable consequence.[6]

To make this practical, I recommend that from time to time, you go back through Part II of this book and reimplement the "Taking Action" recommendations.

In short, the best way to renew your love for Christ is to review His love for you.

The Edge of the Altar

Throughout my Christian life, I've watched young men and women come to the edge of the altar, only to back off because some luring part of the world was knocking at their door.

For some, it was a get-rich-quick scheme. For others, it was a boyfriend or girlfriend who had no heart for Jesus Christ. For still others, it was an opportunity to gain name, fame, or game.

They said "yes" to the world and "no" to the kingdom. These young people lacked the violence for the kingdom that I've been writing about.

Therefore, open yourself up to the love of Christ, and let it compel you. Now and in the future.

Rules Versus Life

In the previous chapters, I've talked about some heavy things, but I've not given you any rules. Nor have I made specific applications. If you have been born from above, you have spiritual instincts. If your heart belongs to the Lord Jesus and His kingdom, you will be able to discern and follow those instincts.

One caveat. If you are sitting under a teacher who is teaching things that run against your spiritual instincts, you will likely turn deaf to those instincts.

Years ago I watched a church sit under a teacher who taught that God wasn't concerned about the lost or the poor. God was only concerned with the church and the people in it.

The result? I saw Christians who once had a heart for the lost and the poor lose interest in both. What happened? Those people replaced the voice of the Holy Spirit with the voice of this teacher. And they ignored their spiritual instincts.

It is for this reason that false teaching is so dangerous. If we ingest a false teaching, it can make us immune to the voice of the Spirit.

If Christ lives in you, you have an instinct to help the poor. You have an instinct to see the lost saved. You also have an instinct to deal with those things that are keeping you from entering into and enjoying the fullness of God's kingdom.

Again, I'm writing this section of the book to open an avenue for you to deal with your Lord. If you have any arguments, take them up with Him. My goal is to see you join the insurgence and make progress in it.

Surviving Failure

One of the marks of those who are part of the insurgence is that they can survive anything. Come dark times or bright times, dry spells or wet spells, their devotion to Jesus Christ is settled and irrevocable. So much so that nothing can blow them over, not even failure.

The Christian life is depicted by a race: Paul rejoiced that he finished the race well (2 Timothy 4:7). Someone cut in on the Galatians and shoved them off the track (Galatians 5:7). The writer of Hebrews exhorts his audience to run the race with endurance (Hebrews 12:1). We also discover that a person can disqualify themselves from the race (1 Corinthians 9:24–27).

Over the last three decades, I've watched Christians, including mighty servants of God, start the race out powerfully, even burning up the track, only to disappear from it years later. One of the reasons is that they were unable to survive failure.

The track is littered with the carcasses of those who couldn't survive failure, so they threw in the towel and disappeared.

The standards I've been raising in this book are high, even impossible. But those who have given themselves utterly to the King and His kingdom keep their hands on the plow, even when they fail.

I call Peter as a witness. It can be argued that no one's sins loomed as large as Simon Peter's. The man who is universally known as "the chief apostle" struggled with the fear of men all his life. He betrayed Jesus during His darkest hour. Not once, not twice, but three times. And not before a political or religious leader, but before a lowly servant girl.

Yet Peter survived his failure. Jesus Christ not only had mercy on Peter, but He commissioned him to feed His sheep just days later.

Years later, Peter, the man who opened the doors of the kingdom to both the Jews and the Gentiles, feared mortal man again. He folded under pressure when certain leaders from Jerusalem urged him to stop eating with the Gentile believers in Antioch. (For this reason, Paul rebuked Peter to his face for his hypocrisy.)

Did Peter throw in the towel then? No. He survived the failure once again.

Finally, at the end of his life, tradition tells us that Peter began to flee Rome to avoid martyrdom. But on his way out of the city, Jesus appeared to him, and Peter asked, "Lord, where are you going?" (*Quo vadis?* in Latin). Jesus replied, saying, "I'm going to Rome to be crucified again."

According to the story, Peter turned around and walked back into the city of Rome, where he was crucified for his Lord.

Just like you and me, Peter was a pile of failures. Yet he obeyed the gospel of the kingdom despite his blunders.

And so it is with all who are part of the insurgence. They treat their failures the same as their successes—*as dung*. What is important to them is not whether they fail or succeed, but that they were counted worthy of the privilege of the fight. And that despite their failures and setbacks, they keep pressing on to know the Lord and finish the race.

> And let us run with perseverance the race marked out for us. (Hebrews 12:1 NIV)

> I have fought the good fight, I have finished the race, I have kept the faith. (2 Timothy 4:7 NIV)

> Let us know; let us press on to know the LORD; his going out is sure as the dawn; he will come to us as the showers, as the spring rains that water the earth. (Hosea 6:3 ESV)

Pushing Reset

. . .

For most of us, to go on with the Lord requires a fresh start. This is what repentance and baptism represented in the first century—a complete break with the past and a new beginning.

If you are a new Christian, what I've said up until this point will give you a strong foundation in your life with Christ. If you've been a Christian for a while, consider this the first day that you were converted. This is an opportunity to reset your Christian life and become an active part of the insurgence.

You're now leaving your old life behind and making a clean break with it. You're shutting the door on your past and setting things right before your God.

Meet Ron

* * *

I met Ron in college.

Ron and I were involved in several on-campus Christian groups, and he was completely devoted to the Lord.

Years later, however, Ron confessed to me and others that he had been highly addicted to pornography ever since he was a teen. He became violent in his pursuit to be free, and the Lord honored it.

What was interesting is that his addiction caused him to compromise his surrender to the Lord in areas that he never realized. Yet after breaking his addiction, he was able to commit every other area of his life to the Lord.

As a result, Ron's hunger for the Lord increased dramatically, and he began to perceive spiritual things like never before. He also experienced God's blessings in his life in ways that exceeded his expectations. The Lord brought a young woman into his life, and they eventually married.

Ron took a violent attitude toward his addiction, and with the Lord's empowerment, he was freed from it. The spiritual benefits that came with that freedom were beyond what he expected.

This experience is available to all who have been radicalized for the kingdom of God.

Meet Shelly

• • •

Shelly grew up in a traditional Christian home. For many years, she was part of one of the world's largest denominations, known for preaching a salvation of grace for the lost and religious duty for the saved.

Years later, she began gathering with a fellowship I was working with. And for the first time in her life, she heard the glorious gospel of the kingdom in one blistering message.

Shelly was arrested by the stunning beauty and majesty of Christ. And she was captured by the piercing message of the kingdom. She opened her heart to the message and began loving the Lord like never before.

As she continued with the fellowship, she learned more about the grace of Christ and the uncompromising nature of His kingdom. One day in a fellowship meeting, Shelly stood up and gave this testimony:

> I have been raised a Christian since I was a child. I've been meeting with you all for about a year now. I was listening to the Christian radio, as I sometimes do, and a song came on. The singer was singing about how unworthy she was and how she needed to try harder to please God. She sang that her righteousness was as filthy rags, and she needed to improve her spiritual walk. I paused and suddenly realized that I couldn't relate to that song anymore. I couldn't relate to it because I've been given new eyes to see myself in Christ. For many years I struggled with a sense of unworthiness, guilt, and condemnation. But that's all gone now. I don't have it anymore, and I feel so free in the Lord's love.

When Shelly shared this testimony, the room erupted. Others began to testify along the same lines.

It was an awesome experience. Shelly had laid hold of the same spiritual reality that the first Christians possessed—that she was in Christ, and Christ was in her. And the gospel of the kingdom—the radical gospel of grace and purity—set her free from all things religious and artificial.

Touching the Throne

I hope that ten years from now, twenty years from now, even thirty years from now you can make this statement: "When I read *Insurgence* in the year [date], I gave my life to Jesus Christ like never before. And He took it."

I urge you before the Lord to wrestle with God until you can make that statement.

In Romans 12:1–2, Paul exhorted the Christians in Rome to offer their bodies as one living sacrifice. But even more, he urged them not to be conformed to this world.

In the next part, I will speak more about the world system and how deep it runs in our veins. But for now, I want you to know that there's not a human alive who has left the world system behind without a violent attitude toward it. Our roots are just too deep. So to leave it behind requires a convulsive uprooting or else we're just fooling ourselves.

Many Christians want a relationship with the Lord halfway between the world and the altar. They want to have all that's pleasurable of the world and all that's pleasurable in God.

But that's impossible. We cannot serve two masters. You cannot live in conformity to the pattern of this world and place yourself on the altar.

In light of all that I've written so far, I ask that you touch the throne of God with me by offering up this prayer to Him:

Lord Jesus, You have every right to me. I want to be considered worthy to be counted among those who have sought Your highest. To be part of a people who can pass through anything and not be moved. A people who have offered themselves to You again and again, totally and without conditions, contracts, or stipulations.

I don't ask for glory, blessings, or even to be used. I am simply grateful for the privilege of the race.

Lord, I want to be part of Your people who exist only for You and Your kingdom.

A people who are Your complete possession.
A transformed people.
A surrendered people.
A cross-bearing people.
A dead people.
A risen people.
An ascended people.
A people who are wholly Yours.
A people who live for You, by You, and to You.
A people who can pass through the depths and the heights.
Lord, make up the gap between where I am and where You are. Deepen Your work in me.
Give me grace and mercy to throw out the clock and forget the calendar. I know this will take time. But I resolve to begin . . . now.
Spare nothing, Lord.
Break up the unplowed ground in my heart.
Allow me to see something higher than I have ever seen before. For Your kingdom and for Your glory.
Amen.

The Lord is calling you into His kingdom (2 Thessaolians 2:12). He wants you to be part of "the people of the kingdom" (Matthew 13:38) and join the insurgence.

So enter in. And welcome home.

TAKING ACTION »

It's never good to hear or read about the high and holy things of the kingdom without taking action on them. In this regard, I recommend you do the following exercise, which includes taking a spiritual inventory of your life and dealing with the Lord violently over each of them. Consider these to be "housecleaning" items.

By God's mercy and grace,

1. Make a list of the things in your life that are immoral and terminate them.

2. Make a list of the things in your life that are idolatrous and destroy them in your heart.

3. Make a list of those things in your life that are improper and end them.

4. Make a list of those things in your life that are stolen and return them, making restitution.

5. Make a list of those things in your life that are unclean and eliminate them.

6. If you have an addiction, make a plan to go through the steps in my online article entitled "How to Break an Addiction" at Insurgence Book.com.

7. If you've never been baptized in water, or you were once baptized but you didn't fully understand what it meant at the time (so you just got wet), read my online article "Rethinking Baptism" at InsurgenceBook .com, and prayerfully consider getting baptized (or rebaptized with your new understanding of what baptism means).

   I've watched many people get rebaptized with great benefit. Jesus even exhorted one of His churches to "do the first works" when that church had fallen away from Him:

   > Remember therefore from where you have fallen; repent and do the first works, or else I will come to you quickly and remove your lampstand from its place—unless you repent. (Revelation 2:5 NKJV)

8. Finally, offer your body, soul, and spirit as a living sacrifice to God. Here is one way I suggest you do it. Write a brutally candid letter to your Lord, Jesus Christ. Begin with the words,

> Dear Lord, this is my life.

After that, write down what your life is made of. The good parts, the bad parts. Your talents and gifts. Your struggles. Your hopes, dreams, and ambitions. The letter may sound like this:

> Lord, this letter is my life. I have an ambition for . . . One of my dreams is to . . . I have a talent in . . . I have a struggle with . . . I have not been able to let go of . . .

Write down everything that makes you up as a person, and write it with sober honesty. It may take you days to write your letter.

When you finish, fold the letter, stick it in an envelope, seal it, and write on the envelope, "The Life of [Your Name]."

With Romans 12:1–2 firmly in mind, find a fireplace (or create a bonfire) which will represent the altar of burnt offering.

You're not vowing to be perfect or to never sin again. Instead, you're saying, "Lord, I consecrate my life to You. So take it. Consume me as a sweet-smelling offering for Your satisfaction. I am crawling on the altar symbolically. I'm giving You my life. All of it."

Having said that prayer, take your letter, throw it in the fire, and watch it burn.

Then celebrate by praising the Lord or worshiping Him with a song.

This is something that must come from your heart—willingly. It's not a rule, a law, or a stipulation. It's a suggestion.

Years ago, I gave this exercise to a local ekklesia, and it was a remarkable and unforgettable experience for all involved—a true milestone in the lives of every believer who did it. The ekklesia came to a fireplace with their sealed letters. And one by one, they threw their letters into the fire. They offered their "bodies" (plural) as "a living sacrifice" (singular).

So you can do this exercise with a group or as an individual. This is a wonderful way to throw your lot in with the insurgence.

But there's still more . . .

Part V
OUR GLORIOUS LIBERTY

In the New Testament, submission to the lordship of Christ goes hand in hand with the liberty of the Spirit. God created us to live freely by His grace. But that freedom is experienced when we live in full dependence upon Jesus and put ourselves under His lordship. In this part, we will explore our full-orbed freedom in Christ and expand some of the threads of legalism and libertinism that were introduced in Part I. A number of chapters will discuss the ongoing battle between the body of Christ and Satan, the kingdom of God and the world system.

Free Radicals

. . .

The difference between a radical religious terrorist and a radical Christian (in the New Testament sense) is that the radical Christian is completely free.

The person who has responded to the gospel of the kingdom is not in bondage to anything. Including religious laws and rules.

She doesn't serve God out of fear, condemnation, shame, guilt, religious duty or obligation. He is free in Christ, yet radically and totally committed to the Lord Jesus Christ and His kingdom.

That which marks the insurgence is total allegiance, total surrender, and total devotion to a living, breathing Person who has won the hearts of fallen humans.

I call these people free radicals.

Regrettably, countless Christians today live like Jews under the old covenant Law or Muslims under the Koran. They are striving to live by the external "letter" of the Law, rather than by the indwelling Spirit (2 Corinthians 3:6). And so they unwittingly turn the New Testament into a dead, cold rule book.

> But to this day whenever Moses is read, a veil lies over their [the Jews'] heart; but whenever a person turns to the Lord, the veil is taken away. Now the Lord is the Spirit, and where the Spirit of the Lord is, there is liberty. (2 Corinthians 3:15–17 NASB)

> For the letter kills, but the Spirit gives life. (2 Corinthians 3:6 NIV)

Such an approach throttles the power of the insurgence, which functions and grows by the Spirit of God and the grace of Jesus Christ.

Contrasts

The gospel of libertinism says, "You are welcome in God's kingdom, and you don't have to change."

The gospel of legalism says, "You are not welcome in the kingdom unless you change."

The gospel of the kingdom and Jesus Christ the King say, "I welcome you into my kingdom, and as a result, you will change."

Fully Accepted, Fully Freed

* * *

The gospel of the kingdom produces liberty, a liberty that Paul exuberantly called "the glorious liberty of the children of God."

> Because the creation itself also will be delivered from the bondage of corruption into the glorious liberty of the children of God. (Romans 8:21 NKJV)

The gospel liberates us from the bondage of the flesh (libertinism) as well as from the bondage of the Law (legalism).

The wonder of the gospel is that you are now in Christ, holy, righteous, and perfect. In Christ, you are fully accepted by a holy God.

> Yet now he has reconciled you to himself through the death of Christ in his physical body. As a result, he has brought you into his own presence, and you are holy and blameless as you stand before him without a single fault. (Colossians 1:22 NLT)

As I set forth in *Jesus Now*, you are under the new covenant. So there is no reason for you to have a guilty conscience or a sense of condemnation. If you are walking in condemnation and guilt, it's because you have turned away from the blood of Christ and have unseated yourself from your high estate in Christ.

Of course, if a person walks in the flesh, the Holy Spirit will illuminate their conscience. But that illumination is redemptive, not condemnatory. And there are few people who are more miserable than a person who is in Christ yet walking contrary to their new nature.

But we don't work *toward* victory, we work *from* it. As I put it in *Revise Us Again*, the Christian life is becoming what you already are.[1]

The truth is, if you're in Christ, you cannot be condemned. Why? Because Jesus Christ has already died for you and paid the full penalty for your sins. But that's not all. Christ has risen and sits at the right hand of God, making intercession for you (Romans 8:34).

Because you are in Christ, God is for you, so who can be against you (Romans. 8:31)? God didn't spare His own Son for you, so He will also freely give you all that you need (v. 32). No one can lay a charge against you (v. 33). And nothing in the universe and no one on the planet can separate you from His love (vv. 35–39).

This is where your life in the kingdom of God begins and this is where it ends.

A Liberated Captive

· · ·

Charles Kingsley was right when he wrote,

There are two freedoms—the false, where a man is free to do what he likes; the true, where he is free to do what he ought.[2]

The Lord Jesus Christ "gave himself for our sins to deliver us from the present evil age, according to the will of our God and Father" (Galatians 1:4 ESV).

The will of God in this verse refers to God's eternal purpose. That purpose is to deliver you from this present evil age, that is, the world system.

That's how Paul began his remarkable letter to the Galatians, which is a letter unfolding our incredible liberty in Jesus Christ.

Remember Lazarus of Bethany, the man whom Jesus loved. I believe Lazarus represents you and me before we met the Lord Jesus.

Like Lazarus, we were dead in our trespasses. Dead to God. Cut off from life. We were hopeless. So much so that we emitted the aroma of death.

Then Jesus came into our lives. And out of His abundant mercy and grace, He called us with the words, "Come forth!" And within that call was a complete and total acceptance. An acceptance with no strings attached.

That's right. God's acceptance of you isn't tied to how much you pray, read the Bible, witness to others, etc.

Lazarus did not earn this calling. He did nothing to deserve it. It was an act of divine mercy and grace. Jesus called Lazarus out of a heart of love (John 11:3, 5).

The sad reality is that countless Christians today, after they come to Jesus, hop on the hamster wheel of religious performance. They are trying to earn brownie points with a God who stopped keeping score. They are living in guilt and condemnation, trying to be "good enough" for God.

Here's the unmovable fact: your acceptance by God is exclusively tied to the fact that you are in His beloved Son by faith alone.

To the praise of the glory of His grace, by which He made us accepted in the Beloved. (Ephesians 1:6 NKJV)

When Lazarus came forth, He was bound in graveclothes. And the Lord said to those around him, "Loose him and let Him go."

In the same way, Jesus not only raised your dead spirit to life, but He freed you from religious bondage. Why? So you can be set free to love Him.

It was for freedom that Christ set us free; therefore keep standing firm and do not be subject again to a yoke of slavery. (Galatians 5:1 NASB)

In short, there is far more freedom under the rule of Jesus Christ than under your own.

Satan's Chief Attack

* * *

Beyond using the tool of deception, Satan's chief tactic against the children of God is to cast a shadow on God's love and unseat them from their holy and perfect status in Christ.

God's enemy seeks to malign the Lord by suggesting things like "God is against you. He's left you. He's not treating you fairly. He doesn't hear you. He doesn't care. He will bless others who are halfhearted while He leaves you out in the cold. It's not worth it to live totally for Him. What has it gotten you?"

Sound familiar?

The enemy constantly maligns God, raising doubts in our thoughts about His love. This was his way in the garden with Adam and Eve, and it was his way in the wilderness with Jesus.

Satan's intention is to get you off the ground of Christ's finished work and onto the ground of your own work.

He seeks to lure you into crawling back onto that religious hamster wheel, striving to make a holy God happy by your conduct.

He will do all he can to put you under condemnation. For this reason, he is "the accuser of the brethren," accusing God's children in their consciences "day and night" (Revelation 12:10).

But please remember that you have an Advocate with God the Father, Jesus Christ the Righteous—the One who gave His life for you. Consider John's words:

> My dear children, I write this to you so that you will not sin. But if anybody does sin, we have an advocate with the Father—Jesus Christ, the Righteous One. He is the atoning sacrifice for our sins, and not only for ours but also for the sins of the whole world. (1 John 2:1–2)

How, then, do we fight against these mental assaults? Simply trust in the blood of Christ and regard it just as the Father does. The blood was enough

217

to forgive, cleanse, and cover your sins. Consequently, the blood of Jesus is the only antidote to a guilty conscience and the sense of condemnation.

It is by "the blood of the Lamb" that we overcome "the accuser of our brethren" (Revelation 12:10–11 NKJV).

> Blessed be the God and Father of our Lord Jesus Christ, who has blessed us with every spiritual blessing in the heavenly places in Christ, just as He chose us in Him before the foundation of the world, that we should be holy and without blame before Him in love, having predestined us to adoption as sons by Jesus Christ to Himself, according to the good pleasure of His will, to the praise of the glory of His grace, by which He made us accepted in the Beloved. In Him we have redemption through His blood, the forgiveness of sins, according to the riches of His grace. (Ephesians 1:3–7 NKJV)

Free for Christ

. . .

Read my words carefully. You have been made free *by* Christ so that you can live *for* Christ. Jesus didn't die so you can be free *to* sin. He died so that you would be freed *from* sin.

Freedom in Christ, then, isn't freedom from Christ.

Freedom is the ability to do what you desire. A true follower of Jesus who has God's life dwelling within him or her wants to live for the kingdom of God. No genuine Christian desires to live in bondage. And no true Christian wants to be gripped by ideas and practices that harm them and others.

But there is a counterfeit freedom, and it enslaves. That counterfeit freedom is bondage operating under the guise of liberty. Peter declared war on this brand of "freedom" when he wrote, "They promise freedom, but they themselves are slaves" (2 Peter 2:19 NLT).

If a man preaches freedom, and worldliness breaks out everywhere among those to whom he preaches, there's a good chance he is not preaching freedom. He's preaching something else.

The Works of the Law

. . .

Some scholars have tried to argue that the phrase "the works of the Law" in Romans and Galatians only refers to certain ceremonial laws in the Old Testament. Specifically, circumcision, the Sabbath, and the dietary laws.*

Upon close scrutiny, however, this argument disintegrates. In Paul's mind, if a person is going to be circumcised to please God, they must also keep the entire Law of Moses.

> Again I declare to every man who lets himself be circumcised that he is obligated to obey the whole law. (Galatians 5:3 NIV)

The phrase "the works of the Law" actually refers to acts done in obedience to the Mosaic Law. It refers to the actions commanded, demanded, and prescribed by the Law. It is the attempt to do everything the Law commands and refrain from everything the Law forbids. And it has in view the entire Law of Moses, not just certain parts of it.

Whenever I stare at a commandment in the Bible and say to myself, "I've got to obey this, and I'm going to do my best to obey it," I've put myself under the works of the Law.

But here's the problem. The Law is a mirror. So if I try to obey it, one of two things is going to happen:

1. I'm going to come under condemnation. Why? Because I will quickly discover that I cannot obey the Law. Paul said that it is by the Law that a person knows that they are a sinner (Romans 3:20; 7:7–20). He also wrote that "sin derives its power from the Law" (1 Corinthians 15:56 Weymouth).

   In other words, if I try to meet the demands of the Law, I will entice the sin that's already in my flesh. This is because the Law

* These scholars hold to what's known as "the New Perspective on Paul." While I agree with some parts of this perspective, especially how it grounds salvation in God's larger purpose, I believe it falls short in its teaching on legalism and "the works of the Law."

exposes and awakens sin, but it gives no ability to keep God's commandments.

Read Romans 7 and you will see the experience (or the biography) of a person who is trying to obey the Law in their own power. They live in perpetual frustration and condemnation.

2. The other thing that may happen is that I will delude myself. Some people imagine that there's no dirt on their face. So they think they are actually obeying the Law when they are not.

What's really happening, however, is that they don't have enough knowledge of what the Law says. Instead, they focus on some of the commandments they believe they are keeping, but ignore others they are actually breaking. So they deceive themselves.

Again, many Christians today live like Old Testament Jews. On this score, F. F. Bruce remarked,

I think Paul would roll over in his grave if he knew we were turning his letters into torah.[3]

If a person is honest, the result of this approach is defeat. If they are dishonest, the result is hypocrisy.

This is what legalism breeds.

The Four Faces of the Legalist

* * *

Every legalist has four faces.

Face 1. The legalist acts out of religious duty or fear of divine punishment. The reason why the legalist attends church gatherings is out of religious duty. The reason why he prays is religious duty. The reason why he reads his Bible is religious duty. He is afraid of divine punishment or divine rejection. He is under the moral obligation of the Law. His motive is selfish. There's no freedom in it. It's simply bondage.

Face 2. The second face of the legalist is that she acts out of self-exerted energy. She tries to be holy. She works hard at being "a good Christian." She grits her teeth, bites her nails, and clenches her fists. She, in effect, is doing her best to make God happy.

Face 3. The third face of the legalist is that he adds his own personal standards and equates them with God's demands. In addition, he pushes those standards on everyone else. "Read your Bible every day. Pray every day. Witness to one person every day. Don't listen to secular music. Don't watch television shows that contain profanity or violence." And on and on. What's interesting is that none of these specific commands are found in the Bible.

Face 4. The legalist is self-righteous and judgmental. She makes a career out of making sure that everyone else is observing her personal standards. Sadly, however, she is deceived. She is out of touch with the fact that she is just as ruined and fallen as everyone she condemns.

This brings us to the problem of sin metrics.

Sin Metrics

• • •

Philip Yancey has a friend who once said, "Christians get very angry toward other Christians who sin differently than they do."[4]

I grew up in a denomination that made homosexuality the gravest of all sins, trumping every other transgression (except murder, maybe).

Many of the people in that church were dutifully self-righteous when it came to certain sins. Those who didn't commit the sins they deemed the worst (externally, that is) saw themselves as more "pure" than their fellow brethren who may have stumbled in those areas.

I regret to say that in my early years as a Christian, I adopted this same attitude. Ironically, these same people winked at the sins of gossip, slander, outbursts of rage, judging the motives of others, and lying. Excuses were routinely made in an attempt to justify these "lesser" sins (so the thinking went). In addition, most of us were monumentally disinterested and unmoved by things like poverty, racism, sexism, genocide, and homelessness.

Later in my journey, I started to give attention to these other problems. And I became friends with a group of Christians who viewed the worst kinds of sins as being societal. These people regarded failure to try to alleviate poverty, stop genocide, and curb homelessness to be the worst kinds of sins, while (unfortunately) sexual sins were almost winked at. Their view on sin was the exact opposite of the first group I mentioned.

In this regard, James makes an eye-opening statement: "For whoever keeps the whole law and yet stumbles at just one point is guilty of breaking all of it" (2:10).

In the same vein, Jesus turns the conversation on its head when He says, "You have heard that it was said to the people long ago, 'You shall not murder, and anyone who murders will be subject to judgment.' But I tell you that anyone who is angry with a brother or sister will be subject to judgment. . . . And anyone who says, 'You fool!' will be in danger of the fire of hell" (Matthew 5:21–22 NIV).

And again: "You have heard that it was said, 'You shall not commit adultery.' But I tell you that anyone who looks at a woman lustfully has already committed adultery with her in his heart" (Matthew 5:27–28 NIV).

Then there's Paul, who places sexual sins in the same list as "fits of rage," "discord," "dissensions," "selfish ambition," and "slander"—all of which bar one from inheriting the kingdom of God if not repented of (Galatians 5:19–21; 1 Corinthians 6:9–10). In these texts, James, Jesus, and Paul level the playing field on sin, showing that every believer is guilty of so-called "dirt" (1 John 1:8).

For Jesus, lust and adultery are on the same par. The same with rage and murder. For Paul, slander and outbursts of rage are no less serious than fornication.

One of my favorite stories underscores this point with clever wit. Allegedly, Charles Spurgeon invited D. L. Moody to speak at an event he hosted. Moody accepted and preached the entire time about the evils of tobacco, and why the Lord doesn't want Christians to smoke.

Spurgeon, a cigar smoker, was surprised at what seemed to be a cheap shot leveled by Moody, using the pulpit to condemn a fellow minister.

When Moody finished preaching, Spurgeon walked up to the podium and said, "Mr. Moody, I'll put down my cigars when you put down your fork."

Moody was overweight.

This story makes the point brilliantly.

George MacDonald famously said, "I understand God's patience with the wicked, but I do wonder how He can be so patient with the pious."

If we're going to play the "your sins are worse than mine" game, we shouldn't be remiss in looking at what made Jesus' blood boil when He walked this earth. Who was He the angriest at? The answer is a lead-pipe cinch for any student of Scripture. It was the self-righteous, pious, condemning, judgmental Pharisees. The self-appointed monitors of other people's righteousness.

The Pharisees reveled in their elite religious status and treated "sinners" with shame, contempt, and exclusion.

Who was Jesus the most patient with? The very people whom my first denomination looked down their noses at as being the worst "sinners." In Jesus, the pyramid is inverted yet again.

The person who is adept at calling "dirt" in others, but fails to see the dirt in himself or herself, is in a very dangerous place. Such is the nature of a Pharisee. Those sins that blind a person from seeing the weight of their own transgressions against that of others are treated as more serious by God.

In short, every sin comes off the same tree. All sin is serious. All sin put Jesus on the cross. Therefore, we are deluded whenever we lessen the sins we've committed and magnify the sins of others . . . whatever they might be.

Thank God that Jesus has paid the price for all our sins and given us the power to walk free from their dominion. Let us, therefore, be harsh with ourselves in the matter of sin and compassionate to everyone else.

When it comes to the issue of sin, the New Testament puts the emphasis on a person's present walk. Is a person continuing in a certain sin? This is where the issue of repentance comes in. (To repent means to stop doing it. It means to "Go and sin no more," as Jesus put it.) So if we know a brother or sister who is "overtaken in a fault" presently, let us seek to restore them in Christ (Galatians 6:1 KJV).

But it is paramount that as we do, we treat them the same way we would want to be treated if we were standing in their shoes, knowing that we are also weak and rely completely on God's grace to save us, "taking heed, therefore, lest we fall into the same thing or worse."

Freedom From the Law

There are two kinds of freedom. The freedom to do what your flesh wants (which is actually bondage), and the freedom to do what God wants (which is genuine liberty).

If a person claims to be free from the Law, but they are handcuffed to the world, they are deluded. They are not free in Christ; they're enslaved.

The Law is a shorthand phrase for the Law of Moses. The Law contains 613 laws; 365 of them are negative and 248 of them are positive.

In Romans 7, Paul said that the Law is good, holy, and just. In Romans 3, Paul said that we who are in Christ do not nullify the Law, we establish it. In 1 Timothy 1, he said that the Law was not made for a righteous person. It was made for the lawless.

God gave the Law to reveal the fact that we are sinners. This is why Paul said in Romans 7, "I would not have known sin except through the law" (v. 7 NKJV).

According to Galatians 3 and 4, the Law is no longer needed for the person who has come to Christ. The Law was our tutor to bring us to Christ (Galatians 3:19). After we give our lives to Jesus, we recognize that the Law serves a different function. It shows us the story of Jesus Christ.[*]

Again, the New Testament is clear that the Law was not made for the righteous but for the unrighteous. It's made for the lost, to bring them to Christ, not for those who are in Christ. This isn't my idea, by the way. Listen to Paul:

> But we know that the law is good if one uses it lawfully, knowing this: that the law is not made for a righteous person, but for the lawless and insubordinate, for the ungodly and for sinners, for the unholy and profane, for murderers of fathers and murderers of mothers, for manslayers, for fornicators, for sodomites, for kidnappers, for liars, for perjurers, and if there is any other

[*] See Sweet and Viola, *Jesus: A Theography* for how the story of Jesus is told in the Old Testament Law.

thing that is contrary to sound doctrine, according to the glorious gospel of the blessed God which was committed to my trust. (1 Timothy 1:8–11 NKJV)

To the believer, Jesus Christ is "the end of the Law" (see Romans 10:4; 8:3–4; 1 Corinthians 15:56; 2 Corinthians 3:6; Galatians 5:18; Ephesians 2:15; Colossians 2:13–14).

Paul sums up his attitude toward the Law by saying,

For through the law I died to the law so that I might live for God. (Galatians 2:19 NIV)

To those under the law I became as one under the law (though not being myself under the law) that I might win those under the law. To those outside the law I became as one outside the law (not being outside the law of God but under the law of Christ) that I might win those outside the law. (1 Corinthians 9:20–21 ESV)

Paul's words "under the law of Christ" are better translated "in-law to Christ." So the point is clear. Paul is free from the Law of Moses, but he is in-law to a Person, the Lord Jesus Christ.

One writer summed up the role of the Law well when he wrote,

> Run, John, run, the law commands
> But gives us neither feet nor hands,
> Far better news the gospel brings:
> It bids us fly and gives us wings.[5]

Those who are part of the insurgence know their freedom from the Law.

The Apostle of Grace

. . .

Grace is the act of God whereby He accepts you in your present condition. Grace is the Father finding favor with you because of the work of Another rather than because of your own. Grace is God receiving you completely and totally apart from your good deeds or bad deeds, your successes or failures.

You know what else grace is? Grace is when God puts up with you! Yes, the Lord will let you do things that are contrary to His will, and He will still love you, care for you, and accept you. Why?

Because you are His child.

Can you think of any earthly father who would disown his son or daughter if they broke one of the house rules? Most fathers would never do that. They would still accept their son or daughter, even when their child is bullheaded and disobedient.

How much more patient is your heavenly Father?

So grace puts up with you. Grace puts up with me. Grace accepts you—not for what you are doing or not doing, but on the basis of what Jesus Christ has done.

But grace also gives you the power to respond to God's will. And that power is not your own. It is *His* power—*His* life.

> For it is God who works in you to will and to act in order to fulfill his good purpose. (Philippians 2:13 NIV)

The gospel of the kingdom is built on the grace of God. That's why it's also known as the gospel of grace. We simply cannot respond to it or obey it outside of God's grace.

Introducing the Libertine

• • •

Paul battled legalism all his life. But he also dealt with the opposite error, libertinism. Jude described libertinism with these words:

> For certain individuals whose condemnation was written about long ago have secretly slipped in among you. They are ungodly people, who pervert the grace of our God into a license for immorality and deny Jesus Christ our only Sovereign and Lord. (Jude 4 NIV)

Peter and Paul also warned against libertinism, saying,

> Act as free men, and do not use your freedom as a covering for evil, but use it as bondslaves of God. (1 Peter 2:16 NASB)

> For you were called to freedom, brethren; only do not turn your freedom into an opportunity for the flesh, but through love serve one another. (Galatians 5:13 NASB)

Libertines turn the grace of God into immorality. They use their freedom in Christ as an opportunity to gratify their flesh.

Libertinism is the idea that because God has accepted you unconditionally, He doesn't care if you go out and sin to high heaven. It doesn't matter what you do because you are "under grace" (so the thinking goes).

But this is a perversion of God's grace. And it merely leads to a different kind of bondage—bondage to the flesh.

While Paul took dead aim at legalism in his letter to the Galatians, he declared war on libertinism in his first letter to the Corinthians.

In 1 Corinthians, Paul came out of the gate swinging blows of grace, declaring, you are "sanctified in Christ Jesus, called holy" (1:3 BLB). Yet he went on to say, "You are not your own; you were bought at a price" (6:19–20 NIV).

As Jesus-followers, we are called to hit the mark. We are called to be a people who are neither legalistic nor libertine, but a people who are under grace and who live by its power.

A Different Kind of Law

• • •

A person who lives by the indwelling life of Christ through the Holy Spirit is a person who is under a law. But it is not the Law of Moses. Nor is it a law that some preacher created from his own personal standards.

No, the law I'm referring to is "the law of the Spirit of life in Christ Jesus" (Romans 8:2 KJV). This law is like the law of gravity; it's a constant force or power.

You and I have an indwelling Lord. The Law of God has been written in our hearts because Jesus Christ lives within us by His Spirit. This is the promise of the new covenant (see Hebrews 8 and 2 Corinthians 3).

Spiritual people are those who live by the Lord's life that indwells them. They know by instinct what the will of God is (1 John 2:27).

When the Spirit leads them, they yield to it (for the most part)—no matter what the cost. And life and peace are the results (Romans 8:6).

The external Law, then, is no longer an outward thing full of dead letters and cold commands. It has been transferred into the indwelling life of Christ.

To live by Christ is our high calling as people of the insurgence.

The Battle of the Ages

· · ·

Since the creation of humans, there has been an ongoing battle over the territory of this earth. Every inch of it has been contested. God's enemy has wanted to dominate the real estate, which rightfully belongs to God.

This cosmic conflict is the reason why there is so much evil in the world.

The central issue of the universe is and always has been, *Who will have the worship? Who will sit on the throne? Who will be in charge?* In fact, those are the questions that stand behind all that happens in the visible creation.

Don't think of worship in terms of attending a church service, singing "praise and worship" songs, or honoring the name of Jesus. The meaning of worship touches much larger questions. Namely, worship is all about who will have the authority over our lives. Who will have our submission? Who will be given first place? Who will win our love, allegiance, and devotion?

True worship is absolute committal, surrender, and submission to God. We only worship in the measure that we are grateful for God's boundless grace and mercy. So worship is based upon deep gratitude for God's grace.

A. W. Tozer had it right when he described worship this way:

> For the Christian, everything begins and ends with worship. Whatever interferes with one's personal worship of God needs to be properly dealt with and dismissed. Keep in mind that above all else, worship is an attitude, a state of mind and a sustained act. It is not a physical attitude, but an inward act of the heart toward God.[6]

Worship, then, is the posture of our lives and the attitude of our hearts. It is the reason why we live, breathe, and have our being. According to Romans 12:1, worship is not an act but a lifestyle.

Drawing a Line in the Sand

• • •

Those who have drawn a line in the sand and decided to worship Jesus Christ have put a target on their back. The enemy will throw everything he can at them, just as he did with Jesus.

If you remember, one of the three temptations that Satan threw at Jesus in the wilderness was the issue of worship. He said to the Lord, "Fall down and worship me and I'll give you all the kingdoms of the world and their splendor" (Matthew 4:8–9, author paraphrase).

Worship of Satan and living for the kingdoms of this world (the world system) go hand in hand.

The devil has been challenging God's authority from the very beginning. All throughout the Old Testament, the enemy used idolatry to dissuade God's people from giving the "worth-ship" to the one true God. Satan does the same today through the attractive elements of the world system that beckon us to worship them.

Dominion Versus Domination

God's goal is world *dominion* through human beings as His image-bearing agents.

Satan's goal is world *domination* through manipulating humans into rejecting the authority of the true God. The all-consuming goal of every cult, false religion, repressive regime, and terrorist group is the domination of the world.

So there are two thrones in contention. And the battle is over your soul.

It seems logical to conclude that when we worship anything other than the true and living God, we give our God-given power to rule over to the enemy. This is precisely why Satan tempted Jesus in the matter of worship. And it's precisely how Satan usurped man's authority when he successfully tempted Adam and Eve in the garden.

All satanic activity in your life and mine is over the matter of worship. The insurgence is all about standing for God's dominion and resisting Satan's domination.

But here's the good news. God's dominion will not only win out in the end, but it will never cease.

> He will proclaim peace to the nations.
> His dominion will extend from sea to sea,
> from the Euphrates River
> to the ends of the earth. (Zechariah 9:10 HCSB)

Jesus Christ, the faithful witness, the firstborn of the dead, and the ruler of the kings of the earth. To Him who loves us and released us from our sins by His blood—and He has made us to be a kingdom, priests to His God and Father—to Him be the glory and the dominion forever and ever. Amen. (Revelation 1:5–6 NASB)

Those who have made the kingdom of God a matter of social activism and reform miss the central issue of the universe.

Systemic sin and individual sin entered the world because humans worshiped a creature instead of the Creator. Consequently, no matter what noble efforts are employed to work for social justice, if the issue of worship isn't resolved, proclaimed, and embodied, those noble efforts will be largely in vain. Why? Because the root of personal and social sin is completely ignored as well as the solution to it.

God's kingdom operates by relationship with the King, not rules or activities. Jesus Christ dealt with the root of systemic and individual sin on His cross. And therein, He also opened the way for true worship to be regained.

Those who stand for the kingdom of God today have given their worshiping allegiance to Jesus, and out of that flows everything else.

The Idolatry of Sin

The word "sin" doesn't just mean wrongdoing. It literally means "to miss the mark." Sin caused humans to forfeit their God-purposed design to bear His image and exercise His authority in the earth.

According to Romans 3:23, sin causes us to "fall short of the glory of God." But God's glory is His expression. Humans are destined to bear the glory, or the image, of God in visible form. This is God's original purpose (Romans 8:28ff.). This is why sin is really a matter of worship. As Paul says in Romans 1:23, humans "exchanged the glory of the immortal God" for the worship of idols.

When humans sinned, they lost the glory of God and handed over their God-given authority to the devil (an entity whom Paul calls "the god of this world" in 2 Corinthians 4).

The nature of all sin is selfishness. And the root of selfishness is idolatry. So idolatry is at the core of all sin. When a person sins, they either worship themselves above God or they worship something in the created order that God has made (Romans 1:23–25).

To be specific, when a person gives their life over to power, they are worshiping the false god Kratos.

When a person gives their life over to wealth, they are worshiping the false god Plutus.

When a person gives their life over to lust, they are worshiping the false god Aphrodite.

These false gods are really spiritual entities in the demonic world (Deuteronomy 32:16–17). They are the demonic spiritual powers that stand behind idols (Psalm 96:5; 106:36–37 ESV; 1 Corinthians 10:19–22). To put it another way, according to the Bible, idols represent evil spirits.

Idolatry is very difficult to recognize in our time. But the truth is, when our hearts become attached to possessions, pleasures, or power, it's effectively the same as an ancient pagan carving a statue out of wood and bowing down to it.

Temptation, therefore, is the enemy's effort to seduce and draw our hearts away from the true and living God to a false god. When that happens, we forfeit some of our power to be God's authority-bearers to an alien entity. And we "miss the mark" of fulfilling God's eternal purpose.

This, in essence, is how Adam and Eve were dominated by the devil. By succumbing to Satan's temptation, the first humans bowed their knees to him and forfeited their God-given power to rule the earth.

The nature of sin is selfishness, the core of sin is idolatry, but the essence of sin is pride. And it is pride that gives birth to rivalries and conflicts. These things have no place in the insurgence.

Sin Remixed

. . .

In the Old Testament, two additional words are used for sin—*transgression* (which means rebellion) and *iniquity* (which means perversion).

Sin is the poison that causes us to miss out on God's eternal purpose. Sin provokes us to rebel against God's intention and pervert our true mission by idolizing ourselves through pride, making us absorbed with self—self-interest, self-pity, self-will, self-sufficiency, etc.

Sin is the enchanting allure of that which kills us. We need a higher beauty, a more compelling loveliness to resist sin. When our eyes are not open to see the Lord's beauty, we are open to spiritual hazards like spiritual boredom.

Martin Lloyd-Jones is known for saying, "Sin is always, in some sense, a life of boredom."

William Blake was dead wrong when he wrote, "The road of excess leads to the palace of wisdom."[7] The road of excess leads to boredom and death. And that road is littered with the bodies of those who have chosen to walk on it.

Sin boils down to independence from God, and it is embodied in the tree of the knowledge of good and evil. "Has God said?" was the tempter's challenge, luring the woman into the illusion of self-sufficiency and independence. And the man followed suit.

So at the end of the day, sin always involves giving away power—a power designed to be used for the exercise of God's eternal purpose. Sin hands that power over to alien forces who have usurped the Lord's rule in the world.

And sin always leads to slavery.

This is made plain throughout the story of ancient Israel in the Old Testament.

In this regard, idolatry is the principal sin of humanity. We fell away from God because we worshiped something (or someone) other than God, and that has led to all kinds of immorality (Romans 1:18–32).

When we behold the beauty of Christ and experience the love shown to us by Jesus, we are drawn to worship Him and give up our false gods, no matter how attractive they may appear to be.

The Lord's beauty stokes the fire of the Christian life. The beauty of Christ is what woos us and fills the affections of our hearts.

Jesus said, "And I, when I am lifted up from the earth, will draw all people to myself" (John 12:32 NIV). Those words refer to Christ's crucifixion. The length that Jesus was willing to go to show His love for us is revealed on the cross.

When we rightly see what Jesus did for us on the cross and how He treats us today, we are drawn to worship Him. And this frees us from worshiping anything else.

A Tale of Two Kingdoms

. . .

The story of the Bible is the tale of two kingdoms that are at war with each other: the kingdom of God and the kingdom of Satan. The kingdom of Satan is also called "the world."

The New Testament author who wrote the most about divine life was John. In the Gospel of John, 1 John, 2 John, 3 John, and Revelation, John's unmistakable emphasis is that Jesus Christ is life—divine, eternal, real, abundant life.

Interestingly, the New Testament writer who wrote the most about the world system was also John.

There is a reason for this. The only way you and I will be able to go forward in Christ is to get clear on what the world is all about. A person who moves deeper in the life of God's kingdom is a person who has insight into what the Bible calls "the world." This is what John teaches us.

The Greek word that is translated "the world" is *kosmos*. John used it approximately 105 times in his writings.

Sometimes *kosmos* means the earth. Other times it means the people who inhabit the earth. But John and Paul often used it to refer to a system that governs fallen humanity.

In classic Greek, one of the meanings of *kosmos* (the world) is an "orderly arrangement" and "the system of human existence in its many aspects."[8] The Greek word *aion*, which is translated "age" and " world," refers to the present age in which the world system dominates (as opposed to the coming age when the kingdom of God governs the whole earth).*

Watchman Nee defined the world system perfectly when he wrote,

Behind all that is tangible we meet something intangible, we meet a planned system; and in this system there is a harmonious functioning, a perfect order.

* *Kosmos* (world) and *aion* (age) are used together in Ephesians 2:2. W. E. Vine, *Vine's Expository Dictionary of New Testament Words* (McLean, VA: MacDonald Publishing Company, 1989), 1256.

. . . There is, then, an ordered system, "the world," which is governed from behind the scenes by a ruler, Satan.[9]

So "the world" is a system that operates on earth and touches everything that's visible and natural. The world system relentlessly pulls in a certain direction. And that direction is always away from God. This is because Satan heads it up. Thus the natural drift of the world is opposed to God's kingdom.

Paul talks about this " drift" when he says that before we trusted Christ, we were "following the course of this world, following the prince of the power of the air, the spirit that is now at work in the sons of disobedience" (Ephesians 2:1–2 ESV).

F. F. Bruce described the world system this way:

On the one hand, the world is God's world, created by God and loved by God, currently alienated from God, it is true, but destined to be redeemed and reconciled to God. On the other hand, the world is dominated by a spirit totally opposed to God, organized in such a way as to exclude God, drawn towards unworthy goals of material status and self-interest, quite different from the goals toward which the Christian way leads.[10]

John Howard Yoder echoes Bruce and Nee, saying,

The "world" of politics, the "world" of economics, the "world" of theater, the "world" of sports, the under-"world," and a host of others—each is a demonic blend of order and revolt. . . . It is creaturely order in the state of rebellion.[11]

Along this line, Clinton Arnold wrote,

Paul's concepts of "world" (*kosmos*) and "this age" (*aión*) correspond most closely with what many modern interpreters describe as structural evil. . . . It is with good reason that Paul calls Satan "the god of this age (*aión*)" who "has blinded the minds of unbelievers, so that they cannot see the light of the gospel" (2 Cor. 4:4). We could legitimately say "Satan is the god of many of the structures that order our existence."[12]

The world system, then, is the order of things that prevails in humankind apart from redemption. It is the systems of this world that operate independent from God.

Let me be blunt. The number one hindrance that will keep you and me from growing in the life of God's kingdom is the world system.

An undivided heart is what the Lord is after. For this reason, may God cause us to be violent with our own hearts until they are free from compromise.

> You cannot drink the cup of the Lord and the cup of demons (1 Corinthains 10:21 NASB)

> You cannot serve both God and money. (Luke 16:13 NIV)

Tozer was on the mark when he wrote,

> Christianity is so entangled with the world that millions never guess how radically they have missed the New Testament pattern. Compromise is everywhere.[13]

Those who are part of the insurgence are allowing God to work in their lives, even through adversity and suffering, so that their hearts are purged to worship Jesus Christ without rival.

To better understand the world system, it's important for us to understand its conception and birth.

The World System Conceived

In the dateless past, one of the highest created beings among the angelic hosts revolted against God and was cast out of the heavenly realms. Pride filled Lucifer's heart and jealousy gripped his soul.

Some have presumed that he was jealous of God's Son and sought to supplant Him, securing God's rule in and for himself.

Others have proposed that Lucifer was jealous of God's new creation (humankind) through which God intended to rule the earth.

Whatever the origin of his pride and jealousy, Lucifer became God's enemy and found his place on God's created earth.

The kingdom of darkness was conceived on earth when the first humans bowed their knee to the devil in the garden. (The kingdom of darkness is another name for the world system.)

God hates the world system with a passion. He hates it because it keeps people away from His Son and thwarts His eternal purpose.

All who are in Christ have been translated from the kingdom of darkness into the kingdom of light (Colossians 1:12–13). It is called the kingdom of darkness because Satan works hidden, in secret, and he blinds the minds of those who are under his influence so they cannot detect his strategies (2 Corinthians 4:4).

Consequently, people who are in the kingdom of darkness don't know it because they are in the dark. It's called the kingdom of darkness because blindness marks it.

> The god of this age has blinded the minds of unbelievers, so that they cannot see the light of the gospel that displays the glory of Christ, who is the image of God. (2 Corinthians 4:4 NIV)

The Birth of the World System

When Adam and Eve rebelled against God in the garden, the world system was conceived. At that time, Satan—a fallen celestial being—became "the god of this world" (2 Corinthians 4:4 NLT) and the "ruler of the kingdom of the air" (Ephesians 2:2 NIV).*

God originally gave humans dominion over the earth (Genesis 1:26–28; Psalm 8:4–6). But in the garden, the first humans surrendered the earth and gave the title deed over to Satan.

By their disobedience, the first humans committed high treason and handed over the dominion God had given them to a fallen celestial creature. As a result, human beings thwarted God's eternal purpose. Satan became "the prince of this world" (John 12:31; 14:30; 16:11 NIV), thus he could offer Jesus all the kingdoms of the world because they are in his control (Matthew 4:8–10; Luke 4:6–7; 1 John 5:19).

Jacques Ellul put it clearly when he wrote,

> And the extraordinary thing is that according to these texts [Matthew 4 and Luke 4] all powers, all the power and glory of the kingdoms, all that has to do with politics and political authority, belongs to the devil. It has all been given to him and he gives it to whom he wills. . . . This fact is no less important than the fact that Jesus rejects the devil's offer. Jesus does not say to the devil: It is not true. You do not have the power over kingdoms and states. He does not dispute this claim.[14]

So when Adam and Eve yielded to the devil, the world system was *conceived*. But the world system was *born* at the hands of Cain, Abel's brother, when he left the presence of God. Consider this text:

> Then Cain went out from the presence of the LORD, and settled in the land of Nod, east of Eden. Cain had relations with his wife and she conceived,

---

* In Ephesians 2, Paul speaks of the air as the domain of the devil. The idea that the air was the realm where evil spirits were active is common in Jewish literature. They were called "aerial spirits."

and gave birth to Enoch; and he built a city, and called the name of the city Enoch, after the name of his son. (Genesis 4:16–17 NASB)

Notice the words: Cain "went out from the presence of the LORD" and "built a city."

Cain built a city that was independent from God.

Incidentally, when Cain left the presence of the Lord, he settled in "the land of Nod," which was located "east of Eden." Interestingly, when the ancient Israelites thought "east," they thought of Babylon, along with Persia and Assyria (the nations that would become Israel's enemies).

Consequently, if Eden was located in what later would be the promised land of Canaan (as we've already pointed out), it's reasonable to believe that Nod was located in Babylon. This idea meshes perfectly with the unbroken narrative of Jerusalem versus Babylon all throughout Scripture. God's presence is located in Jerusalem in Canaan (Eden) while Babylon (Nod) represents exile from God's presence.

As we read further in Genesis 4, we discover that the city Cain built (Enoch) contained the following elements:

- Provision (represented by livestock), Genesis 4:20.
- Enjoyment (represented by musical instruments), Genesis 4:21.
- Security (represented by bronze and iron, which were used to create weapons and fortification), Genesis 4:22.

Provision, enjoyment, and security *apart from God* are the ingredients of the world system. They are the central elements of fallen human civilization. John Nugent has insightfully remarked,

It is not hard to look at this list and see the core essentials of city life: food, entertainment, and industry. It is the beginning of civilization as we know it. . . . The strong connection between metalworkers and warfare is evident in 2 Kings 24:16, where metalworkers are presumed to be capable warriors . . . this account doesn't culminate in the glory of civilization, but in murder and escalating vengeance (Genesis 4:23–24).[15]

The city of Enoch represents the societal life of fallen humanity. Provision, enjoyment, and security are what humans seek to possess in the world apart from God.

Before the Fall

• • •

Before the first humans fell into sin, they lived in the conscious presence of God in the garden. And it was in God's presence that they found their provision, enjoyment, and security.

But when Cain left the presence of God, there was a void inside him that had to be filled. So Cain built the city of Enoch to fill that void.

Whenever a human being leaves God's presence today, there is a void that needs to be filled.

In the Garden of Eden, provision, enjoyment, and security were found in God, and thus they were pure. In the city of Enoch, however, they were distorted and put humans in bondage.

What, then, is the world? The world is the system that takes what is necessary for humanity—provision, enjoyment, and security—and distorts them to the point that they enchain, ensnare, ensnarl, and enslave human beings.

When these three elements are found outside of God's presence, they turn into the lust of the flesh, the lust of the eyes, and the pride of life.

God Starts Over

As we read the biblical story, we learn that the world system overtakes the earth. Humans become more and more depraved, and God destroys the earth with a mighty flood.

Only Noah and his family are saved. And God begins all over again, seeking to recover His eternal purpose.

The Lord's desire is that humans bear His image and exercise His dominion. His desire is for the kingdom of heaven to touch the earth and spread. Interestingly, the commission that God gave to Adam gets transferred to Noah in the new creation.

Noah has three sons. But one of them, Ham, carries with him something of the old world. Ham has a grandson named Nimrod, who builds another city. And that city is called Babel, which is another word for Babylon.

And with Babel, the world system reappears on the earth again.

All the while, the kingdom of the heavenlies doesn't touch earth. It hasn't since the Garden of Eden.

Fallen Human Civilization

. . .

Let's go back and review the story in Genesis 4.

Fallen human civilization is showcased with Lamech, a descendant of Cain. It is in Lamech that we have the first occurrence of unbridled lust in the form of polygamy, vengeance by the sword, and tyranny. Lamech's poem about vengeance in Genesis 4 has been called "The Song of the Sword."*

The sons of Lamech built weapons of war, instruments for entertainment, and the food industry. The world system is simply taking ordinary things (food, music, metals) and systematizing them apart from God until they possess and ensnarl the life of human beings.

John Nugent added further insight, saying,

> In Genesis 4, Lamech's legacy is not framed as progress, but regress. If all of this is so, then "those who seize instruments" could have negative connotations, just like the tent dwellers and metalworkers. Their occupation could refer to the way city dwellers numb their sense of estrangement from God's good creation with the soothing sounds of music. It could refer to the way kings of old commandeered music to serve imperial aims. . . . Cain's descendants merely institutionalized their estrangement from God's good creation, so God's salvation must come from somewhere else.[16]

After God sends the flood and starts over again, fallen human civilization reemerges and even develops. It is with Babel (Babylon) that we have the first use of the term "kingdom" in the Bible (Genesis 10:10).

Babel is the beginning of the nation-state. According to Nugent, "The state is thus a fallen institution that springs from human efforts at self-preservation."[17]

---

* John C. Nugent makes the case that human civilization began in Genesis 4. See *The Politics of Yahweh* (Eugene, OR: Cascade Books, 2011), 23, 34–36; John Nugent, *Polis Bible Commentary, Genesis 1–11*, vol. 1 (Skyforest, CA: Urban Loft Publishing, forthcoming), Genesis 4:17–24. See also Watchman Nee, *Changed into His Likeness* (Fort Washington, PA: CLC Publications, 2007), 23–77, for the history of human civilization from a spiritual perspective.

Significantly, the last time the word "kingdom" is used in the Bible, it's again in reference to Babylon (Revelation 17:17 NASB). Babylon is the outstanding symbol of all that's wrong with human civilization.

(While a discussion of the origins of the nation-state and human hierarchy is beyond the scope of this book, I have traced them in detail elsewhere.)[*]

Recall that when Israel wanted a king "like the other nations," God was severely displeased (1 Samuel 8). Yet the Lord granted Israel's request and used its various kings according to His own purposes, despite the harm they brought to Israel.

As I've traced in *From Eternity to Here*, the Bible is a tale of two cities— Babylon and Jerusalem—the city of the old man versus the city of the new man. These two cities represent the ongoing war between the world system and the kingdom of God.[†]

---

[*] See my online article "The Origins of Human Government and Hierarchy" at Insurgence Book.com. In the article, I present evidence supporting the idea that God made hierarchy for the celestial realm of angelic creatures, not for humans. And the nation-state government was not God's original idea.

[†] See Viola, *From Eternity to Here*, part 2. Jacques Ellul also traces the tale of two cities in his book, *The Meaning of the City* (Eugene, OR: Wipf & Stock, 2011).

False Security

. . .

All throughout the Bible, the city represents humanity's self-alienation from God. Enoch, Babel, Sodom, Ninevah, Egypt, Babylon, etc. all illustrate life without God.

God's original will for humanity was not the city but the garden. Israel—God's pilot project for returning to the life of Eden—was called to be a tribal people rather than a people who lived by the standards of fallen human civilization.*

The city emerged from man's conscious alienation from God. It was built to provide self-preservation and security. *A false security.* Of course, God still uses the city for redemptive purposes, even though it isn't His original will.

However, with respect to leaving God's presence, the disease began with Adam, it became acute with Cain, and it turned terminal with Nimrod.

Even Israel caved and embraced a false security by demanding a king to rule over them. God was sorely displeased with their decision to become like all the other nations and have a king. The Lord's people rejected God as their King and placed their security in a human king who would only disappoint them in the end (1 Sam. 8:1–22).

Putting your trust and hope in a city, country, government, business, or military is a hope misplaced and an evidence of false security.

> No king is saved by the size of his army;
>> no warrior escapes by his great strength.
> A horse is a vain hope for deliverance;

---

* God's design for His people in Torah (the Law) is tribal rather than "high civilization." And God's vision for His people in the New Testament follows suit. Before Israel demanded a king in order to be like all the other nations, the Hebrews lived a tribal life. They had no central government, but a decentralized federation of tribes. Only when the Israelites were dispersed from their land did they live in the fallen cities of men, living under pagan rulership models. See John C. Nugent, *The Politics of Yahweh*, chaps. 2, 3, and 7. The ekklesia—in God's thought—resembles a tribe instead of fallen human civilization. See Viola, *Reimagining Church.*

despite all its great strength it cannot save.
But the eyes of the LORD are on those who fear him,
  on those whose hope is in his unfailing love,
to deliver them from death
  and keep them alive in famine.

We wait in hope for the LORD;
  he is our help and our shield.
In him our hearts rejoice,
  for we trust in his holy name.
May your unfailing love be with us, LORD,
  even as we put our hope in you. (Psalm 33:16–22 NIV)

Jacques Ellul put it this way,

When Jesus says that his kingdom is not of this world, he says clearly what he intends to say. He does not validate any worldly kingdom (even if the ruler be a Christian).[18]

Those who are part of the insurgence have placed their security in Jesus Christ alone. Their trust lies in the power of His Spirit and His cross, not the sword or the vote.

God's Attitude Toward the World System

. . .

While God loves the earth and the people in it, the world system is His enemy. And He hates it with a passion.

> Do not love the world nor the things in the world. If anyone loves the world, the love of the Father is not in him. For all that is in the world, the lust of the flesh and the lust of the eyes and the boastful pride of life, is not from the Father, but is from the world. The world is passing away, and also its lusts; but the one who does the will of God lives forever. (1 John 2:15–17 NASB)

According to John, three chief temptations make up the world system:

- The lust of the flesh (the god of Aphrodite).
- The lust of the eyes—materialism and covetousness (the god of Plutus).
- The pride of life—worldly power and ambition (the god of Kratos).

Consider what James says about the world system:

> You adulteresses, do you not know that friendship with the world is hostility toward God? Therefore whoever wishes to be a friend of the world makes himself an enemy of God. (4:4 NASB)

Interestingly, the temptations that make up the world can be seen in the three temptations that the serpent used to tempt Eve in the garden.

> When the woman saw that the fruit of the tree was good for food [the lust of the flesh] and pleasing to the eye [the lust of the eyes], and also desirable for gaining wisdom [the pride of life], she took some and ate it. (Genesis 3:6 NIV)

These same three temptations showed up in the wilderness when Satan tempted Jesus. The temptation of the second Adam (Jesus) was simply a replay of the temptation of the first Adam.

Thankfully, the second Adam overcame each one.

The Mind Behind the System

. . .

In the New Testament, the mind behind the world system is Satan or the devil. Jesus Christ said so:

> Now is the time for judgment on this world; now the prince of this world will be driven out . . . the prince of this world is coming. He has no hold over me. . . . the prince of this world now stands condemned. (John 12:31; 14:30; 16:11 NIV)

And so did Paul:

> Satan, who is the god of this world, has blinded the minds of those who don't believe. (2 Corinthians 4:4 NLT)

> You used to live in sin, just like the rest of the world, obeying the devil—the commander of the powers in the unseen world. He is the spirit at work in the hearts of those who refuse to obey God. (Ephesians 2:2 NLT)

> For we are not fighting against flesh-and-blood enemies, but against evil rulers and authorities of the unseen world, against mighty powers in this dark world, and against evil spirits in the heavenly places. (Ephesians 6:12 NLT)

John did as well:

> The whole world lies in the power of the evil one. (1 John 5:19 ESV)

Notice John's words: "the whole world" is under the power of the evil one.

Get clear on this. The devil is the head of the world system that dominates this earth.* When you received Jesus Christ, however, you did not receive the spirit of the world. Instead, the Spirit of God who opposes the world system took up residence inside you:

---

* For a scholar's treatment of this point, see Clinton Arnold, *Powers of Darkness* (Downers Grove IL: InterVarsity Press, 1992), 80–82, 92–93, 203–4.

Now we have received not the spirit of the world, but the Spirit who is from God, that we might understand the things freely given us by God. (1 Corinthians 2:12 ESV)

One day the world system is going to end. It will be destroyed at the hand of Jesus Christ, and His unshakable kingdom will completely replace it. This is the hope of the insurgence.

Don't Invest in the World

. . .

Suppose I told you that First Domestic Bank will sink six months from now and everyone who has money there is going to lose it. You would be very foolish to put your money in First Domestic, wouldn't you?

In the same way, the clock is ticking on the world system. One day it will pass away. And that's one of the greatest revelations you and I can have in terms of breaking loose from any attachment we have to it.

The world system is doomed.

Every kingdom within its grip—be it economic, political, educational, military, and even religious—has the word "dethroned" written upon it with the ink of heaven.

Keep that in mind as we continue to explore how much God hates the world system and how much of an enemy it is to your soul.

Love Not the World

. . .

Israel's bones bleached in the wilderness because God's people loved Egypt, which represents the world system. Israel failed to take the high ground of Canaan because her heart was tied to the worldly pleasures of Egypt.

> These things happened to them as examples and were written down as warnings for us, on whom the culmination of the ages has come. (1 Corinthians 10:11 NIV)

Consider the following passages that give us insight into the world system, including its hatred for Jesus and His true followers:

> If the world hates you, you know that it hated Me before it hated you. If you were of the world, the world would love its own. Yet because you are not of the world, but I chose you out of the world, therefore the world hates you. (John 15:18–19 NKJV)

> I have given them Your word; and the world has hated them, because they are not of the world, even as I am not of the world. I do not ask You to take them out of the world, but to keep them from the evil one. They are not of the world, even as I am not of the world. (John 17:14–16 NASB)

> For the grace of God that brings salvation has appeared to all men, teaching us that, denying ungodliness and worldly lusts, we should live soberly, righteously, and godly in the present age. (Titus 2:11–12 NKJV)

> Through these he has given us his very great and precious promises, so that through them you may participate in the divine nature, having escaped the corruption in the world caused by evil desires. (2 Peter 1:4 NIV)

> For if, after they have escaped the pollutions of the world through the knowledge of the Lord and Savior Jesus Christ, they are again entangled in them and overcome, the latter end is worse for them than the beginning. (2 Peter 2:20 NKJV)

Do not conform to the pattern of this world, but be transformed by the renewing of your mind. (Romans 12:2 NIV)

For everyone who has been born of God overcomes the world. And this is the victory that has overcome the world—our faith. (1 John 5:4 ESV)

In addition, the world cannot receive the Spirit of God (John 14:17), and the wisdom of the world is foolishness to God (1 Corinthians 1:20–21; 3:18–19).

To sum up the above passages, we are in Christ and Christ is in us. Therefore, we are to have no attachments to the kingdom of this world.

Consider the words of Jude:

These are the ones who cause divisions, worldly-minded, devoid of the Spirit. But you, beloved, building yourselves up on your most holy faith, praying in the Holy Spirit, keep yourselves in the love of God. (Jude 19–21 NASB)

According to Jude, the antidote to being "worldly-minded" is to keep oneself in the love of God.

This brings us back to Part II of this book. Open yourself up to the Lord's love, and it will overcome your attraction to the world.

The Trend Away from God

The tentacles of the world system are many and varied. They include the systems of education, fashion, politics, entertainment, technology, economics, justice, and religion.

If you pull back the curtain on all these systems, you will discover a greater system. And behind that curtain are systems within systems—an enticing web of relentless activity designed to enslave humans and draw them away from their Creator.

If you pull the curtain back even more, you will realize that behind the world system stands a throne. And the God of Creation is not sitting on it.

Everything that is in the world system has a natural course (Ephesians 2:2). You could say it has its own DNA. And that DNA moves according to a certain trend.

That trend is always away from God because the mind behind it is God's enemy. And he has but one main objective: to lead you and me away from Jesus Christ and tempt us to find our security, enjoyment, and provision outside of His presence.

Detaching Yourself

. . .

As Jesus-followers, we have nothing to do with the world system. We *use* the *things* of this world and seize them for God. But we must not be engrossed by or attached to them.

> Those who use the things of the world should not become attached to them. For this world as we know it will soon pass away. (1 Corinthians 7:31 NLT)

Consequently, a Jesus-follower can make use of art, education, science, business, economics, politics, etc. if he or she employs those things for the Lord without being entangled by the systems they are attached to. Because that system will *always*, without fail, revert back to its natural course away from God.

In speaking about God's people making use of the things in the world, Watchman Nee writes,

> But walk softly, for you are upon territory that is governed by God's enemy, and unless you are on the watch you are as liable as anyone to fall prey to its devices. . . . Unless you tread softly you will be caught up somewhere in Satan's snares and will lose the liberty that is yours as a child of God.[19]

In the hands of those who are completely under the sovereign reign of God's kingdom, the material things of the world can be used as instruments to further His kingdom. In the hands of those who aren't in the kingdom, material things are instruments of the kingdom of darkness.

Put another way, God calls us to detach ourselves from the world system and the false gods that stand behind it, refusing to yield our powers to them.

When it comes to Kratos (the pride of life), those who are devoted to Jesus are learning how to exercise God's power in ways that bring Him glory and further His eternal purpose.

When it comes to Plutus (the lust of the eyes), those who are devoted to Jesus are learning how to use money and give it away wisely rather than to love, hoard, or abuse it. (We can serve God *with* money. But we cannot serve the Lord *and* money—Matthew 6:24.)

When it comes to Aphrodite (the lust of the flesh), those who are devoted to Jesus are learning how to honor and sustain celibacy and/or marriage.

For years, I've watched young Christians begin to follow the Lord. Each one of them was remarkably zealous at first. Then the lure of the world came knocking at their door. And they fell away from God, being roped into some aspect of the world system, whether it was the lusts of the flesh, the ambitions of this life, or the pull of materialism.

The natural course of the world always leads to one of those three things. F. F. Bruce put it brilliantly:

> The Christian is sent into the godless world to reclaim it for its rightful Lord, but while it remains the "godless world" it is an uncongenial environment for the Christian; he cannot feel at home there. . . . This emphasis on being in the world but not of it, involved and detached at the same time, can be found in many parts of the New Testament.[20]

For this reason, those who are part of the insurgence have declared war on the world system.

The World Versus Sin

Sin and the world are not the same. Sin damages; the world possesses.

The world is seeking after you and me. The world never seeks after the lost because it already has them. The lost are already possessed by it.

No, the world seeks after God's people. And it has done so from the beginning. Egypt followed hard after Israel—God's people. So did Sodom. So did Babylon.

Lot pitched his tent near Sodom, and eventually he was captured by it. He ended up in the city of lust. There's a lesson to be learned from Lot. Don't pitch your tent near the world or play games with it. If you do, don't be surprised if you find yourself caught in the riptide of the world system, eventually being drowned by it.

The world is an outward thing. Sin is an inward thing. And worldliness is not recognized as easily as sin.

Consider a drunkard who beats his wife. The bouts of drunkenness and the physical violence the drunkard inflicts on his spouse is blatant sin. It's easy to detect.

But take an architect who is obsessed with his architecture and has an ambition to become famous. Day and night, this goal occupies his heart and mind. The architect has little interest in spiritual things. His obsession with being a *great* architect has smothered his spiritual interests. The world has ensnarled the architect with worldly ambition.

Take a young woman who has a repeated pattern of spreading gossip. She even invents it out of thin air, sowing seeds of discord among her fellow Christian friends. That's blatant sin.

But take a young Christian woman who is obsessed with expensive clothing and fine jewelry. So much so that acquiring these things will determine who she ends up marrying, even if that person has little interest in Jesus Christ or His kingdom. That's worldliness.

So there is blatant sin and there is hidden worldliness (or as John Howard Yoder put it, "respectable worldliness").

The Great Disguise

. . .

The world disguises itself better than sin does. Sin is black. The world is pastel.

If you're going to use the educational system, be aware of a malicious mind behind that system. If you're going to use the political system, know that a malevolent entity is behind that system. If you're going to use the entertainment system, beware of a deceptive personality behind that system.

It is for this reason that countless people who have gotten involved in the systems of this world have become hopelessly embroiled in them. And not a small number have been corrupted by them.

The spiritual power behind these systems is antagonistic toward the Lord's kingdom. This doesn't mean that God cannot lead some of His children into these arenas to be salt and light, but they must understand the dark power behind them. And they should never misplace their hopes and dreams in them.

If the world cannot get you at a low lustful level, it will seek to get you on a higher subtle level. The key characteristic of the world is pollution and possession. It seeks to distract our hearts from the King and His kingdom.

It doesn't matter how long you've been a Christian, the world is still an issue for you. I've been a believer for over thirty-five years, and the world continues to knock at my door.

As we go further in the Lord, we should ask ourselves, "Have I attached myself to anything in this world? Does the world have a place in me?"

The world system is the natural habitat of the unbeliever, just as the ekklesia is the natural habitat of the believer.

As Jesus-followers, our allegiance, identity, security, enjoyment, and provision are in the kingdom of light, not in the kingdom of darkness. It's in the family of God, not in the world system. When we join God's family, we access our true identity and the story of Jesus becomes our story.[*]

This is one of the central features that separates those who have joined the insurgence from those who have not.

---

[*] I discuss this in some detail in *Jesus Manifesto* with Leonard Sweet, chap. 3. That chapter is entitled "If God Wrote Your Biography."

A Polluted River

You can think of the world system as a polluted river. If you get in any part of that river, it sweeps you along. The current is very powerful, and it moves you away from God.

Interestingly, there are different tributaries in that river.

One tributary is the tributary of worldly entertainment. Entire denominations and movements have been built on abstaining from this tributary. They've taken a strong stand against watching certain movies and television programs, and not attending certain events and locations.

Another tributary is the tributary of consumerism. Some Christian movements have taken an uncompromising stand against this tributary, relentlessly assaulting the evils of greed, covetousness, and materialism that mark consumer culture.

Still another tributary in this polluted river is the tributary of empire. Those who have taken aim at this tributary speak loudly about the evils of war, violence, the worship of the state (nationalism), etc.

All of these tributaries are part of the same polluted river. In other words, they are all part of the world system.

The problem, however, is that many who are not swimming in the tributary of worldly entertainment are almost drowning in the tributary of consumerism. Others who are abstaining from the tributary of empire are engulfed in the tributary of worldly entertainment. And some who are abstaining from the tributaries of empire and worldly entertainment, enjoy taking laps in the tributary of consumerism.

But each tributary is part of the world, and to swim in any of them is to be worldly.

The world system—the spirit of the age—is pervasive and its tentacles reach far and wide.

Come Out From Among Them

Pulling out of the world system doesn't mean retreating into the wilderness, storing our money in a safe and ceasing to use soap, shampoo, or running water.

It rather means leaving the ways, habits, values, conduct, and glory of the world behind. And never trusting its goods.

God's word to those who are part of the world system is and has always been "Come out!"

Throughout the entire Old Testament story, the scenes and characters continually change, but the story remains the same.

God judged the world system in Noah's day. The Lord's word to Noah was "Come out!" God then delivered Noah by way of an ark. Eight souls were saved in the ark, passing through the waters of death.

Significantly, eight is the number of resurrection and new beginnings. (Circumcision was on the eighth day. Jesus was resurrected on the eighth day, which is Sunday, the beginning of a new week.)

When Noah and his family emerged from the ark, they stood in a new world—a new creation. The dove, which is a picture of the Holy Spirit, could not find rest until the new earth had fully emerged from the water that buried the old world. In this regard, the ark represents water baptism (1 Peter 3:20–22).

God then called a man named Abraham to leave Ur of the Chaldeans (which is Babylon). The Lord's word to Abraham was "Come out!"

Abraham came out of Ur and built an altar, and he lived in a tent.

The altar that Abraham built was his way of saying, "I am utterly consecrated to the Lord. I have nothing to do with this world. I have left Babylon."

The tent was Abraham's way of saying, "I am not attached to this world. I have no strings here. I can pick up and move whenever and wherever the Lord leads me. I have no roots planted in this world. I live in a tent."

The descendants of Abraham—the children of Israel—found themselves in bondage in the land of Egypt for 400 years. And the Lord's word to Israel was "Come out!" God raised up a man named Moses to deliver Israel from Egypt.

The Lord brought His people out of Egypt by means of two things: a slain lamb and the crossing of the Red Sea.

The eating of the lamb represents partaking of Christ (1 Corinthians 5:7–8) and the crossing of the Red Sea represents water baptism (10:1–2).

With those stories in mind, what is God's call to you and me today?

The Call Today

Notice what the Lord says to His people today, who are under the new covenant.

Do not be yoked together with unbelievers. For what do righteousness and wickedness have in common? Or what fellowship can light have with darkness? What harmony is there between Christ and Belial? Or what does a believer have in common with an unbeliever? What agreement is there between the temple of God and idols? For we are the temple of the living God. As God has said:

> "I will live with them
>   and walk among them,
> and I will be their God,
>   and they will be my people."

Therefore,

> "Come out from them
>   and be separate,
>   says the Lord.
> Touch no unclean thing,
>   and I will receive you."

And,

> "I will be a Father to you,
>   and you will be my sons and daughters,
>   says the Lord Almighty." (2 Corinthians 6:14–18 NIV)

This call is repeated in Revelation:

> "Fallen! Fallen is Babylon the Great!" . . .

> "Come out of her, my people,"
>   so that you will not share in her sins,
> so that you will not receive any of her plagues. (18:2, 4 NIV)

Make no mistake. The Lord hates the world system because it keeps Him from having His lovely bride, the ekklesia. It's no coincidence that the city of Babylon is made up of the same materials as the bride of Christ (Revelation 17:4–5; 21:9–21).

Babylon is a counterfeit of and a poor substitute for the ekklesia.* Babylon represents the apex of human political power, the organization of human self-interest, and the flourishing of human civilization.

With respect to the world system, the Lord's word to you and me is clear. It's still, "Come out!"

---

* As I demonstrated in *From Eternity to Here*, the New Jerusalem in Revelation 21 and 22 is a picture of the bride of Christ, the ekklesia, the Lamb's wife. It's not a physical structure. Jesus isn't returning to marry a physical building.

What Is the World to You?

. . .

I'm not going to name those specific things that are part of the world. I have yet to do that in this book. To do so would make me a legalist. And we'd be back under human rules and regulations.

All I can say is that you already know. And if you don't, ask the Lord with an open heart. If your heart is willing to respond to what He shows you, He will put His finger on what the world is for you.

John told us what the world was in 1 John 2. Later in that same chapter, he told us that we have the anointing of the Spirit who will reveal to us what the world is in our lives.

> As for you, the anointing you received from him remains in you, and you do not need anyone to teach you. But as his anointing teaches you about all things and as that anointing is real, not counterfeit—just as it has taught you, remain in him. (v. 27 NIV)

May God have a people today in every city on this earth who have separated themselves completely from the world system.

A people who are standing in the freedom that Jesus Christ has purchased for all His followers.

A people who have turned their backs on the kingdom of this world and turned their hearts toward the kingdom of God. A people of the altar and the tent.

A people who have passed through the Red Sea and who are eating the real Lamb—not once, but continually.

So ask the Lord what the world is in your life and then "Come out."

Dealing With the World

* * *

Your attitude toward the world system will determine your altitude in Jesus Christ and your usefulness in God's kingdom.

We have a Lord who has defeated Satan and the world system.

The kingdom of darkness (the world) has enslaved and blinded you and me. But Jesus came to "deliver us from this present evil age" (Galatians 1:4 NKJV) and into the kingdom of light, liberty, life, freedom, peace, and joy.

I echo Paul's words to stand fast in the liberty that Jesus Christ has secured for us.

> Stand fast therefore in the liberty by which Christ has made us free, and do not be entangled again with a yoke of bondage. (Galatians 5:1 NKJV)

> But now that you know God—or rather are known by God—how is it that you are turning back to those weak and miserable forces? Do you wish to be enslaved by them all over again? (Galatians 4:9 NIV)

The call to come out of the world and give ourselves utterly and completely to Jesus and His kingdom is being heralded to you right now. Not from a place of duty, guilt, or fear. It's rather a call to respond to the Lord's word graciously, willingly, and lovingly—because of the glorious freedom that Christ has won for you.

The sobering words of William Ralph Inge are fitting:

> Whoever marries the spirit of this age will find himself a widower in the next.[21]

This book is all about moving forward. It's about soaring higher in Christ. The standard I have raised is that there would be a group of people on this earth who would stand against all darkness and declare,

> We will take Christ as our provision, Christ as our enjoyment, and Christ as our security. We have been freed from the world system, and we stand in

the glorious liberty that Jesus Christ has won for us. We are following our Lord without legalism. Without fear. Without guilt or condemnation. His beauty and glory have captured us. We cannot help but bow low and worship Him with all we have.

This is the prayer of the insurgence.

Freedom From Greed

For those who like to count, the sin that's mentioned the most often in the Bible is idolatry. The second is covetousness, which is another word for greed.

John speaks about greed when he uses the phrase "the lust of the eyes" (1 John 2:16). Strikingly, Paul equates covetousness with idolatry.

> Put to death therefore what is earthly in you: sexual immorality, impurity, passion, evil desire, and covetousness, which is idolatry. (Colossians 3:5 ESV)

Greed is common in affluent countries like the United States. And those who are captured by it are often unaware that they are living within its grip.

Indeed, Jesus explicitly warned people to be on their guard against greed, since it's so easy to dismiss.

> Watch out! Be on your guard against all kinds of greed; life does not consist in an abundance of possessions. (Luke 12:15 NIV)

Think about it. When is the last time you heard someone acknowledge that he or she struggles with greed? People admit that they struggle with lust or anger or gossip, but I have yet to hear a person say, "My main temptation is greed."

I once read an interview by a well-known author who happens to be a Christian. In the interview, the author admitted that it's hard for him not to think about his business, even when he's with his family.

This author's whole life is wrapped up in his profession. He rarely if ever talks or writes about the kingdom of God. What dominates his writing and speaking is how people can earn more money.

Is this author in touch with the fact that he has made a god out of money? Perhaps not.

The Deceitfulness of Riches

. . .

It has been said that money is the second most frequently mentioned subject, second to idolatry in the Old Testament and to the kingdom of God in the New Testament.

Jesus talked about "the deceitfulness of riches" for good reason (Mark 4:19 ESV). Riches are deceptive. Those who pay homage to the god of Plutus are rarely aware of the hold money has on them.

> Those who want to get rich fall into temptation and a trap and into many foolish and harmful desires that plunge people into ruin and destruction. (1 Timothy 6:9 NIV)

> For the love of money is a root of all kinds of evil. Some people, eager for money, have wandered from the faith and pierced themselves with many griefs. (1 Timothy 6:10 NIV)

> But mark this: There will be terrible times in the last days. People will be lovers of themselves, lovers of money. (2 Timothy 3:1–2 NIV)

Throughout my life, I've known countless men who started businesses. With the exception of a handful of them, the rest became utterly entangled with their businesses. And Jesus Christ and His kingdom became secondary. These men were owned by their businesses rather than by Christ.

I'm not suggesting that it's wrong for a Christian to start a business. I'm simply issuing a caution, the same caution that both Jesus and Paul issued when they warned that it's incredibly difficult for a rich person to enter the kingdom of God (Matthew 19:23–24).

When business consumes one's mind and governs their decisions, they've made business into an idol. The business absorbs their time and often creates health problems. As a result, the kingdom of God takes a back seat to their earthly "work." The word of the kingdom gets choked out.

The cares of this world, the deceitfulness of riches, and the desires for other things entering in choke the word, and it becomes unfruitful. (Mark 4:19 NKJV)

A good indicator of greed (or any other idol) can be found in what your mind is occupied with most of the time.

A little-known fact is that money is tainted by the world system. That's why Jesus called it "the mammon of unrighteousness" (Luke 16:9 KJV).

Jacques Ellul rightly wrote, "Let us not forget that money, for Jesus, is the domain of Mammon, a satanic domain."[22]

Watchman Nee echoes the point, saying,

The essence of the world is money. Whenever you touch money you touch the world. The question arises: How can we take a thing we know assuredly is of the world, and yet not become involved with the world system? . . . The New Testament key to all finance is that we hold nothing to ourselves. "Give, and it shall be given unto you"; those were our Lord's words (Luke 6:38) and not, "Save and ye shall grow rich"! That is to say, the principle of divine increase is giving, not storage.[23]

While those who are part of the insurgence use money, they are keenly aware of the dangers that are attached to it. It's all too easy to make money an idol. This was as true in Jesus' day as it is in ours. Recall that the Lord said, "You cannot serve both God and money" (Matthew 6:24 NIV).

Note that the Lord's audience was mostly poor. The temptation of the rich is to trust in their wealth, while the temptation of the poor is to covet wealth. Both stand as obstacles to the kingdom of God.

The Story of Money

. . .

In some versions of the Bible, the word *money* is translated "mammon."*

> No one can serve two masters; for either he will hate the one and love the other, or else he will be loyal to the one and despise the other. You cannot serve God and mammon. (Matthew 6:24 NKJV)

Mammon is the Babylonian god of money and riches, similar to the god of Plutus among the Greeks.

The love of money is referred to as "filthy lucre" in some translations (1 Timothy 3:3, 8; Titus 1:7, 11; 1 Peter 5:2 KJV). The love of riches was a problem in the first century, and it's a massive problem today.

The internal story we tell ourselves about money is hugely important. For many, the amount of money one makes is a measure of their value and a piece of their identity.

People tell themselves that if they make a certain amount of money, it means they have value. So it's a measure of their worth.

In Western society, people work harder and longer to gain more "stuff," most of which they don't even need. Such affluence breeds certain epidemics like alienation (from connection and community, because people have no time for it), compulsive addictions, and selfishness.

The real questions that must be settled in our hearts are, *How much money is enough? And what am I willing to trade for it?*

Because there's always a trade.

Years ago, I watched a group of young men leave a rare and beautiful expression of the kingdom of God to relocate to another city to join a new business venture. That venture offered them the promise of becoming wealthy.

At the time, these men felt that their intentions were good. However, they were choosing the world over the kingdom. But they were blind to this fact.

* For example, Matthew 6:24; Luke 16:9, 11, 13 KJV.

Within a year, all of those young men left the Lord and found themselves back in the world system. They were captured by the lure of greed without realizing it. I've watched this same scenario play out numerous times since. Different players, same tragic ending.

Another indicator of greed is found in what you are willing to forsake to gain wealth. Especially when it comes to forfeiting the things of God.

A. W. Tozer nailed it when he wrote,

> I have said that Abraham possessed nothing. Yet was not this poor man rich? . . . He had everything, but he possessed nothing. There is the spiritual secret. There is the sweet theology of the heart which can be learned only in the school of renunciation. . . . Everything is safe which we commit to Him, and nothing is really safe which is not so committed. Our gifts and talents also should be turned over to Him. They should be recognized for what they are, God's loan to us, and should never be considered in any sense our own. . . . If we would indeed know God in growing intimacy, we must go this way of renunciation.[24]

When we have laid all our possessions at the feet of the cross of Christ, our hearts are freed from them. And they no longer constitute a competing idol to the Lord.

If you are held by greed, the antidote is to begin giving away what has a hold on you. This is precisely what Jesus said to a certain rich young ruler (Mark 10:17–31).

The problem isn't that the rich ruler had many possessions. The problem was that those possessions had him.

While I cannot touch the soles of the shoes of John the Baptist, Jesus, Peter, and Paul when it comes to the matter of earthly possessions, I have given away possessions throughout my entire Christian life. And doing so is incredibly liberating.

The issue is not the possessions themselves; it's the spirit of ownership that enslaves us to them. Knowing the difference is a work of God in itself. Those who have joined the insurgence understand this all too well. They also know that with God all things are possible, even when they are impossible for humans (Matthew 19:26).

Only God can break the idol of riches.

The Spirit of Ownership

The kingdom of God makes an exclusive claim on our lives. In God's kingdom, we own nothing. We simply manage what we've been given.

In God's kingdom, we do not work to meet our own needs only. We work so that we "may have something to share with those in need" (Ephesians 4:28 NIV).

As kingdom citizens, Jesus Christ is our first priority in life above every other loyalty, love, goal, or ambition. But there are two things that reflect our values and priorities above everything else: our calendar and our wallet. How we spend our time and money reveals where we stand with the kingdom of God more than anything else.

Those two things reveal whether or not we are part of heaven's culture or the world's. Obsessing over and being consumed with material things is the conduct of those who are part of the world system. Those who are outside the kingdom of God regularly worry about how their needs and wants will be met (Matthew 6:19–34). In effect, Jesus said, "All the nations of the world hustle after these things" (Matthew 6:32). Roman imperial culture was up to its eyeballs in anxiety, alienation, and addiction. The same is true for our society. We are taught from childhood that happiness is found in private wealth and the satisfaction of our appetites.

For kingdom citizens, however, the kingdom of God is our priority in life, even above meeting our own basic needs. Regrettably, the so-called prosperity gospel has distorted the kingdom of God into a funnel for greed.

According to the New Testament, the kingdom is not a bless-me club. We don't enter it to be blessed by God with material goods. Jesus is certainly a good and benevolent king, but He's no Santa Claus.

In Genesis 1, God gave humans dominion, not ownership. When we come into the kingdom, we forfeit and relinquish ownership and become stewards of money and material goods. Understanding this truth produces radical generosity and gratitude because we don't see anything in our possession as our own.

The economics of the kingdom is also radically different from the economics of the world. In the economics of the world, people hoard, save, accumulate, and are gripped by material goods. In the economics of the kingdom, we earn to give. And by giving we receive. Not for our own sake, but for the sake of others. The primitive church took care of each other in ways that startled the world.[*]

In short, we don't live for the pursuit of material things or getting our needs met like the rest of the world.

Remarkably, the economics of the kingdom operates despite what's going on in the world's economy. As a kingdom citizen, you are not under the world's government or economic system. For this reason, you can have peace during recessions, economic crises, and even depressions.

The economics of the kingdom ensures that those who are in God's kingdom do not go without food, clothes, or shelter.

According to Jesus, nothing you give for the kingdom of God is really lost. You simply receive it back in a different form and in a multiplied way (Luke 18:28–30).

[*] See Viola, *Reimagining Church*, chap. 5 for details.

The Peril of Riches

. . .

The four people in the New Testament who preached the gospel most forcefully each teach us a valuable lesson about the kingdom of God.

John the Baptist only owned a coat made of camel's skin, a leather belt, and sandals.

The One who created the earth and lived a perfect life couldn't find a place to lay His head (Matthew 8:20). Jesus of Nazareth only possessed a seamless robe and sandals. And He died owning neither.

Peter, who was married, had his expenses met by the Jerusalem church. But he himself appeared to have spent everything on the kingdom of God after meeting the needs of his family. Recall Peter's words to a lame beggar, "Silver and gold have I none" (Acts 3:6 KJV).

Paul of Tarsus worked for a living as a tentmaker (more accurately, a leatherworker). Yet everything he earned beyond meeting his basic needs went toward his apostolic ministry, even supporting the men he trained in Ephesus (Acts 20:34).

Like Jesus, Paul died without owning anything except for a cloak and some sacred scrolls. And Paul would have had them in his possession only if Timothy visited Paul in prison before Paul was beheaded (2 Timothy 4:13). In the same spirit, when Jesus sent out His disciples, He told them not to take a money purse with them (Luke 10:4).

These men raised an incredible standard. They lived as strangers, foreigners, and pilgrims on this earth. They had no earthly attachments. Nothing in this world controlled or hindered them.

A Disturbing Observation

I live in the United States of America where there is no shortage of rich people. Ever since I began following Jesus, I've known only a small number of people whom I would describe as being "rich" or "wealthy."

All of them profess to be Christians.

They all attend church and read their Bibles. All of them talk about God now and then, but not a great deal. What occupies their speech mostly is their careers, which is the source of their wealth.

Over the years, I've spent time with each of them in person. And I've never heard any of them talk about the kingdom of God or the cost of the kingdom.

To be candid, I seriously doubt any of them are reading this book. The reason is because they seem to only be interested in reading books on business or leadership.

My point in mentioning this is not to condemn others. It's to bring home a neglected truth. God doesn't have a very pleasant attitude toward riches in the New Testament. (As I've explained elsewhere, the riches in the Old Testament were shadows of our wealth in Christ. They aren't a prescription for how God's people can become rich in this world.)

Can a rich person enter the kingdom of God? Yes. But according to Jesus, it's not terribly easy (Matthew 19:24). And if you really want to read something scary about how riches detract people from God's kingdom, read what James had to say to the rich believers to whom he was writing (James 5:1–6). If you are wealthy, it should curdle your blood.

> Again I tell you, it is easier for a camel to go through the eye of a needle than for someone who is rich to enter the kingdom of God. (Matthew 19:24 NIV)

> Look here, you rich people: Weep and groan with anguish because of all the terrible troubles ahead of you. (James 5:1 NLT)

I don't write these things to put you under a pile of guilt for owning material goods or for gaining a sizable income. Rather, I write them to stir your heart about how you *view* and *use* your money and possessions. I write to challenge you about how much your job, your career, your income, and your earthly goods capture your heart and mind.

How much time do you spend on these things in comparison to how much time you spend seeking Jesus Christ and living for His kingdom? (Living for the kingdom includes the time you spend in, for, and with the ekklesia, the kingdom community.)

All told, your priorities determine how you use the four currencies of life: time, money, energy, and attention. Radical generosity prevents the things you own from owning you.

Relentless generosity is the fruit of the kingdom and the result of making the King and His kingdom first priority in your life. Extravagant generosity dethrones greed and causes us to be detached from this world's goods.

In speaking of the principle of detachment to material things, Watchman Nee wrote,

> What, then, is the secret of holding our material things in the will of God? Surely it is to hold them *for God*, that is to say, to know we are not hoarding useless valuables, or amassing vast bank deposits, but laying up treasures to his account. You and I must be perfectly willing to part with anything at the moment. It matters not whether I leave two thousand dollars or merely two. . . . What matters is whether I can leave whatever I have without a twinge of regret. . . . I keep nothing because I love it, but let it go without regret when the call comes to leave it all behind. That is what it means to be detached.[25]

God doesn't want us to feel guilty about having money. He wants us to feel grateful so that our gratitude will overflow into generosity to those in need.

Having money isn't the problem. The problem is that all too often, money has us.

This is one of the most challenging truisms of the insurgence.

Breaking Out of Christian Suburbia

· · ·

Warning: this chapter may incite defensiveness. So tread with an open heart.

In the US, the typical lifestyle of the average Christian is based on scarcity. A scarcity mentality believes that material things are scarce; therefore, the name of the game is to get more stuff at the cheapest possible price. To those of this mentality, Black Friday is one of the highlights of the year.

Countless American Christians have adopted this mentality. These individuals live to secure a better house, nicer cars, swell their savings accounts and retirement funds, all with the goal of sending their kids to college, raising grandchildren, and teaching them to continue the cycle of acquiring more stuff. (Living with a boatload of debt to maintain this consumerist lifestyle is also a common characteristic of this mentality.)

Some Christian teachers have even built untenable theologies to justify their lust for more stuff based on proof-texting certain verses of the Bible.

For most of these Christians, "going to church" is a convenient supplement to their already busy lives—lives that are marked by maintaining their cherished possessions, spending endless hours on mindless entertainment, and living in isolation from others.

I call this lifestyle "Christian suburbia."

Those who have hearts for the insurgence are extremely uncomfortable with this lifestyle. They know in their bones that there has to be a higher way to live.

Such people crave a kingdom lifestyle. A kingdom lifestyle is based not on scarcity but on abundance. Kingdom-minded people are convinced that God will meet their physical and material needs out of the abundance of His love and "the riches of His glory" (Philippians 4:19).

When they buy an item for themselves, it's only out of need or if it will enable them to become more effective agents for the kingdom. To the kingdom-minded person, the name of the game is not getting more stuff but making connections.

For this reason, kingdom-minded believers have been known to do things that disrupt the social status quo. They've been known to sell their homes, quit their jobs, and relocate to where other kingdom-minded believers are sharing their lives together to proclaim, embody, and display God's rule in a given city.

Whenever kingdom-minded people own a possession, they don't view it as their own property. Instead, they are keenly aware that everything they own belongs to the Lord as well as to their fellow sisters and brothers in Christ.

Their lives are marked by radical generosity. Not just in religious rhetoric, but in practical reality.

Consequently, a kingdom-minded believer is unattached to anything in this world. So much so that he or she is ready to sell one's possessions and live in common with other believers should the season or the need arise. The ekklesia in Jerusalem lived in common during its early years in response to a crisis.*

In addition, the ability of the early Christians to move money across the Roman Empire to help one another was remarkable (Acts 11:27–30; 1 Corinthians 16:1–4; 2 Corinthians 8).

In the first century, the ekklesia was its own "civilization" within the civilization of the world. It had its own life, culture, and conduct that was drastically different from the world's. And I believe God desires to recover this dynamic in the body of Christ again.†

---

* The crisis was that some 3,000 Jews from all over the Roman Empire had just been saved, and they decided to stay in Jerusalem where the apostles lived rather than to return to their homes and jobs. Consequently, this presented an immediate financial crisis. So the believers pooled their resources together and lived in common (Acts 2:44–45; 4:32–35). While living out of a common purse was an experience unique to the Jerusalem church in the New Testament, the principle that lies under the practice is that of financial equality. And that principle was observed by all the churches in the first century (see 2 Corinthians 8:13–15 and Ephesians 4:28). In 2 Corinthians 8, Paul refers to the "manna economy" sketched out in Exodus 16. That economy prohibited hoarding and resulted in everyone having their needs met. Those who had more gave away their surplus to those who had a shortage (2 Corinthians 8:14ff.). For the early ekklesia, security lay not in money or possessions but in the social network of the community of God's people who cared for each other from cradle to coffin. The principle of God's economy was and still is "enough for all." See Ched Myers, *The Biblical Vision of Sabbath Economics* (n.p.: Tell the Truth, 2002); Gene Edwards, *The Early Church* (Goleta, CA: Christian Books, 1974); Christian Smith, *Going to the Root* (Scottdale, PA: Herald Press, 1992); Hal Miller, *Christian Community* (Ann Arbor: Servant Books, 1979); and Howard Snyder, *The Community of the King* (Downers Grove, IL: InterVarsity Press, 1977).

† See Frank Viola, *Finding Organic Church* (Colorado Springs: David C. Cook, 2009), for details. Again, I'm using the word "civilization" with respect to the ekklesia metaphorically. It's better described as a tribe rather than high civilization.

The Witness of Church History

. . .

The instinct of the early Christians to not regard their possessions as their own—to take care of each other as well as the poor—can be found throughout church history.

Here are some examples:

They [Christians] despise all worldly goods alike, regarding them merely as common property.

Lucian (2nd century)

They [Christians] love one another. They do not overlook the widow, and they save the orphan. He who has ministers ungrudgingly to him who does not have.

Aristides (2nd century)

So a great work of love burns a brand upon us in regard to some. *See,* they say, *how they love one another....* They are furious that we call each other brothers.... So we who are united in mind and soul have no hesitation about sharing property. All things are common among us except our wives.

Tertullian (2nd–3rd century)

Most of our brother Christians showed unbounded love and loyalty; never sparing themselves and thinking only of one another. Heedless of danger, they took charge of the sick, attending to their every need and ministering to them in Christ, and with them departed this life serenely happy; for they were infected by others with the disease, drawing on themselves the sickness of their neighbors and cheerfully accepting their pains. Many, in nursing and caring for others, transferred their death to themselves and died in their stead.... The best of our brothers lost their lives in this manner.

Dionysius (3rd century)

These impious Galileans [Christians] not only feed their own poor, but ours also; welcoming them into their *agapae* [love feasts], they attract them, as children are attracted, with cakes. Whilst the pagan priests neglect the poor, the hated Galileans devote themselves to works of charity, and by a display of false compassion have established and given effect to their pernicious errors. See their love-feasts, and their tables spread for the indigent. Such practice is common among them, and causes a contempt for our gods.

Emperor Julian (4th century)[26]

The early believers redefined private wealth into common wealth. The ekklesia embodied a security system that lasted from birth to old age. These Christians saw themselves as family and took care of one another.

In this respect, they constituted the third largest "bank" during the first three centuries. Their ability to move money throughout the Roman Empire in an effort to help one another was exceeded only by the State treasury and the Jewish Temple treasury.

Our Boast

. . .

Those who are part of the insurgence have died to the world. So as a member of God's kingdom, you have no place in this world system, and the world has no place in you.

But here is good news: Jesus Christ has already delivered us from the world system!

> I have told you these things, so that in me you may have peace. In this world you will have trouble. But take heart! I have overcome the world. (John 16:33 NIV)

The Lord has given us this freedom already. Our job is simply to appropriate it.

Paul of Tarsus was a man who did not boast of his own work in the Lord. But if you ever found him boasting, he boasted in Christ and in His cross, by which he was dead to the world.

> May I never boast except in the cross of our Lord Jesus Christ, through which the world has been crucified to me, and I to the world. (Galatians 6:14 NIV)

Religion causes us to boast in something regarding ourselves. The gospel leads us to boast in the cross. And wherein did Paul boast? The great apostle boasted that the cross crucified the world to him and crucified him to the world.

God forbid that you and I should boast in anything else.

Double Vision

. . .

Consider the story of the Exodus. When the children of Israel passed through the Red Sea, the Egyptians pursued them. Not knowing that the Israelites had escaped on dry land, the remaining Egyptians looked at the Red Sea and said, "We cannot locate them. They've disappeared."

Because of the death of Christ, the world has not been able to locate you. In the world's records, you don't exist. You have been crucified to the world.

Yet when God looked at the same Red Sea after He caused it to bury the Egyptians when they tried to pass through it, He said, "The Egyptians have died and drowned. Egypt is no more."

In God's records, Egypt—which represents the world system—has died.

So get behind the eyes of God and get behind the eyes of the world and look. Behind the eyes of the world, you don't exist. And behind the eyes of God, the world doesn't exist.

The world system was crucified 2,000 years ago on the cross of Jesus Christ. So from God's viewpoint, it is dead and its power over you has been stripped.

Those who are part of the insurgence are dead to the world, and the world is dead to them.

The Shadow Government

· · ·

A shadow government is the idea that the real and actual political power resides not with publicly elected representatives but with private entities who exercise political power behind the scenes.

As we've seen, the government that runs the world and its systems is in fact a shadow government. It's spiritual, invisible, and headed up by God's enemy.

The good news is that there is another government operating above and beyond the shadow government.

That government is located in heavenly realms, and it is progressively gaining ground on the shadow government as it continues to break into the earth.

Jesus of Nazareth is the absolute ruler of this heavenly government, and it's destined to overturn all other kingdoms, both visible and invisible.

Those of us who have given ourselves to the insurgence are giving ground to God to visibly defeat the shadow government with His own—the kingdom of God

What an exciting prospect!

An Unshakable Kingdom

The kingdom of heaven was shaken when a certain celestial being revolted against God and other angelic beings left the presence of the Almighty.

The kingdom of darkness was shaken when Jesus Christ destroyed Satan's power on the cross (Colossians 2:14–15; Hebrews 2:14).

But there is a kingdom that will never be shaken! *It is the kingdom of Jesus Christ.*

> Since we are receiving a Kingdom that is unshakable, let us be thankful and please God by worshiping him with holy fear and awe. (Hebrews 12:28 NLT)

People today are in search of meaning, identity, significance, and belonging. This universal search is the reason why gangs and cults abound and why extreme terrorist groups exist. These groups recruit people who are desperately searching for these fundamentals.

The kingdom of God is the true answer to these longings. All other offers to fulfill them are counterfeits.

Whether you are already a follower of Jesus or not, I urge you: Enter the kingdom of God. Surrender your life to it. Abandon yourself to it wholly, completely, and fully. Give your utter loyalty and allegiance to it.

It is in the kingdom that you will find meaning, identity, significance, and belonging, as well as cohesion and purpose. You will also find security, for God's kingdom cannot be shaken, crushed, or toppled.

> The God of heaven will set up a kingdom that will never be destroyed, nor will it be left to another people. It will crush all those kingdoms and bring them to an end, but it will itself endure forever. (Daniel 2:44 NIV)

> His kingdom is an eternal kingdom; his dominion endures from generation to generation. (Daniel 4:3 NIV)

> For when you [David] die and are buried with your ancestors, I will raise up one of your descendants, your own offspring, and I will make his kingdom

strong. He is the one who will build a house—a temple—for my name. And I will secure his royal throne forever. I will be his father, and he will be my son. (2 Samuel 7:12–14 NLT)

He will be great and will be called the Son of the Most High. The Lord God will give him the throne of his father David, and he will reign over Jacob's descendants forever; his kingdom will never end. (Luke 1:32–33 NIV)

In Daniel 2:35, the kingdom of Jesus Christ is symbolized by a "rock" that "became a huge mountain and filled the whole earth" (NIV).

Every other kingdom of this world will be shaken and fall. And every kingdom built by human hands cannot be the kingdom of God (Daniel 2:34). All other allegiances bring bondage.

Only the kingdom of God brings freedom and joy. So bow low at the King's feet and you will stand high above everything else.

Such is the nature of the insurgence.

Meet Pam

Pam grew up in a Christian home. She attended church every Sunday and read her Bible faithfully.

I knew Pam when she fell in love with a young man. Shortly thereafter, she began sleeping with her boyfriend. Her boyfriend accepted Jesus into his heart and he also attended church. But he was living for the world.

As Pam continued this relationship, I watched her heart grow colder toward the things of God and more warm toward the things of the world. Her interests shifted to luxurious possessions, high fashion, and earthly comforts.

One day Pam attended a gathering of Jesus-followers who had an informal meeting in a home. A man who was part of the group unleashed the gospel of the kingdom, preaching it like a house on fire.

Pam was deeply moved. Her eyes were opened to see the fraudulent promises of happiness that the world offered to her.

She was so touched that she asked to be baptized with the full understanding of what baptism meant—death to the world system and its ways.

Pam had been radicalized for the kingdom of God. She broke up with her boyfriend and gave her life completely to Jesus Christ. Even though she desired to be married, she decided that she would not compromise her devotion to Jesus for a man who would derail her from the kingdom.

Pam remained single for several years, serving as a living example to other women and men of what it means to devote oneself entirely to Christ.

As the years passed, she met a man whose heart was fully given to God's kingdom, and they eventually married. The last I heard, they were active participants in the insurgence.

Meet Tim

From an early age, Tim was taught that God wants His children to be wealthy. He was part of a movement that built its theology on certain biblical texts that promise prosperity to God's people, overlooking the passages that bring balance to those Scriptures and ignoring countless others that teach the opposite. Tim's parents put him through college, and Tim majored in business. At a young age, Tim started his own enterprise, which grew quickly. By the time he was in his midthirties, he was a multi-millionaire. Every material need he had was met. The "American dream" became a reality for him.

But there was one problem. His business obsessed him day and night. The pursuit of more clients, the hiring and firing of new workers, the resolution of endless problems in his business had become his daily pursuit. His health went downhill, and he even developed an ulcer. What is more, Jesus Christ was left out in the cold of his life.

Tim regularly went to church with his wife and children. He said his prayers and even read his Bible on occasion. But his heart was full of something else besides the Lord Jesus. His business loomed larger.

One day he heard the gospel of the kingdom, and the message pierced his heart. From that point on, the Lord began to deal with Tim about what following Jesus Christ meant for him. As the weeks rolled by, Tim had the distinct sense that the Lord was asking him to sacrifice his business for the kingdom.

He grappled, he struggled, and he went back and forth in his mind about the matter. He shared his turmoil with his wife. And although she loved the material things Tim's business provided, the Lord began to deal with her heart as well.

Finally, Tim laid hold of the violence necessary to cast off that which had been an obstacle between him and his Lord—*his wealth*. He sold his business, and he and his wife divested themselves of many of their possessions—downsizing their lifestyle considerably.

They also generously gave an enormous amount of their savings to several ministries that aided the poor. Tim invested the rest of his money so he and his wife could support themselves and continue to fund the Lord's work.

After simplifying their lives, the couple threw themselves wholeheartedly into the kingdom with a group of other kingdom-minded believers, seeking active ways of displaying God's loving reign to those in need. In so doing, Tim and his wife became part of the insurgence.

Stand Fast in Your Liberty

. . .

Because of the death of Jesus Christ, the world has no actual grip on you. But you can put *yourself* back into its bondage, just like you can put yourself back under the Law if you choose.

As the Lord's life expands in you, your understanding of the world system will also expand. And your break with it will increase.

You cannot detach moving further into God's kingdom from being separated from the world. The two go hand in hand. You will get only so far in Christ and His kingdom until you break with the world.

Again, God hates the world system. It's the tool of His enemy to derail you from living in and expressing His kingdom. And since the world system is God's enemy, it is also yours.

For this reason, Paul said, "Do not be conformed to this world" (Romans 12:2 NASB).

John said, "Love not the world" (1 John 2:15 KJV).

James said, "Keep oneself unspotted from the world" (1:27 NKJV).

Jesus said, "If the world hates you, you know that it hated Me before it hated you" (John 15:18 NKJV).

The world has enough people who are enslaved to it. It has enough people who serve its agenda. It has enough people who love its waning treasures and empty promises.

Consequently, the world will go on just fine without you. So why not let it? And let Jesus Christ have someone who refuses to be part of this world's enslaving system.

Let that someone be you.

A Prayer for the Kingdom

. . .

Lord, my prayer for myself and every reader is that You would give us all grace and mercy to obey Your gospel. We confess that this is simply beyond us. So we lean hard on You to make us worthy agents of Your unshakable kingdom and its explosive message—one that is free of legalism on the one hand and free of compromise on the other.

May You have a people on this earth one more time who obey Your gospel. A people who can stand before any mortal, no matter how high or low, armed with Your incredible gospel.

Show us how to obey the gospel of the kingdom in its totality and in its every dimension. Show us where we need to make a clean break with the world.

Open our eyes and give us the power both to will and do Your good pleasure, just as You promised. Give us abundant grace to respond to Your gospel.

Amen.

TAKING ACTION »

To make this part of the book practical, I recommend you do the following:

1. Listen to "For God So Loved the World vs. Love Not the World" at InsurgenceBook.com.

   When you finish listening to the message, spend some time praying over those things that stirred your heart.

2. Read these texts and consider them in the light of God's kingdom: 1 Timothy 6:8; Hebrews 13:5; Philippians 4:12.

3. Obedience to the kingdom of God means rethinking our relationship to money and possessions. In Luke 3:11, John the Baptist said, "Anyone who has two shirts should share with the one who has none, and anyone who has food should do the same."

   In Luke 19:8–9, when Zacchaeus met the Lord Jesus, Zacchaeus gave away half his possessions. Jesus responded by saying that salvation had come to Zacchaeus's house.

   Dorothy Day said, "If you have two coats, you have stolen one from the poor."

   John Chrysostom wrote, "Not to enable the poor to share in our goods is to steal from them and deprive them of life. The goods we possess are not ours, but theirs."[27]

   Basil, the bishop of Caesarea, wrote, "When someone steals another's clothes, we call them a thief. Should we not give the same name to one who could clothe the naked and does not? The bread in your cupboard belongs to the hungry; the coat unused in your closet belongs to the one who needs it; the shoes rotting in your closet belong to the one who has no shoes; the money which you hoard up belongs to the poor."[28]

   We'll never know just how attached we are to our possessions until we begin sharing them or giving them away.

   Some Christians barely get by. They live paycheck to paycheck. They have no extra money to spend on kingdom projects like helping those in need, attending conferences for equipping and connection, and kingdom resources (even as inexpensive as this book). If you are one of these individuals, I urge you to seek the Lord for wisdom and provision on how to increase your income without becoming a slave to your job.

Make this text your motivation: "Anyone who has been stealing must steal no longer, but must work, doing something useful with their own hands, that they may have something to share with those in need" (Ephesians 4:28 NIV).

In God's kingdom, we gain so that we might give.

At the same time, lots of Christians have large sums of money in their savings accounts, CDs, stocks, and bonds. And there's no real purpose for it.

Here are two discipleship exercises I encourage you to put into practice:

Exercise 1—Go through all of your possessions room by room, closet by closet, drawer by drawer. If something you own is not being actively used or it's excessive, donate it to the poor. Or sell it and give the money to the poor.*

In 1 Timothy 6:17, Paul wrote, "Teach those who are rich in this world not to be proud and not to trust in their money, which is so unreliable. Their trust should be in God, who richly gives us all we need for our enjoyment" (NLT).

In Matthew 6:19–21, Jesus said, "Do not store up for yourselves treasures on earth, where moths and vermin destroy, and where thieves break in and steal. But store up for yourselves treasures in heaven, where moths and vermin do not destroy, and where thieves do not break in and steal. For where your treasure is, there your heart will be also" (NIV).

Exercise 2—If you're someone who has a savings of some kind, consider before the Lord if you're "storing up treasures on earth"

---

* As I write this book, there's a recent trend called "minimalism." People in the world who don't know Jesus have promoted it. It has nothing to do with the kingdom of God. It's actually just another consumer choice. Decluttering, minimalizing, and downsizing are the new "buying" and the new economic status symbol. Consequently, "minimalism" is just as worldly as acquiring wealth. What I'm talking about in this chapter is not "minimalism." I'm talking about obedience to the gospel of the kingdom.

and act accordingly. Ask Him what you should do with your finances and respond.

4. Take a spiritual inventory of your life. Specifically, identify those things that are part of the world system and have a hold on your life. (Once we name something accurately, we take away much of its power. So naming those things that are part of the world is half the victory.)

Write each one of them down. Then, trusting in the Holy Spirit's power, renounce each one in your heart before the Lord. Make your renouncement verbal to God.

Your renouncement should be followed by definitive action. It may mean pulling out of some organizations. It may mean changing careers or jobs. It may mean ending a relationship where there exists an "unequal yoke" and the person you are relating to is dragging you back into the world. It will certainly mean letting go of those things that are derailing you from seeking God's kingdom first in your life.

Make a violent break with the world. This is the only way to appropriate the freedom that Jesus Christ has given you from the world system, enabling you to give your life to the insurgence.

If you are married, discuss your decisions with your spouse and seek agreement when it comes to your lifestyle, standard of living, the possessions you share together, and what you will give to those in need.

Part VI
ADVANCING THE KINGDOM

From the beginning of Acts to the end of Revelation, the main terms that describe our relationship to the kingdom of God are *enter*, *proclaim*, and *inherit*. The Gospels, however, talk about the kingdom of God growing and spreading. In this book, I'm using the word *advance* to describe the expansion of God's kingdom on the earth. Precisely how the kingdom of God advances, however, is a subject of much debate. But the Scriptures give us insight into this question, and we will explore it now.

First Things

. . .

Before we explore how the kingdom of God spreads and advances in the earth, I want to raise a piercing question.

If the gospel of the kingdom is not changing your life, how can you expect it to change the lives of others?

This is why I began this book with the issue of loving the Lord and entering His kingdom ourselves.

But the point remains. Those who co-work with the Lord in advancing His kingdom must first experience and enjoy it in their own lives.

To put it another way, if the gospel of the kingdom isn't transforming you, how can you expect it to transform anyone else?

How the Kingdom Comes

* * *

Some segments of the Christian world teach that the church exists to make the world a better place. This usually involves the pursuit of political power and engagement in social activism.

Terms like "building the kingdom" are typically employed to describe this work.

Interestingly, the New Testament never teaches us to "build" the kingdom. In fact, nowhere in Scripture are we told to build, grow, or even advance the kingdom of God.

This work is done by God alone. However, we co-labor with Him in this work.

In one of his letters, Paul mentions his "co-workers for the kingdom of God" (Colossians 4:11 NIV). Paul also described himself and others as "co-workers in God's service" (1 Corinthians 3:9 NIV). In the same spirit, Mark tells us that "the Lord worked with" the disciples after His ascension (Mark 16:20 NASB).

So God is the One who advances His kingdom, but we have a role in co-working with Him for its advance.

I submit that while the people of God certainly have an influence on the world, especially when we are living under the lordship of Jesus, we are not called to fix the problems of the world.

Those Christians who have tried to make the world a better place through their own efforts have sometimes made it worse. And they've often burned themselves out in the process. The fact is, we are incapable of fixing the countless problems that plague our society.

So how does the kingdom come? How does God advance it in the earth? And what role do we—the members of the ekklesia—play in that advancement?

Those are the questions that will occupy us throughout the rest of this book.

The Source of the Kingdom

• • •

For the last 1800 years, Christians have been trying to build the kingdom in the energy of their own flesh. The result? *Profound failure, frustration, and eventual burnout.*

As I've argued many times before, the only way to live this thing called "the Christian life" is to stop trying and discover the secret of letting Christ live His life in and through us.

Regrettably, many Christians who are interested in "seeing the kingdom" have zero interest in learning anything about living by the indwelling life of Jesus Christ, a truth that stands at the very heart of the New Testament.

Consider these texts:

Now may the God of peace, who through the blood of the eternal covenant brought back from the dead our Lord Jesus, that great Shepherd of the sheep, equip you with everything good for doing his will, and may he work in us what is pleasing to him, through Jesus Christ, to whom be glory for ever and ever. Amen. (Hebrews 13:20–21 NIV)

For it is God who is at work in you, both to will and to work for His good pleasure. (Philippians 2:13 NASB)

I have been crucified with Christ; and it is no longer I who live, but Christ lives in me; and the life which I now live in the flesh I live by faith in the Son of God, who loved me and gave Himself up for me. (Galatians 2:20 NASB)

There remains therefore a rest for the people of God. For he who has entered His rest has himself also ceased from his works as God did from His. (Hebrews 4:9–10 NKJV)

Remarkably, even Jesus Christ could not live the Christian life by His own power and initiative.

So Jesus explained, "I tell you the truth, the Son can do nothing by himself. He does only what he sees the Father doing. Whatever the Father does, the Son also does." (John 5:19 NLT)

By myself I can do nothing. (John 5:30 NIV)

Then He turned around and told us the same thing.

Apart from me you can do nothing. (John 15:5 NIV)

As the living Father hath sent me, and I live by the Father: so he that eateth me, even he shall live by me. (John 6:57 KJV)

What the Father was to Jesus, Jesus is to you and me. *He's our indwelling Lord.*

Independence, which is living by our own initiative, is an essential aspect of sin. Dependence upon the Lord's life is an essential aspect of righteousness. For this reason, Satan tempted Jesus to act on His own initiative and do something outside of God's will (Matthew 4:3, 5, 9). Satan's temptations against us are of the same nature.

Sin is the dethroning of God in one's life. Righteousness is bringing God back into His rightful place.

The one Seed—Jesus—fell into the earth and died in order to bear many seeds (John 12:24). Those many seeds are you and me. We are the undoing of the enemy as we live by the life of Christ, which is the life of God's kingdom.

The cross of Christ has made all of this possible. The cross was the undoing of the enemy, making possible the inauguration of the new creation by Christ's resurrection.

Elsewhere I've spoken about how to live by the life of Christ.* But the first step is to understand that it's both necessary and possible. Anything less will never advance the kingdom.

The reason is because the source of the kingdom is spiritual, not physical. And even though the kingdom has tangible manifestations, its essence is heavenly.

---

* See my "Living by the Indwelling Life of Christ" course at InsurgenceBook.com.

Hungry for Justice

• • •

Recently, one of my email subscribers unsubscribed from my blog, a blog where I glorify Christ and discuss the implications of living by His life.

When I asked her why she unsubscribed, her answer was, "I'm into social justice. I'm hungry for justice and that's my passion."

This person is an example of those who have made the kingdom of God the equivalent of social justice, wherein Jesus Christ has gotten short-changed in the process.

It's actually idolatrous to make "social justice" one's passion above the Lord Jesus Himself. It's idolatrous because our allegiance has shifted from Christ to serving the world.

Tragically, there are countless Christians today who are more interested in making the world a better place than they are in knowing and living by Christ, who is the very incarnation of God's kingdom.

While engaging in humanitarian efforts is good and noble, such efforts are being done in spades by wealthy entrepreneurs and philanthropic celebrities, many of whom are atheists and agnostics. These efforts are not exclusive to Christians (though it can be argued that philanthropy in the West was originally influenced by Christianity).

Humanitarian efforts alone cannot be rightly called "kingdom work." Not in any biblical sense, anyway.

"Kingdom work" is only done when those engaged in the labor have surrendered to Jesus as King. If that hasn't happened, it can be called "good" work, "noble" work, "humanitarian" work, but not "kingdom" work.

Kingdom work proclaims, embodies, or demonstrates the sovereign kingship of Jesus Christ. To put it bluntly, you cannot make something that's worldly spiritual by slapping the word "kingdom" on it.

Another Brand of Worldliness

. . .

As I was writing this book, someone asked me what I thought about a particular "movement" that is focused on bringing justice to a certain slice of Americans. My response was that the movement—which is headed up by a human organization (not the ekklesia)—is dedicated to a cause. The cause is noble; however, neither the organization nor the movement is preaching the gospel of the kingdom of Jesus Christ. Therefore, it's not an instrument of God's kingdom.

Here's the harsh reality. Serving the world can actually become another brand of worldliness. The "social gospel"—which focuses on fixing the problems of the world—began over a century ago. But it has failed to solve the problems of wickedness, corruption, violence, and oppression.

Yet more tragically, the social gospel has emptied the gospel of the kingdom of its spiritual power. When the end game becomes trying to make the world a better place by our own efforts, the need for worship goes out the door. So does the need for living by the indwelling life of Christ and warring against the invisible, spiritual forces that run the world. This is why many of the early proponents of the social gospel have argued that it often leads to unbelief.

In describing the liberal bent of the social gospel, H. Richard Niebuhr insightfully wrote,

> A God without wrath brought men without sin into a Kingdom without judgment through the ministrations of a Christ without a Cross.[1]

The truth is, we cannot do kingdom work without worshiping the King. And we cannot do kingdom work apart from living by the King's life. And both of those elements are based on the cross of Jesus Christ.

The gospel of the kingdom and the cross of Jesus Christ cannot be separated. It is for this reason that Paul used "the cross" and "the gospel" interchangeably (1 Corinthians 1:17–18).

A. W. Tozer rightly said, "I will never be able to love other people in the world until I have first mastered my love for God."[2]

New generations of Christians are attracted to the social gospel because they are disillusioned with the idea that the gospel is only about retreating to heaven after death. But they are unaware of the social gospel's long track record of failure. They are also unaware that there is another alternative to it—*the gospel of the kingdom.*

Again, the idea that the kingdom of God is the equivalent of social justice completely misses worship. Think about it. Why do we need to worship God and learn to live by Christ's indwelling life if we can bring the kingdom by our own efforts?

We can't.

The kingdom of God advances when the kingdom of darkness is pushed back, and this requires that our entire lives are submitted to Jesus as Lord and we are living by His indwelling life. Only the Holy Spirit in us can push back the darkness, not the best efforts of fallen human life.

Unfortunately, many today want a theology and a social cause without the living Person of Jesus. They take His teachings and even cite them. But they treat Christ Himself as though He were dead. Such people are not doing the work of the kingdom of God, no matter how noble their deeds may be.[*]

Those who are part of the insurgence "hunger and thirst for righteousness." But they understand that Righteousness is a living Person who is still active in the world. And His name is Jesus (1 Corinthians 1:30).

Whenever we live by the life of Christ, we proclaim, embody, and demonstrate the righteousness of Jesus Christ in the world.

On the contrary, any efforts done in our own natural strength, regardless of the motive, will have very little spiritual impact and will eventually lead to burnout.

So we have to begin in a brand-new place.

---

[*] Leonard Sweet and I address this common problem in our book *Jesus Manifesto.*

The Secret of the Kingdom

• • •

Jesus is the master key to the kingdom of God. He's also the open secret of the kingdom.

In Matthew 13 and Mark 4, Jesus unfolds what He calls the "secret"—or mystery—of the kingdom of God.

The principal secret of the kingdom is that it's here now as a present reality, but in a largely hidden way.

Instead of overturning the political rule of this world, the kingdom of God declares war on the unseen rule of God's enemy.

Instead of trying to overthrow governments, the kingdom of God effects change in the spiritual lives of human beings.

The kingdom is a gift that's offered to all, but it works secretly, imperceptibly, below the surface.

The kingdom belongs to the future, but it's brought into the present. The kingdom is part of the age to come, but it has arrived in this age. The kingdom belongs to tomorrow, yet it's here today.

The kingdom is found wherever Jesus is manifesting God's ruling presence. It's where God's will is done on earth as it is in heaven. It appears wherever the followers of Jesus enact the Lord's will in the world. While the kingdom is here now, its full flowering will be manifested when Jesus returns to earth at His second coming.*

The kingdom is active in the hearts and lives of those who submit to its rule now, but it shall dominate the whole earth later.

The kingdom doesn't force itself on people, so it can be rejected. It's like a man sowing seed in the ground, only bearing fruit in fertile, receptive ground. And like a seed in the ground, it works quietly, secretly, and out of view.

---

* A detailed discussion of the second coming of Christ can be found in chap. 16 of my book with Leonard Sweet, *Jesus: A Theography*, "The Return of the King."

The Hidden-to-Visible Kingdom

· · ·

The kingdom of God is like wheat sown among weeds. The wheat and weeds grow together until the final harvest comes when the last separation reveals the difference.

The kingdom is small and insignificant like a mustard seed, but it will eventually grow into a large shrub.

The kingdom is like leaven, which is mostly imperceptible. But the leaven will eventually permeate the entire batch of dough.

The kingdom is like a treasure and a pearl, worth forfeiting everything a person has to obtain it. Yet the treasure is hidden and the pearl is created outside the sight of humans.

The kingdom is like a dragnet, working underneath the water, unseen. But it will be pulled ashore so the fish it has caught will be revealed to all.

The point of all the parables in Matthew 13 and Mark 4 is that the kingdom of God lives in a hidden-to-visible tension. It works quietly and unobtrusively, beyond the perception of mortals. But it grows slowly and steadily until finally, when the King returns, it will overcome the entire world.

For this reason, if you follow the daily news, you may be tempted to ask, "Where is the kingdom of God in the midst of all this chaos?"

Rest assured. The kingdom is advancing, but mostly in secret.

But as more people join the insurgence, that advance will escalate and become more noticeable.

Radical Reversals

• • •

Much of what Jesus did was countercultural. He ate with all the wrong people. He chose those on the margins to be His closest associates. He routinely turned sacred traditions inside out. This got Him in constant trouble with the religious and political elites of His day. His teaching and practices were revolutionary.

The reason is because the kingdom of God doesn't operate like the world operates. In the upside-down kingdom of Jesus, power is redefined and values are reversed.

In the kingdom, those who serve are exalted, and those who exalt themselves are humbled (Matthew 23:12; Luke 1:52; 14:11).

In the kingdom, those who lose gain, and those who seek to gain lose (Matthew 10:39; 16:25–26; Luke 17:33).

In the kingdom, the proud are debased while the humble in heart are blessed (Matthew 18:2–4; Luke 14:11).

In the kingdom, truth is hidden from the wise and prudent, but it is revealed to babes (Matthew 11:25).

In the kingdom, the greatest serve and those who seek to be great are humbled (Matthew 23:11–12).

In the kingdom, leadership is not set up like a top-down, chain-of-command hierarchy nor is it based on titles; it's based on service and humility (Matthew 20:26–28; 23:5–9; Luke 22:25–26).

In the kingdom, the last will be first, and the first will be last (Matthew 20:16; Mark 10:43–44).

In the kingdom, those who were hungry and mourn will eat and be merry (Luke 6:25).

In the kingdom, those who have received evil will receive good (Luke 16:25).

The countercultural, counterintuitive nature of God's kingdom explains why the most religious people of Jesus' day understood the message the least and why the least religious of His day got it the most.

The kingdom of God is a beautiful and blessed thing. The domain of God's rule causes people to be blessed, satisfied, and happy. For this reason, God's intention has always been to extend His kingdom from heaven to earth, from eternity to here, which is essentially the expansion of the Garden of Eden that we find in Genesis 2.

It is no surprise, then, that Eden means "delight."

The Cross and the Insurgence

. . .

The New Testament tells the story of the kingdom of God coming to earth just as it is in heaven. And the cross of Christ is central to that story. The cross is also the basis of our sacrifice to the Lord, which is best articulated in this timeless hymn:

> When I survey the wondrous cross
> On which the Prince of glory died,
> My richest gain I count but loss,
> And pour contempt on all my pride.
> Were the whole realm of nature mine,
> That were a present far too small;
> Love so amazing, so divine,
> Demands my soul, my life, my all.[3]

The Community of the King

. . .

Rightly understood, the ekklesia is a group of people who are learning to live by the life of Christ, which is the life of God's kingdom. This life is also called divine life and eternal life.

Eternal life is the life of the age to come. It's the life of the kingdom of the heavens. When you and I live by that life, we bear the image of God and exercise His authority.

The ekklesia is none other than the community of the King. In every city where she is found, she lives as a microcosm, a signpost, a foretaste and foregleam of the kingdom of God. (I use "she" to describe the ekklesia because Paul did—see Ephesians 5:25–27. The ekklesia is the bride of Jesus Christ.)

The ekklesia is the firstfruits of the final harvest in the resurrection, the pilot project of what the kingdom of God is all about.

> He chose to give us birth through the word of truth, that we might be a kind of firstfruits of all he created. (James 1:18 NIV)

> Not only so, but we ourselves, who have the firstfruits of the Spirit, groan inwardly as we wait eagerly for our adoption to sonship, the redemption of our bodies. (Romans 8:23 NIV)

> But we ought always to thank God for you, brothers and sisters loved by the Lord, because God chose you as firstfruits to be saved through the sanctifying work of the Spirit and through belief in the truth. (2 Thessalonians 2:13 NIV)

The firstfruits are the promise of the full harvest. And they are the beginning of that harvest. In this regard, the Holy Spirit has been given to us as the down payment of the future resurrection and the full glory of God. Because the Spirit is the down payment, we can experience the power of the Holy Spirit right now in this evil age.

As the writer of Hebrews puts it, we are those who have "tasted the . . . powers of the coming age" (6:5 NIV). A taste is a real experience. But it's also the promise of the full meal.

The ekklesia—when she's living as God intended—reveals to the lost that God has already changed the world. We, the body of Christ, are the embodiment of God's triumphant and sovereign rule here and now. For we have come under that rule ourselves, and we are learning to live it out. And God's sovereign rule is a reign of grace (Romans 5:21), which we live by and display.

So if you wish to find the sovereign rule, dominion, authority, and government of Jesus Christ, you will find it in the ekklesia when she is functioning properly.

The Collective Expression of Christ

· · ·

The ekklesia of God is called to exercise and manifest the authority of Jesus Christ in the earth (Matthew 16:19; 28:18). The ekklesia is the collective expression of Jesus; therefore, the ekklesia embodies the kingdom of God.

In 1 Corinthians, Paul uses the human body as a metaphor for the ekklesia. And then he makes this shocking statement:

> For even as the [human] body is one and yet has many members, and all the members of the body, though they are many, are one body, so also is Christ. (1 Corinthians 12:12 NASB)

Notice the words "so also is Christ." Paul didn't make a mistake in that statement. Jesus Christ is one with His ekklesia. The ekklesia is the corporate (collective) expression of Jesus in the earth. It's the manifestation of the age to come in the midst of this present age of rebellion.

Those who are part of the insurgence long to be in face-to-face community with others who are learning to have the character of Christ formed in them and who are revealing that character where they live, "on earth as it is in heaven."

Chiefly, the ekklesia is a people whose lives are marked by forgiveness, the meaning of the Jubilee of God, where all of Israel's debts were forgiven. (Remember, Jesus made reference to the Jubilee when He referred to "the year of the Lord's favor" in Luke 4:19.)

Jesus Christ is our Jubilee who has come to earth in the form of the kingdom of God. And the ekklesia is called to live that Jubilee by her lifestyle.

Through the Holy Spirit, we experience the life of the age to come in the present as well as in the future during the coming age.

As F. F. Bruce put it,

> And it is by the Spirit's operating that the people of Christ, instead of being left as isolated individuals, are unified not only to Him but one to another,

to form the reconciled community which, in God's eternal purpose, is the model for the reconciled universe.[4]

God's plan is to use the ekklesia as His instrument to advance His kingdom in three chief ways: proclamation, embodiment, and demonstration.

Whenever the body of Christ carries out these three tasks, its members consciously walk in the invisible geography of the kingdom of God. And just as the kingdom appeared wherever Jesus walked when He was on the earth, the kingdom appears wherever the body of Christ proclaims, embodies, and demonstrates the King.

Jesus said that only those who are born from above are able to "see" the unseen kingdom of God (John 3:3). Those who are part of the insurgence attune themselves to this "seeing" and act accordingly.

Proclaiming the Kingdom

• • •

One way that God's kingdom advances is through the apostolic proclamation. This proclamation began with John the Baptist (Matthew 3:1–2) and Jesus (Luke 4:43).

And he sent them out to proclaim the kingdom of God. (Luke 9:2 NIV)

Following in the footsteps of John and Jesus, the early apostles and evangelists proclaimed the gospel of the kingdom and summoned people to repent and believe it (Acts 2:38; 3:19; 8:12; 19:8; 20:21, 25; 28:31).

Just as a Roman emperor's messengers traveled to the territories in which he was enthroned as lord to bring the good news of his accession to the throne, so the apostles (messengers) of Christ were sent out to herald the good news that Jesus was now the enthroned Lord of the world.

What does it require to proclaim the gospel of the kingdom? Not much. Just a pound of flesh and a pint of blood. The gospel of the kingdom demands that those who preach it first obey and experience it themselves.

If a person tries to proclaim the gospel of the kingdom without obeying it, their words will have little effect.

The apostolic proclamation continues today as the Holy Spirit anoints and sends members of His body—those who have obeyed and experienced that gospel themselves—to proclaim it in a way that's totally uncompromising.

The gospel of the kingdom is the message of the insurgence.

The Witness of the Kingdom

• • •

Another word for the apostolic proclamation of the kingdom is "witness." The apostles lived as "witnesses" of Jesus' accession to the throne of God in heaven and they summoned others to believing obedience to Jesus, the new King (Acts 1:8; Luke 24:44–48).

To proclaim the kingdom is to announce that the dark powers that enslave people have been defeated. It's to proclaim that people can be free of those powers if they surrender to the One who triumphed over them.

To announce the kingdom is to declare that God is with us in the person of Jesus, and forgiveness of sins, restoration, deliverance from oppression, new life, and knowing God as our Father are all available.

> Now this is eternal life: that they know you, the only true God, and Jesus Christ, whom you have sent. (John 17:3 NIV)

The apostles and evangelists weren't witnessing about how to go to heaven when you die, although that's part of the meaning of eternal life. They were rather witnessing to the fact that Jesus of Nazareth has been installed as Lord of the world and we can enter His kingdom here and now as well as in the future.

The gospel of the kingdom the apostles announced was a gospel of transformation, which invites people into a present reality that will become fuller and more widespread when Jesus returns. This is in contrast to the gospel of evacuation, which encourages people to believe in Jesus so they can go to heaven when they die.

While the book of Acts shows us how the apostles and evangelists proclaimed the gospel of the kingdom all throughout the Roman Empire as Jesus commissioned them to, we don't see a great deal of emphasis placed on proclaiming the gospel of the kingdom in the epistles of the New Testament, which were written to the ekklesias.

Instead, we see abundant encouragements to God's people to witness to the kingdom of God by the testimony of their lives. Peter exhorts the believers in the ekklesias to live in such a way that unbelievers are provoked to ask them questions about why they live so differently.

> But in your hearts revere Christ as Lord. Always be prepared to give an answer to everyone who asks you to give the reason for the hope that you have. But do this with gentleness and respect. (2 Peter 3:15 NIV)

Paul makes a similar point:

> Be wise in the way you act toward outsiders; make the most of every opportunity. Let your conversation be always full of grace, seasoned with salt, so that you may know how to answer everyone. (Colossians 4:5–6 NIV)

But as important as the proclamation of the gospel is, it's not enough to advance the kingdom. The kingdom of God also needs to be embodied and demonstrated.

Embodying the Kingdom

. . .

The ekklesia is called to embody the kingship of Christ, not just in word, but also in deed.

Like any other kingdom, the kingdom of God has its own culture. In the realm of human and natural things, it's easy to discern someone's citizenship by their accent, dialect, and the way they pronounce certain words. Sometimes their dress will give it away too.

In the same way, those who live under the sovereign rule of God have a vocabulary that reflects their citizenship. Jesus taught that what comes out of our mouths is a reflection of what's in our hearts (Matthew 12:34). Make no mistake about it. Those who live by the life of the kingdom will talk differently than people in the world (Ephesians 4:29; 5:4; Colossians 3:8).

Our values will also be different. The same with our hobbies and pastimes. While some of these may overlap, kingdom citizens will also have different hobbies and pastimes than those practiced by the citizens of the world.

In addition, the way kingdom citizens conduct themselves in relationships and business will diverge from those who are part of the world.

> Yet we urge you, brothers and sisters, to . . . make it your ambition to lead a quiet life: You should mind your own business and work with your hands, just as we told you, so that your daily life may win the respect of outsiders and so that you will not be dependent on anybody. (1 Thessalonians 4:10–12 NIV)

People who live exactly like the world will never provoke people to ask questions about the "hope that lies within them" (as Peter puts it). But those who talk, act, and live differently often will. Hence the words of Paul:

> Only conduct yourselves in a manner worthy of the gospel of Christ. (Philippians 1:27 NASB)

The Better Place

. . .

While some Christians are trying to make the world a "better place," God's way of advancing the kingdom is to make the ekklesia the "better place" on earth as it is in heaven.

[He] made us to be a kingdom. (Revelation 1:6 NIV)

As members of the body of Christ, we are not called to transform the world. We are called to *be* a transformed world.

John Nugent put it brilliantly when he wrote,

> Our responsibility from God is not to make the world a better place, but to be the better place God has begun in this world through Christ. We are His kingdom work. We are ambassadors who proclaim what God has done, is doing, and will do. God's strategy is for His people not to fix this world but to plant a new world right in the midst of the old one and to woo the old world to Himself through it. As followers of Jesus, the body of Christ, the new humanity and new creation is us. We are the new world that has already broken into the old. A new creation has already begun in the midst of the old world that remains. It is the new world of God's kingdom and its people.[*]

Nugent is correct. When the ekklesia was born in the first century, the Roman Empire saw something that was not human. It saw something that was divine. The empire witnessed a people who were embodying and demonstrating self-sacrificing, self-giving love, which is the DNA of divine life.

Nugent took the idea deeper when he wrote,

> God's people are not responsible for making this world a better place, but for being the better place that Christ has already made. . . . The early believers were vocal in proclaiming the gospel of God's kingdom and visible in living

---

[*] John Nugent develops these ideas in his book *Endangered Gospel* (Eugene, OR: Cascade Books, 2016).

it out as a community. . . . The church's calling centers on being the better place God began in Jesus.[5]

Notice that Jesus Himself made the same point,

By this everyone will know that you are my disciples, if you love one another. (John 13:35 NIV)

. . . so that they [My followers] may be brought to complete unity. Then the world will know that you sent me and have loved them even as you have loved me. (John 17:23 NIV)

Indeed, when the ekklesia was born, the world saw a piece of heaven on earth. By its robust life together as the body of Christ, the unbelieving world was given a glimpse into the new creation. The kingdom of God was showcased by the loving fellowship the early Christians had with one another.

When Jesus Christ rose again from the dead and indwelt His followers at Pentecost, a new power was unleashed in the world. It was the power of God's nature deposited in human beings (2 Peter 1:4). And that nature was one of self-giving love lived out in face-to-face community. That love was so powerfully expressed in the ekklesia's life together that it shook the Roman Empire to its foundations.*

Here was a people who were living as though God was calling the shots. They lived as though Jesus the Messiah was running the show. And they believed that they were living in the presence of the future.

Our life together as God's people is the only evidence the Lord left in this world that He has inaugurated a new world through Jesus. God uses His kingdom community, the ekklesia, to model the new social order that Jesus brought in through His ministry, death, resurrection, and ascension.

My question to you and every other Christian who is part of a church today is this: *Is your life together embodying God's kingdom to the world around you? If so, how?*

---

* See my online article "You Shall Not Taste Death" at InsurgenceBook.com for my thoughts on what happened on the day of Pentecost.

The Centrality of the Ekklesia

The most political and revolutionary thing that God's people can do today is to learn to gather together under Christ's lordship and embody the life of the kingdom collectively. This is what "church" was in the first century. The ekklesia was a kingdom society that embodied God's sovereign reign before a watching world.

The ekklesia told an alternative story by her life together, a story radically different from the narrative told by the world.

Let me be blunt. God's people who want justice, peace, and forgiveness for their country should be spending their energies embodying these virtues in their local assemblies. If they aren't doing those things in the context of the ekklesia, their "work" in the world for these values simply rings hollow.

The ekklesia doesn't join the world system in trying to improve the world. The ekklesia lives a life that's contrary to the world system and calls those in the world to submit to Jesus as Lord.

As I've argued in *From Eternity to Here*, the ekklesia is God's heartbeat. It's also the center of His work in the earth. From the beginning, God purposed to have a bride, a house, a body, and a family.

This is why the issue of "church restoration" is so vitally important. Despite the attacks against it by those who fight tooth and nail to retain the status quo and settle for rearranging the chairs on the *Titanic*, the call of the Spirit to face the issue of radical church restoration remains.

We can hide our heads in the sand and ignore those prophetic voices who are calling for such restoration today. But as we do, the world will remain monumentally unimpressed with "church" as it bears little resemblance to the kingdom of God, the very thing the ekklesia was designed to be in the earth.

The primary purpose of the ekklesia is to be the presence of Christ in the world and manifest the earth-shaking power of the gospel of the kingdom before a watching world. And that showcasing naturally leads to blessing the world, just as Jesus blessed it while He was on earth.

As I put it elsewhere,

The gospel of Luke is a record of what Jesus Christ "began to do and to teach" (Acts 1:1). It's a record of the beginning of Christ's life and ministry on earth. The book of Acts is a record of the continuation of Christ's life and ministry on earth through His body. As John the apostle said, as Jesus was in this world, so now is the church (1 John 4:17).[6]

Demonstrating the Kingdom

In the year 2008, I released a book entitled *Reimagining Church*. In it, I sketched out a vision of what the local ekklesia can look like when the members of the body of Christ are submitted to Christ as their head (Colossians 1:18).

The book was not built on theory but from my own experience. It was also solidly rooted in the New Testament.

In short, *Reimagining Church* cast a clear vision on how the local ekklesia can proclaim, embody, and demonstrate the kingdom of God today in ways that break with the status quo.

Because I covered a great deal of terrain in that volume, I won't repeat it here. Suffice it to say that some who first read that book were threatened by its revolutionary message. Why? Because it challenged numerous sacred cows about church practice.

Interestingly, many who first attacked the book wrote me letters years later to the tune of, "I was wrong about your book. I now see the need for rethinking our church practices in the light of God's eternal purpose. The kingdom of God is suffering because our practice of church is not rooted in the New Testament. When the lost visit most churches today, they don't see or experience the presence of Jesus Christ."

One of the key points I made in that book is that the ekklesia, when functioning under the headship of Christ, will shame the cosmic principalities and powers by showing that a fallen human race can be led by an invisible, resurrected Lord who has conquered them.

> His intent was that now, through the church, the manifold wisdom of God should be made known to the rulers and authorities in the heavenly realms. (Ephesians 3:10 NIV)

Also, the undeniable love and care that the brothers and sisters in the ekklesia have for one another when they are living by the indwelling life of

Christ spills over to the lost as a tangible, visible, locatable signpost that the kingdom of God has in fact come. In addition, the hostile cosmic powers as well as God's faithful angels witness God's multicolored wisdom and glory by the presence of the ekklesia.[*]

In this way, those who are part of the insurgence stand for God's eternal purpose as a witness to both earthly and heavenly realms.

[*] Angels observe human affairs. They look and learn (1 Corinthians 4:9; 1 Peter 1:12).

What Does the Kingdom Look Like?

. . .

The kingdom of God looks like a people who are taking care of each other. It looks like a people who are laying their lives down for each other. It looks like a people who are living as an extended family. It looks like a close-knit, functioning body where each member is affected by what happens to the other members.

> If one part [of the body] suffers, every part suffers with it; if one part is honored, every part rejoices with it. (1 Corinthians 12:26 NIV)

But it also looks like

Feeding the hungry.

Clothing the naked.

Blessing the poor.

Giving sight to the blind.

Caring for the sick and infirm.

Delivering those who are bound by Satan.

Forgiving others and preaching the forgiveness of sins through Christ's death and resurrection.

Proclaiming the gospel of the kingdom to the poor and showcasing it by our lives.

In other words, the ekklesia does all the things that Jesus did while He was on earth. And she does it in the name of Jesus Christ and by the power of His Spirit.

Why? Because Jesus is the kingdom of God yesterday and today (Luke 4:16–19; Acts 10:38). And the ekklesia is Christ in corporate (collective) expression (1 Corinthians 1:12–13; 12:12; Acts 9:1–4).

Herein lies the power of the insurgence.

The Authority of the Believer

. . .

Some have suggested that Jesus' authority over Satan was exclusive to Himself. Therefore, the ekklesia has no such authority. But this idea fails to take into account the fact that the body of Christ has been anointed by the same Spirit who anointed Jesus (2 Corinthians 1:21–22; 1 John 2:20, 27; Luke 10:17–19).

Jesus Himself exhorted us that He will continue to work in and through us:

> I tell you the truth, anyone who believes in me will do the same works I have done, and even greater works, because I am going to be with the Father. (John 14:12 NLT)

The anointing oil that poured on the head of our Great High Priest flows down to His body (Psalm 133). Consequently, the body of Christ continues the earthly ministry of Jesus in the world with the same authority that was given to Jesus. This is the meaning of praying and healing in "the name of Jesus," which we find all throughout the book of Acts.

In fact, Acts and the Epistles are full of examples of the body of Christ doing the same works that Jesus did in delivering those who were oppressed by the devil (Mark 16:17–18; Acts 3:6; 5:15; 6:8; 13:6–11; 16:16–18; 19:11–12; Romans 15:19).

> You, dear children, are from God and have overcome them, because the one who is in you is greater than the one who is in the world. (1 John 4:4 NIV)

When Jesus handed the keys of the kingdom of God to the ekklesia, He sent it into the world to carry on His ministry with the same authority (John 20:21–23).*

Notice the wording of God's call to Paul:

---

* A discussion of the miraculous gifts of the Holy Spirit is well beyond the scope of this book; however, I have addressed the subject in detail in *There Must Be More*, which can be found at InsurgenceBook.com.

> For this purpose I have appeared to you, to appoint you a minister and a witness . . . rescuing you . . . from the Gentiles, to whom I am sending you, to open their eyes so that they may turn from darkness to light and from the dominion of Satan to God. (Acts 26:16–18 NASB)

God continues to use the members of His body to turn the lost "from the dominion of Satan to God." Jesus' power-filled words to His disciples still apply to you and me today.

> Behold, I give you the authority to trample on serpents and scorpions, and over all the power of the enemy, and nothing shall by any means hurt you. (Luke 10:19 NKJV)*

As incredible as it sounds, God has bestowed on the ekklesia "the immeasurable greatness of his power" in accomplishing this task (Ephesians 1:18–19 ESV). As a member of the body of Christ, you are in Christ in a position of power and authority far above all cosmic principalities and powers (Ephesians 2:6; 1:19–22). That power can only be *fully* expressed, however, collectively as the body of Christ. It is the body, not an individual member, that is Christ's expression on the earth.

T. Austin-Sparks was correct when he wrote,

> Two saints, simple, humble and unimportant in this world, but really meeting together in the Spirit, can be a functioning instrument of Him to whom has been committed all authority in heaven and on earth. With them all these old limitations can be dismissed and they can at one moment touch all the ends of the earth. Do you believe that? That is really the meaning of our glorying in Christ risen.[7]

---

* Serpents and scorpions are symbols of the satanic realm. One of the best treatments of the believer's authority over Satan and the biblical teaching about spiritual warfare is Clinton Arnold's *Powers of Darkness* (Downers Grove, IL: InterVarsity Press, 1992). See also Greg Boyd's *God at War* (Downers Grove, IL: InterVarsity Press, 1997), 269–93.

The Signposts

. . .

Human kingdoms advance by coercion, force, and violence. But God's kingdom advances by forgiveness, suffering, stories, proclamation, demonstration, and example.

The kingdom of God doesn't move forward by slitting the throats of Romans nor by withdrawing from sinful society. It doesn't come by the extermination of the King's enemies, but by the death of the King Himself and the self-sacrifice of His followers.

As we've already seen, the kingdom grows quietly, slowly, and under the surface, like yeast in a bowl of dough or seed inside of soil. The kingdom gains ground when the subjects of the King forgive, love, and bear the cross of their Lord.

The miracles of Jesus were signposts of the kingdom. Healing deaf people symbolized hearing the truth with the ears of the heart. Healing the blind symbolized seeing the truth with the eyes of the human spirit. Raising the dead symbolized newness of life.

The signs and wonders that Jesus performed revealed that the God of creation was becoming King. And that He is a good and benevolent King, present in the mess of the world, bringing forgiveness, peace, justice, liberty, and wholeness to all who submit to Him.

> For this purpose the Son of God was manifested, that he might destroy the works of the devil. (1 John 3:8 KJV)

Whenever Jesus cast out a demon or healed an oppressed person, He was foreshadowing the ultimate defeat of Satan's kingdom at the cross, where God would cut off the root of evil once and for all.

When the ekklesia continues the ministry of Jesus in the earth today, it is carrying on the same work.

Through the insurgence, Christ's ministry continues.

Kingdom Cells

· · ·

While those who have entered the kingdom of God have been "radical-ized," they don't act like hidden "sleeper cells." They are active, visible, and engaged—proclaiming, embodying, and demonstrating the kingdom on earth as it is in heaven.

Some of the ekklesias I've worked with marked out seasons in their shared life together to create small "kingdom cells" which sought creative ways to demonstrate the kingdom of God in their local communities.

Some of those smaller "kingdom cells" served the poor in their city, others helped widows and widowers, others aided the homeless, others ministered to drug addicts, others helped pregnant teens, and others served those caught in the sex-trafficking industry.

Some of these groups came alongside other groups and organizations that were already doing this work in their cities. They cooperated without compromising their convictions. They also brought Jesus Christ into those places by their witness and testimony.

Because they were led by the Spirit of Christ in these endeavors and did their work in the name of Jesus and by the energy of the Spirit, their work truly was "kingdom work"—even in those cases when the organizations they partnered with were not part of God's kingdom.

These believers were not trying to fix the problems of the world. They were instead showcasing the ministry of Jesus before a watching world and witnessing to the fact that the ekklesia is the better place that God has made.

Breaking Good

* * *

The term "break bad" is verbiage used in the American South that means to go wild and defy moral authority. I'm using the term "break good" to convey the opposite.

In the New Testament, the phrase "good works" or "good deeds" has in view the alleviation of human suffering. The ekklesia, when she is living by the life of Christ, carries on the ministry of Jesus who "went about doing good, and healing all that were oppressed of the devil" (Acts 10:38 KJV, see also John 10:32).

The body of Christ does the same today. Paul said to the Galatia Christians,

> So then, as we have opportunity, let us do good to everyone, and especially to those who are of the household of faith. (Galatians 6:10 NIV)

The words "Let us do good to everyone" are often skipped over by those who believe that God's people should only take care of their own. But Paul made the same point in 1 Thessalonians:

> May the Lord make your love increase and overflow for each other and for everyone else. (1 Thessalonians 3:12 NIV)

> Make sure that nobody pays back wrong for wrong, but always strive to do what is good for each other and for everyone else. (1 Thessalonians 5:15 NIV)

Peter breathed the same air when he wrote,

> Live such good lives among the pagans that, though they accuse you of doing wrong, they may see your good deeds and glorify God on the day he visits us. . . . For it is God's will that by doing good you should silence the ignorant talk of foolish people. (1 Peter 2:12, 15 NIV)

Peter also exhorts his readers to show respect to everyone, not just believers (1 Peter 2:17).

All throughout the New Testament, God's people are exhorted to do "good works" (alleviate human suffering) wherever, whenever, and to whomever.

These works are to be done to and for God's people first (Galatians 6:10), but also to "everyone else" (see Matthew 5:16; Ephesians 2:10; 1 Timothy 2:10; 5:10, 25; 6:18; 2 Thessalonians 2:17; Titus 2:7; 3:8, 14; Hebrews 10:24).

> With this in mind, we constantly pray for you, that our God may make you worthy of his calling, and that by his power he may bring to fruition your every desire for goodness and your every deed prompted by faith. (2 Thessalonians 1:11 NIV)

Keep in mind that the good works spoken about in these texts do not refer to deeds that we do in our own natural energy. Rather, good works are like fruit falling off a tree. They are the product of living by the life of Christ who dwells in us. Interestingly, God has prepared the good works that we will walk in before we ever showed up.

> For we are His workmanship, created in Christ Jesus for good works, which God prepared beforehand, that we should walk in them. (Ephesians 2:10 NKJV)

Indeed, the ekklesia of God is marked by good deeds that flow naturally out of faith and love for her King. Such good works give people who aren't in the kingdom a taste of God's loving reign and the beauty of the King (Titus 2:14).

Those who are part of the insurgence have dared to "break good" in the world.

Beautifying

* * *

We are discovering that while the kingdom of God is spiritual and invisible, it has tangible manifestations.

If you recall, in the first part of this book, we reflected on the stunning beauty of the King. The remarkable thing about conversion is that Jesus Christ, by the Holy Spirit, is in the business of beautifying us with His own beauty.

> For the LORD takes pleasure in His people;
> He will beautify the humble with salvation. (Psalm 149:4 NKJV)

> He did this to present her to himself as a glorious church without a spot or wrinkle or any other blemish. Instead, she will be holy and without fault. (Ephesians 5:27 NLT)

> I saw the Holy City, the new Jerusalem, coming down out of heaven from God, prepared as a bride beautifully dressed for her husband. (Revelation 21:2 NIV)

> To console those who mourn in Zion,
> To give them beauty for ashes. (Isaiah 61:3 NKJV)

To demonstrate the kingdom of God, then, is to express the beauty of the King. The Lamb's wife—the ekklesia of God—reflects the beauty that Jesus Himself possesses.

As Jesus ravishes our hearts and beautifies us with His own beauty, those outside the kingdom detect the radiant beauty of Christ in and through us. This is especially true when we plot good deeds which show forth the glory of God's life.

The insurgence, therefore, knows and reflects the beauty of Christ.

Not a Bless-Me Club

· · ·

Some have taught that Jesus only ministered to His fellow Israelites and didn't demonstrate good works to those who weren't Jewish. Accepting this viewpoint, they suggest that the ekklesia is not called to do good works to the lost but *only* to fellow members of the ekklesia.

While it is true that Jesus was "sent to the house of Israel" and sought to re-create Israel around Himself, it is not true that He did good works only to those who were fellow Israelites.

Some examples are when Jesus healed a Roman centurion's son (Luke 7:1–10), when He ministered life to a Samaritan woman and her friends (John 4), when He delivered a demon-possessed man in the region of the Gerasenes (Mark 5:1–20), and when He healed and fed many sick people in Gentile territory (Matthew 15:29–39).

Jesus didn't do these good deeds among the Gentiles simply because He was a "nice guy." Jesus Christ is Compassion incarnate, and He did these deeds as signposts of the kingdom.

> But if I drive out demons by the finger of God, then the kingdom of God has come upon you. (Luke 11:20 NIV)

> How God anointed Jesus of Nazareth with the Holy Spirit and power, and how he went around doing good and healing all who were under the power of the devil, because God was with him. (Acts 10:38 NIV)

Jesus' ministry of casting out demons was a manifestation of the victory of God's kingdom over Satan's.

In addition, the ministry of Jesus was for the whole world, not just for Israel (Matthew 28:19; John 10:16). Jesus came to destroy the works of the devil, and those works have affected all human beings, not just Israelites (1 John 3:8). Like the gospel, the ministry of Christ was given "first to the Jew, then to the Gentile" (Romans 1:16).

In the same way, while those who follow Jesus primarily show the world what it looks like when Jesus is Lord by taking care of one another in the ekklesia, Jesus-followers are also called to demonstrate the kingdom by doing good works for the lost.

To remove this aspect of the kingdom turns the ekklesia into a bless-me club, a holy huddle of those who care only for their own and are dismissive toward the rest of the world for whom Jesus died.

Whenever this happens, the ekklesia replays the sin of ancient Israel. God's promise concerning Israel was that through her, all the nations of the earth would be blessed. But instead of being the light she was called to be for the world, Israel retained God's blessing for herself, turning its windows into mirrors.

As we saw from the previous chapter, "good works" have everything to do with the kingdom of God. And we do them for the lost as well as for the fellow members of the body of Christ.

Humanitarian Aid

. . .

It must be understood that there's a profound difference between the humanitarian aid and philanthropic "good" deeds that the world engages in and the "good works" that the New Testament speaks about.

While it may appear the same to the naked eye, to the invisible realms of God, it's significantly different.

The good works that the New Testament refers to are always done in the name (or presence) of Jesus Christ and in the power of the Holy Spirit. And the motivation and source of each "good work" is Christ Himself.

> For the kingdom of God is not a matter of talk but of power. (1 Corinthians 4:20 NIV)

So, in effect, the "good works" that the ekklesia carries out—together or as individual members who represent her—are the activity of the community of the King carried out in His person and by His power.

For that reason, they are a living testimony that the kingdom of God has come and a signpost of what the kingdom embodies.

This is not the case when the world engages in humanitarian deeds nor when Christians do such deeds in their own power and strength.

The Fellowship of the Reconciled

As I write this book, the problem of racism is a hotbed issue. Despite all the progress that has been made in the West, racist attitudes and ideas still loom large.

But the problem of racism is not new. It's embedded in the warp and woof of fallen humanity.

The world of the first century was littered with racism and oppression. In the mind of a first-century Jew, Gentiles (Africans, Romans, Greeks, Syrians, Asians, etc.) were created to fuel the fires of hell.

When a Jew called a Gentile "uncircumcised," he spit it. It was a name of profound contempt.

If a Jewish person married a Gentile, the Jewish parents held a funeral service for their child. In their eyes, their child was dead.

On the flip side, Gentiles regarded Jews to be subhuman. Historically, the Jews have been an oppressed people, living under the thumb of one Gentile nation after another (e.g., Egypt, Assyria, Babylon, Greece, Rome).

In all of human history, there has never been so much animosity, hatred, and violence between two groups of people as there has been between the Jew and the Gentile. But alas, in the first century, there emerged a group of radicals on the planet who transcended this entrenched racial hostility.

Here was a group of people who saw themselves as members of the same family . . . a people made up of Jews, Gentiles, slaves, free, rich, poor, male, and female.

These were the early followers of Jesus. The Roman world stood in awe as they saw a people who hated each other begin to love one another and do life together in the name of Jesus.

Watch them walking into the marketplace together, arm in arm, singing with joy in their hearts.

Jew and Gentile.

Slave and free.

Rich and poor.

Male and female.

Look at them closely. Jew and Gentile eating together, working together, greeting one another with a holy kiss, raising their children together, taking care of one another, marrying one another, and burying one another.

This fact blew the circuitry of every person living in Century One. It shook the Roman Empire to its very foundations.

The church of Jesus Christ was a classless society. Its members didn't regard social status, color, or position. For them, there was no Jew or Greek in the body of Christ. There was no slave or free. There was no rich or poor.

> Here there is not Greek and Jew, circumcised and uncircumcised, barbarian, Scythian, slave, free; but Christ is all, and in all. (Colossians 3:11 ESV)

For the first two hundred years, the Christians only addressed each other by their first names. The reason?

Because their last names indicated their social position in society.

Here was a classless, raceless society where all social distinctions were erased.

To their minds, Jew and Gentile, slave and free, rich and poor no longer existed. The early believers saw themselves as part of the same family. They were a new race . . . a colony from another realm, not *of* or *from* this earth. Yet *for* this earth.

By His resurrection, Jesus brought forth a new humanity out of Jew and Gentile, destroying the wall of division and hostility that separated them.

> For he himself is our peace, who has made the two groups one and has destroyed the barrier, the dividing wall of hostility. . . . His purpose was to create in himself one new humanity out of the two, thus making peace, and in one body to reconcile both of them to God through the cross, by which he put to death their hostility. (Ephesians 2:14–16 NIV)

Jesus Christ became the firstborn of a new creation (Romans 8:29).

In 1 Corinthians 10:32, Paul mentions three races: Jew, Gentile, and the *ekklesia* of God. For this reason, the second-century Christians called themselves the "third race" as well as the "new race."

The body of Christ, then, is the restoration of God's original image that creation was designed to bear. An image where there is no Jew or Greek, slave or free, male or female.

> There is neither Jew nor Greek, there is neither slave nor free, there is neither male nor female; for you are all one in Christ Jesus. (Galatians 3:28 NKJV)

Within this new non-ethnic community, the dividing lines of gender, race, class, and social status are wiped away. And new distinctions of spiritual gifting are bestowed. The ekklesia of God, then, is called to be a raceless, genderless, classless society.

Think. If Jesus can bring Jew and Gentile together to form a new humanity, He can bring any group of races together. Or in the words of F. F. Bruce,

> The removal of the Jewish-Gentile barrier carries with it the promise of the removal of other barriers which keep various parts of the human family apart.[8]

Bruce accurately described the church as "not only God's masterpiece of reconciliation here and now, but also God's pilot scheme for the reconciled universe of the future."[9]

Political solutions will only go so far. Adjustments to our laws will always be limited. Nuances to the justice system won't do enough. Only the ekklesia, when she is living by the unified life of Christ, can show forth what a world without racism looks like.

Again, Bruce nailed the matter clearly:

> If the church is to be an effective instrument in promoting the divine work of universal reconciliation, she must be seen to be the fellowship of the reconciled. She cannot convincingly proclaim the gospel of reconciliation to others if the barriers of creed, class, race or colour which are found in the world are tolerated within her own confines. If they are so tolerated, she has fallen into crass wordliness; her witness is nullified; the salt of the earth has lost its savour and has become good for nothing.[10]

John Howard Yoder echoed the same thought:

> The church must be a sample of the kind of humanity within which, for example, economic and racial differences are surmounted. Only then will

it have anything to say to the society that surrounds it about how those differences must be dealt with. Otherwise preaching to the world a standard of reconciliation which is not its own experience will never be honest nor effective.[11]

There is no racism in the kingdom of God. Those who are part of the insurgence understand that they are part of a new humanity that's void of racism, sexism, ageism, classism, etc. And they walk accordingly.

The gospel of the kingdom, when received, ends all racism and racial tension among those who receive it. God's kingdom includes a vision for social justice. That vision is to fill this world with communities of Jesus-followers who reflect God's economics, God's justice, and God's politics. None of which are part of this world.

Those who are part of the insurgence seek to flesh out this vision in their lives, homes, and assemblies.*

* This chapter is an excerpt from an article published on my blog (frankviola.org) called "The Race Card of the Early Christians" written with Derwin Gray. The excerpt is my contribution.

A Collusion of Powers

. . .

The New Testament uses the phrase "principalities and powers," which is also translated "rulers and authorities." This phrase refers to hostile cosmic powers (evil spiritual forces) as well as earthly governmental rulers.

The principalities and powers include human rulers, kingdoms, social structures, governing systems, and spiritual entities.[*]

Despite the players involved, the political and governmental systems of this world are heavily influenced by the evil cosmic principalities and powers ("rulers and authorities") in the spiritual realm. Paul wrote,

> For we do not wrestle against flesh and blood, but against principalities, against powers, against the rulers of the darkness of this age, against spiritual hosts of wickedness in the heavenly places. (Ephesians 6:12 NKJV)

The cosmic principalities and powers use human authorities (governments, political leaders, etc.) as their instruments in "this present evil age" (Galatians 1:4; 1 Corinthians 2:8).

In the New Testament, the spiritual principalities and powers that run the world system are intertwined with the earthly rulers and powers who wield power. This doesn't mean that all politicians and governmental officials are owned by Satan.

Nor does it mean that governments cannot do good things. They often do. But it does mean that the political and governmental systems of this world are governed by hostile cosmic forces in the present evil age.

---

[*] In the New Testament, the terms "principalities" and "powers" are often used together as pairs in Scripture. See Luke 12:11; 20:20; 1 Corinthians 15:24; Colossians 1:16; 2:10, 15; Ephesians 1:21; 3:10; 6:12; Titus 3:1. I agree with Scot McKnight who affirms that the principalities and powers emphasize "supernatural beings more than structures" and "the powers refers to dark cosmic forces that are at work in the *structures* of God's world." Scot McKnight, *The Letter to the Colossians*, NICNT (Grand Rapids: Eerdmans, 2018), "Excursus: The Powers as Polluted Structures," 252–61. See also Clinton Arnold, *Powers of Darkness*, chaps. 6–15; and Greg Body, *Crucifixion of the Warrior God*, vol. 2 (Minneapolis: Fortress Press, 2017), chaps. 21–23.

This explains why Satan could offer Jesus the kingdoms of this world during the wilderness temptation (Matthew 4:8). It explains why Scripture tells us that the nations are under the power of satanic princes (Daniel 10:13–20); why Paul called Satan "the god of this world" (2 Corinthians 4:4 ESV); and why Jesus called him the "prince of this world" (John 12:31; 14:30; 16:11). It also explains why so many politicians (even righteous ones) eventually become corrupted by the system.

So regardless of which political party is in power at a given time, hostile spiritual entities operate behind the scenes, manipulating earthly rulers. At the same time, God is sovereign over the conduct of these rulers. And He orders and arranges them to accomplish His own ends (Daniel 2:21; 4:32; 5:21; Psalm 33:10; Proverbs 8:15).

> The LORD has established His throne in the heavens,
>   And His sovereignty rules over all. (Psalm 103:19 NASB)

God used the Assyrians (Isaiah 10); Cyrus, king of Persia (Isaiah 45); the Chaldeans (Habakkuk 1); and Nebuchadnezzar, king of Babylon (Jeremiah 27) to accomplish His purposes. He also uses human governments to bring order to society, even though He didn't engineer them.*

The good news is that because of the death and resurrection of Christ, the cosmic hostile powers that are behind the fallen political structures have no spiritual authority over us as God's people (Colossians 2:15; Ephesians 6:14–18).

Satan is an accuser (Zechariah 3:1; Job 1:9–11; Revelation 12:10). But because of the shed blood of Christ, he can no longer accuse or condemn the children of God nor paralyze them with fear (Hebrews 2:14; Romans 8:34, 38; Revelation 12:9–11).

All that to say: never put your hope in any government, no matter who is in power (your "guys" or someone else's).† Because during this present evil age, despite the players involved and their level of spiritual awareness, all governments "are in collusion with hostile foreign powers." Jesus and Paul are proof.

---

* See my online article "The Origins of Human Government and Hierarchy" Insurgence Book.com.

† See my online article "A Word About Political Elections" at InsurgenceBook.com.

Dethroning Principalities and Powers

· · ·

Let's look again at the cross of Jesus Christ and peer into the invisible realm.

Look at Him, the innocent Man from Galilee, hanging on a Roman cross, bloodied beyond recognition.

The earthly rulers and authorities had stripped the Son of God of His clothes and displayed Him contemptuously to public view.

But that's not what was happening in the spiritual realm. Jesus, by His death, was doing those very same things to the rulers and authorities who put Him to death. Listen to Paul in Colossians 2:15:

> He [Jesus] stripped the rulers and authorities of their armour, and displayed them contemptuously to public view, celebrating his triumph over them in him. (NTE)

This fact throws fresh light on Paul's words in 1 Corinthians where he wrote,

> None of the rulers of this age understood it, for if they had, they would not have crucified the Lord of glory. (2:8 NIV)

Why does Paul say this?

It's because by putting Jesus to death, the cosmic rulers of this age brought about their own undoing. The Lord Jesus Christ unmasked, shamed, disarmed, dethroned, and defeated the principalities and powers through His unjust death.

The worldly rulers were furious at Jesus' challenge to their sovereign reign. So they stripped him naked and held him up to public contempt, celebrating their victory over the Galilean prophet.

But just like the ancient kings stripped their defeated foes of their weaponry and paraded them through their streets in triumph, so Jesus Christ, the true King, triumphed over the principalities and powers. Paul portrays Jesus as a victorious general leading the ones He's conquered, dragging them to their imprisonment.

You see, the cosmic principalities and powers that rule this age influenced the Jewish and Roman rulers to put Jesus to death. And it was those cosmic rulers that were dethroned by the death of Christ! Our Lord turned the tables on them.

The cross was a display of spiritual jujitsu against the cosmic powers, in which Jesus used their own moves against them. He exposed them for what they were—wrongful usurpers of God's authority.

The cross, then, was the ultimate Trojan horse. Jesus now has primacy over the powers, so we are not at their mercy or beck and call.

> Jesus Christ . . . has gone into heaven and is at the right hand of God, with angels, authorities, and powers having been subjected to him. (1 Peter 3:21–22 ESV)

> According to the working of His mighty power which He worked in Christ when He raised Him from the dead and seated Him at His right hand in the heavenly places, far above all principality and power and might and dominion, and every name that is named, not only in this age but also in that which is to come. And He put all things under His feet, and gave Him to be head over all things to the church. (Ephesians 1:19–22 NKJV)[*]

Consequently, the cosmic principalities and powers have no spiritual power over the children of God. Despite what the spiritual rulers of darkness do, they cannot take us captive or separate us from God's love (Romans 8:38). Nor can they oppress us with the fear of death (Hebrews 2:14). We have also been given authority to cast evil spirits out of the possessed (Luke 10:19).[†]

---

[*] See also Colossians 2:10; Matthew 28:18; Luke 22:69; Philippians 2:5–11.

[†] In the Gospels, demons appear to be distinct from the cosmic principalities and powers. Throughout those documents, demons oppress and possess people, usually in the wilderness and territories associated with the Gentiles. In Paul and the other writers of the New Testament, the word "demon" is used more generally to refer to any malevolent spiritual entity. As we'll shortly see, the cosmic principalities and powers are fallen celestial beings that influence earthly governments. As we've previously pointed out, Satan fell before or at the same time the first humans were created. There is no scholarly consensus on the origin of demons. Detailing the various theories are beyond the scope of this book, but a theory based on Genesis 6 can be found in Archie T. Wright, *The Origin of Evil Spirits* (Minneapolis: Fortress Press, 2015); Annette Yoshiko Reed, *Fallen Angels and the History of Judaism and Christianity* (Cambridge Unversity Press, 2005); Michael Heiser, *Reversing Hermon* (Crane, MO: Defender Publishing, 2017). For details on Satan, demons, and the devil in the Gospels, see G. H. Twelftree, "Demon, Devil, Satan," *Dictionary of Jesus and the Gospels*, ed. Joel B. Green and Scot McKnight (Downers Grove, IL: InterVarsity Press, 1992). Regardless of their origin, demons appear to work for Satan. The devil is connected with demons in Luke 10:17–20; Matthew 9:34; Mark

The seventy returned with joy, saying, "Lord, even the demons are subject to us in Your name." (Luke 10:17 NASB)

Yet even though Satan and his allies have been defeated and dethroned, they've not yet been annihilated. By His cross, Jesus put out the warrant for their arrest. And when Christ returns to the earth, He will initiate the arrest and remove them from power.

Another illustration is the interval between D-Day (when the Allied forces defeated Germany) and V-Day (when Germany actually surrendered).* Jesus defeated the fallen cosmic powers at the cross (D-Day), but He will wipe them out forever at His second coming (V-Day).

Then comes the end, when he delivers the kingdom to God the Father after destroying every rule and every authority and power. (1 Corinthians 15:24 ESV)

Clinton Arnold put it succinctly when he wrote,

The church continues to live in this "mopping up" period. Final victory is assured, but it is still a dangerous time, and there are many battles to be fought. Satan and his powers continue to attack the church, hold unbelieving humanity in bondage and promote every kind of evil throughout the world.[12]

So paradise is now and not yet. We live in the overlap of two ages. Even though all things have been put under the feet of the son of Man, "we do not yet see all things put under him" (Hebrews 2:8 NKJV).

This is part of the "already, but not yet" tension of the kingdom of God. The world system is still part of Satan's kingdom, yet it's also restricted by God's sovereignty.†

3:22; Luke 11:18. In Matthew 25:41, Jesus mentioned "the devil and his messengers" (YLT). Revelation 12:9 also mentions the messengers (or "angels") of Satan. Since Satan is "the god of this world" and "the prince of the power of the air," he has dominion over demons and the other fallen celestial beings.

  * Oscar Cullmann deserves credit for this illustration. I've further explored the tension between Jesus' victory over the powers and their present operation in chap. 7 of *Jesus Now*, "Lord of the World" as well as in chap. 8, "Jesus Christ Today."

  † I discuss the principalities and powers in more depth in my online article "The Origins of Human Government and Hierarchy," which you can read at InsurgenceBook.com.

The Powers Behind the Actors

Jesus confirmed that it was the cosmic rulers of this age who worked through the Jewish religious hierarchy to put Jesus to death when He said,

> Every day I was with you in the temple courts, and you did not lay a hand on me. But this is your hour—when darkness reigns. (Luke 22:53 NIV)[*]

However, Jesus also told Pilate that it was God who allowed the Roman ruler to wield his power:

> You would have no authority over me at all unless it had been given you from above. (John 19:11 ESV)[†]

Scripture is clear that it was the Father's will for Jesus to die (Luke 22:42; Romans 8:32).

The crucifixion of Jesus, then, gives us a window into how God uses the evil activity of the principalities and powers to bring about His perfect will. Peter weaves these two forces together in this statement:

> This man [Jesus] was handed over to you by God's deliberate plan and foreknowledge; and you, with the help of wicked men, put him to death by nailing him to the cross. (Acts 2:23 NIV)

Because God permits the governmental rulers of this age to exist—and even uses them—He calls His people to submit to them, even though they are part of a fallen world system and often produce evil. Note the following texts:

[*] In like manner, Satan entered Judas, provoking him to betray Jesus (John 13:2, 27). This is yet another example of how fallen cosmic powers influenced wicked humans to carry out the crucifixion of Jesus. See also 1 Corinthians 2:8.

[†] Jacques Ellul has argued that Jesus was speaking of the hostile principalities and powers of darkness who operate in the air when He said "from above." However, when Jesus uses the phrase "from above" throughout John, He is always speaking about God. Jacques Ellul, *Anarchy and Christianity* (Grand Rapids, MI: Eerdmans, 1988), 68–69.

Remind them to be submissive to rulers and authorities, to be obedient, to be ready for every good work. (Titus 3:1 ESV)

Submit yourselves for the Lord's sake to every human authority: whether to the emperor, as the supreme authority, or to governors, who are sent by him to punish those who do wrong and to commend those who do right. (1 Peter 2:13–14 NIV)

The exception, of course, is when those rulers command us to do something that is against God's will. In that case, we are to obey God rather than man (Acts 5:27–32; Daniel 3, 6).

In Romans 13:1, Paul makes the following statement:

Let every person be subject to the governing authorities. For there is no authority except from God, and those that exist have been instituted by God. (ESV)

A better translation of "instituted" ("established" in the NASB) in this verse is "ordered" or "arranged." The same is true for the Greek word translated "appointed" (ESV) and "instituted" (NIV) in verse 2. John Howard Yoder explained it this way:

God is not said to *create* or *institute* or *ordain* the powers that be, but only to *order* them, to put them in order, sovereignly to tell them where they belong, what is their place. It is not as if there was a time when there was no government and then God made government through a new creative intervention; there has been hierarchy and authority and power since human society existed. Its exercise has involved domination, disrespect for human dignity, and real or potential violence ever since sin has existed. Nor is it that by ordering this realm God specifically, morally approves of what a government does. The sergeant does not produce the soldiers he drills; the librarian does not create nor approve of the book she or he catalogs and shelves. Likewise God does not take the responsibility for the existence of the rebellious "powers that be" or for their shape or identity; they already are. What the text says is that God orders them, brings them into line, providentially and permissively lines them up with divine purposes. This is true of all governments. It is a statement both *de facto* and *de jure*. It applies to the government of dictators and tyrants as well as to constitutional democracies. It would in fact apply just as well to the government of a bandit or a warlord, to the extent to which such would exercise real sovereign control.[13]

Jacques Ellul rightly points out that even though the kingdoms of this world are part of the world system, God can still use them for good. Speaking of the authority of the state, Ellul wrote,

> These products of the spirit of power can be deflected from what the prince of this world expects of them and can be used for other ends. The state can become a servant and law an instrument of justice when they are permeated by grace and evangelical truth. But this is the exception. Similarly money can be deflected from the use intended by Mammon and used for giving, that is, of grace. This is a sign (and perhaps can be no more) that God has not given us up to the prince of this world.[14]

Lifting the Curtain

* * *

Whenever you see a government oppressing, tormenting, and victimizing a people, lift the curtain and you'll see fallen human beings who are pulling the strings.

But lift the curtain again, and you will see hostile spiritual entities operating behind the government and the fallen humans who are in charge of it.

Lift the curtain yet again, and you will see the hand of God permitting the evil to occur, yet using it to write straight with crooked lines, working out His eternal purpose in spite of the free will of fallen entities (Ephesians 1:11; Romans 8:28).

Imagine the world as a three-dimensional chessboard. God controls the chessboard, but each piece has its own free will. God, the master chess player, doesn't force the pieces to move wherever He desires. But He's twenty moves ahead of each piece. He not only anticipates their every move, but He wisely uses the moves of His opponents against themselves, out-strategizing them in the process. And then bringing about something good and glorious out of the wreckage.

The intersection between God's sovereignty and the fallen powers is like that. At the same time, it's a divine mystery that Scripture never fully explains. But we have clues all throughout the Bible showing how God anticipates and oversees the moves of His enemies.

In the book of Acts, we can see the interplay of God's sovereign ordering and the wickedness of those who put Jesus to death:

Him [Jesus], being delivered by the determined purpose and foreknowledge of God, you have taken by lawless hands, have crucified, and put to death. (2:23 NKJV)

For truly against Your holy Servant Jesus, whom You anointed, both Herod and Pontius Pilate, with the Gentiles and the people of Israel, were gathered together to do whatever Your hand and Your purpose determined before to be done. (4:27–28 NKJV)

Notice that God the Father "delivered" Jesus to the lawless to be cruci-fied, but it was according to the "determined purpose and foreknowledge of God."* This same interplay between God's leading and the devil's activity is seen in the wilderness temptation of Jesus:

> Then Jesus was led up by the Spirit into the wilderness to be tempted by the devil. (Matthew 4:1 NASB)

Notice the Spirit "led" Jesus to be "tempted by the devil."

In short, we are called to trust Christ as the supreme Lord over heaven and earth, and regard all earthly powers as lesser underlords under His absolute authority.

On this score, Paul issues a hope-filled word about the future of the insurgence.

> In the sight of God, who gives life to everything, and of Christ Jesus, who while testifying before Pontius Pilate made the good confession, I charge you to keep this command without spot or blame until the appearing of our Lord Jesus Christ, which God will bring about in his own time—God, the blessed and only Ruler, the King of kings and Lord of lords, who alone is immortal and who lives in unapproachable light, whom no one has seen or can see. To him be honor and might forever. Amen. (1 Timothy 6:13–16 NIV)

The author of Revelation agrees:

> These [the kings in league with Babylon] shall war against the Lamb, and the Lamb shall overcome them, for he is Lord of lords, and King of kings; and they also shall overcome that are with him, called and chosen and faithful. (Revelation 17:14 ASV)

---

* The interplay between God allowing Satan to operate under His sovereignty is also reflected in texts like 2 Samuel 24:1 and 1 Chronicles 21:1. In 2 Samuel, Satan moves David to number Israel. In 1 Chronicles 21, it is God who does it.

Layers of Rule

. . .

Putting together the content of the previous pages, we can state it this way.

God is the *ultimate* ruler of creation; Jesus is the *rightful* ruler of the universe (since His ascension); Satan is the *functional* ruler of the world during this present age.

When this present evil age comes to its close, the Lord Jesus Christ will functionally rule over all things. He will then hand the kingdom over to His Father, and God will be all in all.

If you're looking for a footnote, you can find it in 1 Corinthians 15:20–28.

The Cosmic Story

* * *

Up until this point, we've looked at the story of the kingdom of God beginning with the heavenlies, to the fall, to the conception of the world system, to the call of Abraham, to the forming of Israel, to the coming of Christ, to the birth of the ekklesia, and to the role of cosmic principalities and powers on human governments.

In this chapter and the next two, I will retell the story through a completely different vantage point. In so doing, many of the themes we've already established will be reassembled to create a brand-new picture.

In Genesis 6, the earth had become full of increasing wickedness, so God judged it through the great flood. After the flood, God started over again. Noah built an altar in honor of God, and God blessed Noah and his sons. God commissioned Noah with the same commission that He gave Adam: "Be fruitful and multiply, and fill the earth" (Genesis 9:1, 7 NKJV). He also reminded Noah that humankind was made in God's image (Genesis 9:6).*

So with Noah, the Lord was beginning afresh to establish His kingdom on the earth.

As time went on, something of the wickedness that marked the days before the flood was carried over with one of Noah's sons, Ham. The wicked Canaanites were descendants of Ham. And so were the Egyptians, the Babylonians, the Assyrians, and the Philistines—Israel's worst enemies. Nimrod, the man who built the first worldly kingdom—Babel—was also a descendant of Ham.

I've written about the spiritual meaning of Babel elsewhere.[15] But God's judgment came on the people of Babel because of their pride and disobedience. Instead of being fruitful and multiplying throughout the earth

---

* The original Adamic commission is found in Genesis 1:22, 28. It was repeated to Abraham (Genesis 17:2; 22:17–18); to Jacob (Genesis 35:11–12; 28:3–4); and to Noah. From the beginning, God's eternal purpose has been to fill the earth with His image. You can find the language of the Adamic commission ("be fruitful and multiply") in the New Testament as well (Acts 6:7; 12:24; 19:20; Colossians 1:6, 10).

(as God commanded), they opted to create a centralized government that reached heaven in order to make a name for themselves.*

The Lord condemned the whole enterprise. He confused their languages and dispersed them throughout the earth. And then He divided the nations according to the number of one class of celestial beings in heaven.

So new nations sprung up all over the world. Then God did something incredible. *He, in effect, disinherited the nations.* Instead of ruling over them directly, He appointed some of the celestial beings He created to be in charge of them.

You can find this in Deuteronomy 32:8. The most accurate version of this text reads,

> When the Most High gave to the nations their inheritance,
>   when he divided mankind,
> he fixed the borders of the peoples
>   according to the number of the sons of God. (ESV)†

This passage is referring to what took place at Babel in Genesis 10–11. The phrase "sons of God" refers to the celestial beings who are part of God's heavenly host (Job 1:6; 2:1; 38:4–7; Psalm 29:1; 89:6 ESV). The NLT translates the latter part of the verse, "according to the number in his heavenly court."

God was essentially saying, "I'm through with the human race. I have scattered them into new nations throughout the earth. But I'm disinheriting them all. And I'm putting my heavenly host in charge of each nation. My heavenly host will be responsible for the people of the world from now on. However, I'm not giving up on My eternal purpose. I'm starting all over again, and I will create a new nation for Myself. I will call a man

---

* In Genesis 11, the inhabitants of Babel sought to make "a name" for themselves. Nimrod, the city's founder, is described as being a "mighty" man. Interestingly, when the earth rose to its highest level of wickedness in Genesis 6, the Nephilim are described as being "mighty" men of "name" [renown], Genesis 6:4 ESV. I owe this connection to John Nugent, *Polis Bible Commentary, Genesis 1–11*, vol. 1, Genesis 11:1–9. The writer of Genesis is telegraphing that Genesis 11 is something of a replay of Genesis 6. The line of the old man wasn't wiped out in the flood but reappeared through the lineage of Ham.

† The Septuagint (the Greek Old Testament) and the Dead Sea Scrolls confirm this translation. Many scholars agree that this is the most accurate rendering. The newer translation, "sons of Israel," doesn't make sense because Israel didn't exist during the Babel story in Genesis 10, which Deuteronomy 32:8 is pointing to.

named Abraham, and through Abraham's seed, I will create this new nation. That new nation will be My people, My portion, My inheritance. And I will care for them."

This is confirmed by the next verse:

> For the people of Israel belong to the LORD;
> Jacob is his special possession. (Deuteronomy 32:9 NLT)

So God put the nations under the administration of lesser beings, while He would create a brand-new nation for Himself. This explains why God called Abraham (the father of the new nation of Israel) in Genesis 12 immediately following His judgment on the people of Babel in Genesis 11.

> But as for you [Israel], the LORD took you and brought you out of the iron-smelting furnace, out of Egypt, to be the people of his inheritance, as you now are. (Deuteronomy 4:20 NIV)

Israel would be God's inheritance and special possession (Psalm 28:9; 33:12; 74:2; 79:1; 1 Samuel 10:1; Jeremiah 10:16).

More Tragedy

. . .

Even though God disinherited the nations at Babel, He would not abandon them forever. Instead, He promised to one day reclaim them and bring them under His reign (Isaiah 66:18–23). And Israel would play a major role in that endeavor.

But tragedy struck again. The celestial beings that God put over the nations rebelled against Him. Their corrupt administration is recorded in Psalm 82.[*]

> God presides over heaven's court;
>   he pronounces judgment on the heavenly beings:
> "How long will you hand down unjust decisions
>   by favoring the wicked?" (vv. 1–2 NLT)

In Psalm 82:6–7, God judged the heavenly hosts whom He put over the nations, promising to take away their immortality.

> But you will die like mere mortals;
>   you will fall like every other ruler. (v. 7 NIV)

But the psalmist ends on a high note, confirming that God will one day inherit the nations again.[†]

> Arise, O God, judge the earth;
>   for you shall inherit all the nations! (v. 8 ESV)

Daniel 10 talks about "the prince of Persia" and "the prince of Greece" fighting the archangel Michael and another angel who were faithful to

---

[*] This reading is confirmed by *The Jewish Study Bible*, 2nd ed. (Oxford, NY: Oxford University Press, 2014), 1361.

[†] I owe this specific narrative to Michael Heiser's book *The Unseen Realm* (Bellingham, WA: Lexham Press, 2015), 110–15. Heiser provides scholarly academic support for each point I've made, and he answers common objections to it as well. If you're skeptical about any piece of the narrative I've told in this chapter, consult Heiser's book. Time and space will not permit me to detail all the scriptural and historical support for it here.

God. In that chapter, Daniel is speaking about the geopolitical enterprise. Michael and another angel who are caring for Israel are warring against the celestial powers of darkness who are over the other nations.

These fallen celestial beings are the "false gods" and pagan "idols" that the Old Testament speaks about. (Paul says as much in 1 Corinthians 10:19–22.)

In Psalm 2, we get another glimpse into the hostility of the nations against God and "His Anointed."

> Why do the nations rage,
> And the people plot a vain thing?
> The kings of the earth set themselves,
> And the rulers take counsel together,
> Against the LORD and against His Anointed, saying,
> "Let us break Their bonds in pieces
> And cast away Their cords from us." (vv. 1–3 NKJV)

But the tragedy didn't end there. Israel, God's inheritance, was also seduced by the celestial beings who ruled the nations, and God's own people began worshiping them.

> They [Israel] went and served other gods and worshiped them, gods whom they have not known and whom He had not allotted to them. (Deuteronomy 29:26 NASB)

> They [Israel] sacrificed to false gods, which are not God—
> gods they had not known. (Deuteronomy 32:17 NIV)

Even though God warned His people against worshiping the heavenly hosts that He put over the nations, they still did.

> And beware lest you raise your eyes to heaven, and when you see the sun and the moon and the stars, all the host of heaven, you be drawn away and bow down to them and serve them, things that the LORD your God has allotted to all the peoples under the whole heaven. (Deuteronomy 4:19 ESV)

> I am making this covenant with you so that no one among you—no man, woman, clan, or tribe—will turn away from the LORD our God to worship these gods of other nations. (Deuteronomy 29:18 NLT)

Interestingly, Paul refers to these fallen celestial entities over the nations as the principalities, powers, rulers of darkness of this age, and spiritual hosts of wickedness (Ephesians 6:12). These are terms indicating geographical authority and territorial dominion.[16] Paul is referring to the hostile heavenly beings who have dominion over the nations. And they too are under Satan's dominion.*

But the story doesn't end there, thank God. In our next chapter, we'll explore how God sets in motion a plan to reclaim the nations for Himself.

---

* Satan has dominion over the principalities and powers because he is "the god of the world" and "the prince of the power of the air" (compare 2 Corinthians 4:4; Ephesians 2:2; 6:12). Adam handed his right to rule the earth over to Satan in the garden. Since that time, the devil has power over fallen humans, the fallen celestial powers, and the demons, all of which reside under his domain.

Eden Restored

* * *

Michael Heiser points out that the Old Testament is the story of Israel against the nations, the God of Israel against the false gods of the world.*

God's kingdom project has always been to restore Eden where God dwells with humans, and they bear His image and exercise His authority.

The impulse to get back to the garden is not only found in the heart of God's people, but even nonbelievers possess this instinct. The lyrics of Joni Mitchell's timeless song "Woodstock" is an example: "And we've got to get ourselves back to the garden."

Well, no Woodstock concert could ever bring us back to the garden. So how does God bring us "back to the garden" and recover the nations that are under the thumb of the fallen powers of darkness?

Let's look at the ministry of Jesus through a different lens. At one point during His ministry, Jesus sent out seventy of His disciples to preach the gospel of the kingdom (Luke 10:1, 9).

Why seventy? Because seventy nations were created after the dispersion at Babel.† The seventy disciples simply mirrored the seventy nations that were under the domain of the enemy.

The message is clear. Jesus was bringing the gospel of the kingdom to all seventy nations that God disinherited. The Lord's disciples went into those nations to deliver them from the fallen powers and begin reclaiming them for God's kingly reign. It's no accident, then, that the disciples waged war against the powers of darkness during this kingdom mission trip (Luke 10:17–20).

---

* This is a paraphrased quote. Heiser actually said, "The rest of the Old Testament pits Yahweh [the God of Israel] against those [false] gods and Israel against their nations." Heiser, *The Unseen Realm*, 123.

† Some translations of Luke 10 say that Jesus sent out seventy-two. In the same way, Genesis 10 in the Greek Old Testament (Septuagint) says there were seventy-two nations in the "table of nations" at Babel. Whether it was seventy or seventy-two, the point remains. Jesus' disciples were beginning to reclaim the nations with the gospel of the kingdom. See Leon Morris, *Luke: Tyndale New Testament Commentaries* (Grand Rapids: Eerdmans, 1998), 198.

After it was over, Jesus (standing in Israel) prayed to His Father and called Him "Lord of heaven and earth" (Luke 10:21). Connect the dots. God was beginning to reclaim the nations which were under the domain of the enemy.

Jesus' last commission to His disciples before He ascended was a continuation of this effort to reposses the nations.

> And Jesus came and spoke to them, saying, "All authority has been given to Me in heaven and on earth. Go therefore and make disciples of all the nations." (Matthew 28:18–19 NKJV)

Clearly, the Lord's objective is to lay claim on every nation with the gospel of the kingdom.

> And this gospel of the kingdom will be proclaimed throughout the whole world as a testimony to all nations. (Matthew 24:14 ESV)

Why does Jesus want the gospel of the kingdom proclaimed to every nation? Is it just so the people of the nations can go to heaven when they die? No. The purpose of the apostolic commission was—*and still is*—to deliver the nations from Satan's dominion and reclaim them for God's kingdom (Acts 26:18). It's to restore Eden "on earth as it is in heaven."

After He commissioned His apostles, Jesus ascended into heaven. But on the day of Pentecost, He descended in the form of the Holy Spirit, no longer limited by space and time (John 14–16). This brings us to the story of Pentecost in Acts 2.

As I've pointed out elsewhere, what happened on the day of Pentecost was a reversal of what took place at Babel.* As Luke (the author of Acts) describes the event, he wants his readers to remember Babel. For example,

- In Acts 2:3, the same Greek word used for "divided" tongues (ESV) is used in Deuteronomy 32:8 (when God "divided" humankind) in the Greek version of the Old Testament.[17]
- In Acts 2:6, the word "bewildered" (ESV) is the same Greek word used in Genesis 11:7 ("confuse" their language) in the Greek version of the Old Testament.[18]

---

* For details, listen to my audio message "Vantage Point: The Story We Haven't Heard—Part II" at InsurgenceBook.com.

- The nations mentioned in Acts 2 correlate with the nations mentioned in Genesis 10, only their names were updated.[19]
- At Babel, sinful men tried to achieve unity, and God confused them by scrambling their languages. At Pentecost, God unites the people, they speak in other tongues, and they understand one another.

The fire that appeared on the heads of the believers at Pentecost is reminiscent of the fire that fell from heaven on the temple when it was dedicated (2 Chronicles 7:1–3). The message is unmistakable.

At Pentecost, God began building His new temple in the earth—the ekklesia, the people of the insurgence who would take the nations back for the Lord.

For this reason, those who are part of the ekklesia are under God's domain, and those who are put outside the ekklesia are under the domain of the enemy (1 Corinthians 5:4–13; Ephesians 2:1–3).

It's no accident that Israel's return from exile—which was fulfilled through the death and resurrection of Christ—is depicted in the Old Testament as a restoration of the Garden of Eden (Isaiah 51:2–3; Ezekiel 36:35).*

---

* The return from exile also includes the language of the Adamic commission, "Be fruitful and multiply" (Ezekiel 36:10–11, 29–30).

To the End of the Earth

· · ·

When Jesus showed up, He began to undo the grip of the hostile fallen powers over mortals. When Jesus died and rose again, He undermined the power of the false gods over the nations, advancing His own kingdom on the earth.

In Acts 2:9–11, Luke lists all the nations that were represented on the day of Pentecost. Those nations correspond to the nations listed after Babel in Genesis 10. If you locate all those nations on a map, you will discover that they move from east to west.*

Interestingly, the Garden of Eden was planted in the east (Genesis 2:8; 3:24). And the entrance of the temple of God was also in the east (Ezekiel 40:6).

When Jesus commissioned His apostles to witness to the gospel of the kingdom, He told them to begin in Israel and then move "to the end of the earth."

> You shall be witnesses to Me in Jerusalem, and in all Judea and Samaria, and to the end of the earth." (Acts 1:8 NKJV)

> Go therefore and make disciples of all the nations. (Matthew 28:19 NKJV)

> That repentance and remission of sins should be preached in His name to all nations, beginning at Jerusalem. (Luke 24:47 NKJV)

Significantly, in the first part of Acts (chaps. 2–12), we see the gospel of the kingdom brought to Israel (Judea and Samaria). In the second part of Acts (chaps. 13–28), we see Paul of Tarsus taking the gospel to the nations. And just like the list in Acts 2 moves east to west, Paul moves east to west (from Antioch to Galatia to Greece to Rome).

---

* Michael Heiser provides maps comparing the nations listed in Acts 2 with the nations listed in Genesis 10. There is an unmistakable correlation. *The Unseen Realm* (Bellingham, WA: Lexham Press, 2015), 300–301.

In Romans 15, Paul indicates that he feels compelled to go to Spain after he visits Rome (vv. 24 and 28). Why Spain? First, Spain is west of Rome, so Paul was still pushing west. But more striking, when the "table of nations" is recorded in Genesis 10, the nation that's located farthest west is Tarshish.

Tarshish is Spain.[20]

Paul was tracing the nations mentioned in Genesis 10, from east to west, until he came to "the end of the earth" in his day.* His goal is mentioned in Romans 11:25, which was to bring in what he called "the fullness of the Gentiles" (ESV) or "the full number of the Gentiles" (NIV).†

This meshes nicely with what Jesus said in Matthew 24:14. That when the gospel of the kingdom is preached to all nations, the end shall come.

So we can clearly see that the gospel of the kingdom is not just for the Jews, as some have wrongly alleged. The Messiah has claim to all earthly turf. *The gospel of the kingdom is for all nations.*

It is for both Jew and Gentile.

After this I looked, and there before me was a great multitude that no one could count, from every nation, tribe, people and language, standing before the throne and before the Lamb. They were wearing white robes and were holding palm branches in their hands. (Revelation 7:9 NIV)

It shall be that I will gather all nations and tongues; and they shall come and see My glory. (Isaiah 66:18 NKJV)

He [one like the son of Man] was given authority, glory and sovereign power; all nations and peoples of every language worshiped him. His dominion is an everlasting dominion that will not pass away, and his kingdom is one that will never be destroyed. (Daniel 7:14 NKJV)

Thus the Old Testament promise that the Messiah would "inherit" the nations is fulfilled in Jesus.

---

* I owe this insight to Michael Heiser. (*The Unseen Realm*, 303). Note that "the end of the earth" is different for our time. The ancients weren't aware of North and South America, for example.

† Heiser, *The Unseen Realm*, 303–4. This is the fulfillment of God's promise that Abraham's seed would bless all the nations of the earth (Genesis 22:18). That seed is Christ, and He came from Israel, Abraham's seed (Galatians 3:16).

I will declare the decree:
The LORD has said to Me,
"You are My Son,
Today I have begotten You.
Ask of Me, and I will give You
The nations for Your inheritance,
And the ends of the earth for Your possession." (Psalm 2:7–8 NKJV)

Great and marvelous are Your works,
O Lord God, the Almighty;
Righteous and true are Your ways,
King of the nations!
Who will not fear, O Lord, and glorify Your name?
For You alone are holy;
FOR ALL THE NATIONS WILL COME AND WORSHIP BEFORE YOU,
FOR YOUR RIGHTEOUS ACTS HAVE BEEN REVEALED. (Revelation 15:3–4
NASB)

Since Pentecost, God has been reclaiming the nations. And He will continue to do so until the end of the age. The kingdom of God, in effect, is all about Jesus Christ taking back the earth, which is rightfully His (Colossians 1:16). As the prophet foresaw,

"Sing and rejoice, O daughter of Zion! For behold, I am coming and I will dwell in your midst," says the LORD. "Many nations shall be joined to the LORD in that day, and they shall become My people. And I will dwell in your midst. Then you will know that the LORD of hosts has sent Me to you. (Zechariah 2:10–11 NKJV)

The people of the insurgence take part in this global reclamation.*

---

* Isaiah 54:3–5 says, "And your descendants will inherit the nations. . . . For your Maker is your husband. . . . He is called the God of the whole earth" (NKJV). This is a prophetic statement promising that Jesus Christ will inherit the nations through His seed, His bride, the ekklesia. And the Lord will be called the God of the earth as well as heaven.

The Need of the Hour

. . .

We live in a politically charged era. The atmosphere is so radioactive that countless Christians divide from one another simply because they are engaging the political dialogue through the same lens that the world utilizes.

All those political smackdowns that Christians engage in every day on Facebook reflect a complete misunderstanding of what the kingdom of God is. It also underscores that we have completely lost sight of the gospel that was preached in the first century—what Jesus called "the gospel of the kingdom."

Let me be clear. Don't make the mistake of confusing the kingdom with the conservative right. The gospel of the kingdom will make the conservative right livid.

Don't confuse the kingdom with the progressive left. The gospel of the kingdom will make the progressive left furious.

Don't confuse the kingdom with the libertarian movement, the Tea Party, Black Lives Matter, Occupy Wall Street, or any other political movement.

The gospel of the kingdom leaves all of these entities standing in the dust of an insurgence.

The gospel of the kingdom is heavenly. It has nothing to do with the systems of men, be they political or religious.

The lordship of Jesus Christ is at the helm of that gospel. It's in the center, along the circumference, and in the margins. Its outstandingly unmistakable message (meaning, you can't miss it) is that Jesus of Nazareth is the rightful King and Lord of the world. So submit to Him. Give your life to Him, not to a noble cause (the two aren't the same).

If you live in the West, the two main idols or false gods are nationalism and capitalism. I live in America, and these two idols have this nation in its grip.

People kill, sacrifice, and die for these idols. Anything is justified for love of country (nationalism) and love of money (capitalism). And this mindset has even bled into the Christian community.

The teachings of Jesus are ignored or diluted in the name of these two false gods.

In the USA there's a real strong spirit of nationalism, especially if you're over forty years old. Then if you're under forty, there's a strong spirit of globalism.

Make no mistake: Both nationalism and globalism are at variance with the kingdom of God. Because both pledge one's allegiance to the kingdoms of this world.

According to the Scripture, you're a citizen of another kingdom. Your citizenship is in the heavens. And your complete allegiance belongs there as well.

The major idols or false gods in the East are education and business on the one hand, or socialism and communism on the other.

Scores of people can't think beyond those things.

But the insurgence obliterates all idols.

Unplugging From the Matrix

* * *

The 1999 movie *The Matrix* is a great illustration of what I'm writing about. The world system, the kingdom of darkness, permeates everything on this earth. It's interwoven into the very existence of humankind. It is part and parcel of all of us.

So your need is not just to get your sins forgiven. You need something far greater. You need to be delivered from this corrupt tyrannical system. To cut all ties to the world system. To unplug from the Matrix.

The kingdom of this world distracts us from the compelling, consuming obsession on God's heart. For this reason, Jesus Christ is totally opposed to this world system.

There are men and women on this earth who name the name of Jesus Christ who are totally and absolutely consumed with business.

There are men and women on this earth who name the name of Jesus Christ who are totally and absolutely consumed with education.

There are men and women on this earth who name the name of Jesus Christ who are totally and absolutely consumed with entertainment.

Am I saying it's wrong to have a business? That's not the point. If you have a business, why do you have it? And how much of your life is chained to it?

If you're getting an education, what is it for? Most people who get an education do so to acquire wealth.

I'm exhorting us all to let the Lord expose and deal with our worldliness and our attachment to the things of this earth.

The person who has given themselves to the kingdom of God can declare, "I don't care about wealth. And I don't care about poverty. I don't care about position, ambition, or educational credentials. I care only for Christ and His kingdom."

May God have a people on this earth who can stand before rulers, kings, presidents, politicians, and multitudes to proclaim the gospel of the kingdom, uncompromising and unflinching. A people who live for the insurgence.

Abandoning Identity Politics

. . .

"Identity politics" refers to the tendency for people of a particular religion, race, or social status to vote for a certain political party. For this reason, it's highly divisive and reflects an allegiance to the world system rather than to Jesus Christ and His kingdom.

Let me give you an example.

For decades, Anna's family voted for a certain political party. Her family also finds their identity in their shared race. The same is true for Anna's friends.

One day Anna heard the gospel of the kingdom, and she discovered that in Christ Jesus, she's part of what the early Christians called "the third race"—the new humanity where there is no Jew, Gentile, Black, White, Asian, Latino, etc. (Colossians 3:11).

Anna wholeheartedly received that gospel, and since that day, she no longer finds her identity in her race or the political party she was raised with.

As a result, Anna began embracing people of different races who believed the same kingdom gospel, and she began treating them like her own flesh and blood. She also came to the conclusion that the hope of the world doesn't lie in any political party, including the one she was raised with.

Anna's new passion became the kingdom of God—a kingdom that recognizes no race except the new creation and that upholds no political agenda except the lordship of Jesus Christ.

The result: Anna's friends and family have effectively ostracized her. They now view her as betraying her own race and political party.

But this hasn't dissuaded her from complete devotion to Jesus and His kingdom.

Now here's the kicker: *Anna's family and friends all claim Jesus as their Savior.*

This is how deep identity politics runs. And it's an example of the disturbing things that Jesus said about the cost of the kingdom when it comes to one's family.*

I can multiply examples like Anna's from different races and political parties, but I trust you get the picture.

The gospel of the kingdom dismantles identity politics.

* See my online article "The Radical Cost of the Kingdom" at InsurgenceBook.com.

Speaking to Earthly Power

God's way of advancing His kingdom is never through wielding physical violence or political power. Nor is it by asking for a seat at Caesar's table. The Lord advances His kingdom through the poor in spirit, the meek, the merciful, the mourners, the pure in spirit, the peacemakers, and the persecuted (Matthew 5:3–10).

God arms His own people with a divine capacity to lay their lives down and suffer—the same way Jesus ushered in the kingdom initially.

Because the earth now is rightfully under the lordship of Jesus Christ, sometimes His servants will bear prophetic witness to those who hold earthly power. And they do so through the Holy Spirit.

> When he [the Holy Spirit] comes, he will prove the world to be in the wrong about sin and righteousness and judgment: about sin, because people do not believe in me; about righteousness, because I am going to the Father, where you can see me no longer; and about judgment, because the prince of this world now stands condemned. (John 16:8–11 NIV)

Through the ekklesia, the Spirit of God calls the entire world to account.

You see, since Jesus ascended, He is now rightfully in charge of the earth. This includes its political leaders. Consequently, if a government official acts in a way that runs contrary to the true Lord of this world, that official is usurping the power that God has given to him or her.

In such cases, God's people will sometimes be compelled to prophetically speak God's mind to the official, rebuking him or her for abusing their power—a power given by God to accomplish good and not evil (Romans 13:1–5).

An example of this is when Paul rebuked the officials in Philippi for their abuse of power when he was unlawfully beaten (Acts 16:37–39).

> The Most High is sovereign over all kingdoms on earth and gives them to anyone he wishes. (Daniel 4:32 NIV)

Again, God intended to rule the world through humans, and He's never abandoned that purpose (Genesis 1:28). Jesus came to set humans free from the curse so that they may rule the earth in the way that God originally intended (Revelation 5:9–10).

That said, whenever a person announces that Jesus is Lord, they are speaking truth to power.* Through the ministry of God's people, the Holy Spirit convicts the world of sin, of righteousness, and of judgment (John 16:7–11).

This is the message that the insurgence bears.

* The term "speaking truth to power" is commonly used to refer to the act of speaking God's truth to those in political power. Apparently, the phrase was coined by the Quakers in the mid-1950s.

The Ruled Shall Rule

• • •

Those who rule in God's kingdom are those who have been ruled. Therefore, those who exercise God's authority must first know submission to His authority in their own lives.

David could not rule until he was first ruled. And Jesus didn't bear the authority of God until He was first fully subject to His Father (Philippians 2:6–10; Hebrews 5:8).

Unfortunately, countless Christians have been brainwashed, hoodwinked, and tricked into thinking that they are powerless over their circumstances. But the truth is, because you have the Spirit of God, you are far more powerful than you think you are.

It is through the cross and the indwelling Spirit that Jesus puts His kingdom achievement into operation. This is why Jesus called the Twelve to carry on His work. God the Father worked through Jesus, and now Jesus works through His followers.

When we live by the Lord's indwelling life, we become Christ's witnesses. Tragically, the word "witness" has been reduced to the idea of telling others that Jesus died for their sins. But as I've said before, the New Testament uses the word to mean telling others that Jesus is the Lord of the world. And to say "Jesus is Lord" means that no one else is.

Put another way, Jesus exercises His rule in the world through the ekklesia, which is the new creation, His body and presence in the earth.

Consequently, the body of Christ will sometimes proclaim the kingdom to those in power as well as to the powerless. This is yet another way that the ekklesia demonstrates the kingdom of God, wielding the spiritual authority that the Lord has given her.

Even before the kingdom touched the earth with Jesus, John the Baptist preached the kingdom of God with an emphasis on repentance. That gospel led John to speak truth to power, which eventually got him killed.

The people of God will sometimes be compelled to speak to those in power by the Holy Spirit's leading. But this brand of "speaking to power" will rarely look like the talking points of the political right and left. It will pull that trigger when "the powers that be" are found usurping the lordship of Christ and subverting the values of His kingdom. And it will bring Jesus Christ into view.

Accordingly, those who speak to power today should be prepared for the backlash. But this is how the insurgence gains strength.

Salt and Light

* * *

Jesus said that the people of the kingdom will "produce its fruit." The kingdom of God, once entered, enjoyed, and embodied, produces visible fruit to demonstrate its life.

> Therefore I tell you that the kingdom of God will be taken away from you *and given to a people who will produce its fruit*. (Matthew 21:43 NIV)

Another way of describing the fruit of the kingdom is through the terms "salt" and "light" (Matthew 5:13–15).

Salt preserves and light illuminates. Salt flavors food; light eradicates darkness. Salt works in a hidden way; light works out in the open.

Again, when Jesus spoke of salt and light, He was referring to good deeds which alleviate human suffering:

> In the same way, let your light shine before others, that they may see your good deeds and glorify your Father in heaven. (Matthew 5:16 NIV)

The ekklesia of the first century was salt and light, fulfilling God's commission to Israel through Abraham that "by your descendants all the nations of the earth shall be blessed" (Genesis 26:4 NASB).

The resurrection and ascension of Jesus are more than proofs that God still does miracles or that Jesus is returning again. They are the beginning of God's re-creation project where His people colonize earth with the life of heaven. This, in fact, is the meaning of the Lord's prayer,

> Your kingdom come,
> your will be done,
>   on earth as it is in heaven. (Matthew 6:10 NIV)

From this text we learn that the kingdom of God is the earthly manifestation of God's sovereign will. And God's will is expressed when His people love one another. The first-century ekklesia of God "turned the world upside down" because of the love they had for one another. This was also true in the second century, when one pagan gave a report about the Christian community to a Roman emperor, saying, "Behold, how they love one another."

As I've argued elsewhere, she—the ekklesia of God—when functioning as God intended her to, is the world's greatest evangelist.

The three elements of God's sovereign rule are righteousness, peace, and love. When the world beholds the *peace* of God operating in the lives of God's people, the *love* that they have for one another, and the *righteousness* they display, the world can't help but be impressed.

In this way, the ekklesia testifies that Jesus is Lord. She is the concrete witness that Christ is on the throne.

Jesus said that the world will know that the Father sent Him when His disciples are unified and love one another (John 13:35; 17:23).

Because the ekklesia is the concrete evidence of the lordship of Christ in the world, God's enemy has fiercely attacked and assaulted her wherever she has been established. Simply read the book of Acts and the letters of Paul and you will see this attack and assault at every turn.

The same is true today whenever a group of believers take a stand to be God's house in their city, expressing His kingdom through having a shared life together.

Salt is useless when confined to the saltshaker. The Lord's call is for His people to come out of the saltshaker and display their good deeds in public.

Those who are part of the insurgence don't just talk about "loving the brethren." They lay their lives down for them.

Seeking the Kingdom First

. . .

One of the most often quoted sayings of Jesus about the kingdom of God is this:

> But seek first his kingdom and his righteousness, and all these things will be given to you as well. (Matthew 6:33 NIV)

The Lord's reference to "all these things" in this text refers to those things that people worry about when their hearts have not made the kingdom of God their top priority in life. Those things include money, clothing, food, housing, etc.

To seek first the kingdom means, among other things, to view everything in light of how they serve God's rule. It means that the interests of Christ become preeminent in our lives. It means we seek to possess the character of the King, a King who "shall reign in righteousness" (Isaiah 22:1 KJV).

The interests of Christ and His kingdom come before even our own interests. Paul bemoaned the problem of priority when he spoke well of his co-worker Timothy, saying,

> For I have no one like him [Timothy], who will be genuinely concerned for your welfare. For they all seek their own interests, not those of Jesus Christ. (Philippians 2:20–21 ESV)

To seek first the kingdom—to seek the interests of Jesus Christ—is to seek the welfare of God's house, His people, His ekklesia. It means to care for His body, because caring for the Lord's body is caring for the King and His kingdom.

When we seek His kingdom first, our lives are arranged according to His interests. Therefore, God promises to look after our own interests in return.

So the question before you and me in every decision we make is, How does this serve the interests of the sovereign rule of God?

God's enemy will do all he can to divert our attention from that question and replace it with some other interest. The enemy seeks to bring the children of God into toilsome bondage and anxious care over earthly things.

But Jesus says, "Seek first My kingdom and My character and I will relieve you of your cares and anxieties over the necessities of life."

Interestingly, the New Testament spends far more time explaining how to be citizens of God's kingdom than it does about the issues of work and home life.

Consequently, those who are part of the insurgence seek to bring the interests of God's reign and character to bear on every situation in which they find themselves.

The Least of These

. . .

In the following text, Jesus gives us some insight into what is going to happen at the last judgment:

> Then the King will say to those on his right, "Come, you who are blessed by my Father; take your inheritance, the kingdom prepared for you since the creation of the world. For I was hungry and you gave me something to eat, I was thirsty and you gave me something to drink, I was a stranger and you invited me in, I needed clothes and you clothed me, I was sick and you looked after me, I was in prison and you came to visit me."
>
> Then the righteous will answer him, "Lord, when did we see you hungry and feed you, or thirsty and give you something to drink? When did we see you a stranger and invite you in, or needing clothes and clothe you? When did we see you sick or in prison and go to visit you?"
>
> The King will reply, "Truly I tell you, whatever you did for one of the least of these brothers and sisters of mine, you did for me." (Matthew 25:34–40 NIV)

Note the words, "Truly I tell you, whatever you did for one of *the least of these brothers and sisters of mine*, you did for me."

Some believe "the least of these brothers and sisters of mine" refers to any human being. So when Jesus referred to visiting the sick and the prisoner, feeding the hungry and thirsty, etc., He was talking about every individual, including the lost.

This interpretation is based on a theological teaching called "the Fatherhood of God and the brotherhood of Man," which asserts that every human being—even the unregenerate—are equally God's children.

Others have adopted a certain brand of eschatology and assert that "the least of these brothers and sisters of mine" refers to Israel. These teach Matthew 25 within a specific end-time scheme where Christians will care for persecuted Jews.

Let me say emphatically that visiting prisoners, caring for the sick, feeding the hungry—regardless of their standing with the Lord—is a commendable act of mercy. We've already discussed this in previous chapters.

But I don't believe Jesus had this in mind in Matthew 25.

Consider the following texts that clearly identify who the "brothers and sisters" are:

> Then Jesus' mother and brothers arrived. Standing outside, they sent someone in to call him. A crowd was sitting around him, and they told him, "Your mother and brothers are outside looking for you."
>
> "Who are my mother and my brothers?" he asked.
>
> Then he looked at those seated in a circle around him and said, "Here are my mother and my brothers! Whoever does God's will is my brother and sister and mother." (Mark 3:31–35 NIV)

> Now that you have purified yourselves by obeying the truth so that you have sincere love for each other, love one another deeply, from the heart. For you have been born again, not of perishable seed, but of imperishable, through the living and enduring word of God. (1 Peter 1:22–23 NIV)

> We know that we have passed out of death into life, because we love the brothers. Whoever does not love abides in death. (1 John 3:14 ESV)

> If anyone has material possessions and sees a brother or sister in need but has no pity on them, how can the love of God be in that person? (1 John 3:17 NIV)

> What good is it, my brothers and sisters, if someone claims to have faith but has no deeds? Can such faith save them? Suppose a brother or a sister is without clothes and daily food. If one of you says to them, "Go in peace; keep warm and well fed," but does nothing about their physical needs, what good is it? In the same way, faith by itself, if it is not accompanied by action, is dead. (James 2:14–17 NIV)

> Therefore, as we have opportunity, let us do good to all people, especially to those who belong to the family of believers. (Galatians 6:10 NIV)

> Meanwhile, Saul was still breathing out murderous threats against the Lord's disciples. He went to the high priest and asked him for letters to the synagogues in Damascus, so that if he found any there who belonged to the Way,

whether men or women, he might take them as prisoners to Jerusalem. As he neared Damascus on his journey, suddenly a light from heaven flashed around him. He fell to the ground and heard a voice say to him, "Saul, Saul, why do you persecute me?" (Acts 9:1–4 NIV)

All of these texts make plain that the "brothers and sisters" (or "brethren") in the New Testament always refers to the members of the body of Christ, the children of God by new birth (not just physical birth).

What's more striking is that Jesus doesn't distinguish Himself from His body. The head and the body are fully united; therefore, what happens to the members of the body of Christ happens to Him.

Consequently, to treat the body one way is to treat the Lord the same way.

Taking Care of Jesus Christ

Because Christ is unified with His body, it is not a small thing to take care of your fellow members of the Lord's body. It's also a serious thing to do harm to a child of God.

Put another way, the most cared-for people on this earth should be God's people, the members of the ekklesia, the disciples of Jesus Christ.

Why? Because taking care of your sisters and brothers in Christ is the closest you'll ever get to caring for the Lord Jesus Himself.

The kingdom is embodied when we take care of one another—body, soul, and spirit. And the kingdom is demonstrated when the world sees this embodiment.

So take care of your brothers and sisters in the Lord. For in so doing, you're taking care of the Lord and ministering to Him.

You will never have a higher honor in your life than to care for another child of God. Especially the least of them.

This is kingdom experience.

In 1 John, the apostle argues that those who love "the brethren" have eternal life. In Matthew 25, Jesus essentially says that those who love the brethren inherit God's kingdom. Those are two ways of saying the same thing.

Therefore, learn to view your sisters and brothers in Christ as part of Christ Himself. For that is how God sees them.

Echoing Jesus, Peter wrote,

> Therefore, brothers, be all the more diligent to confirm your calling and election, for if you practice these qualities you will never fall. For in this way there will be richly provided for you an entrance into the eternal kingdom of our Lord and Savior Jesus Christ. (2 Peter 1:10–11 ESV)

As I stated in a previous chapter, our care for one another (which is our priority in the kingdom) should flow out to our care for those who are in the world. But our chief priority is to care for those in God's house, the members of Jesus Christ our Lord, the people of the insurgence.

A Colony of Heaven

Many Christians believe that God's people shouldn't take care of the earth because they belong to heaven. Here is the text they use to support this belief:

> We are citizens of heaven, where the Lord Jesus Christ lives. And we are eagerly waiting for him to return as our Savior. (Philippians 3:20 NLT)

But this concept is built on a misreading of that text.

According to the Moffatt translation of the Bible, Philippians 3:20 says, "We are a colony of heaven on earth."

I believe Moffatt is correct. "Colony" is a better translation of this text. Let me explain.

When I was a young believer, I took this passage to mean that I'm a citizen of heaven. Therefore, my home isn't here. I'm just passing through, waiting to go to heaven (my real home).

But this isn't what Paul had in mind.

Paul is writing to the Christians in Philippi. Philippi was a Roman colony. As such, the city reflected the ideals of Roman life. A Roman colony was "a little bit of Rome away from Rome." Although Rome was far away, if you were in Philippi, it was as if you were in Rome. You heard people speaking Latin. You saw the Roman way of life. And Caesar was regarded as the savior and lord of the world.

As a Roman colony, Philippi was an outpost, an extension, a small re-production of the imperial city of Rome. Philippi was a miniature Rome, over 700 miles away in the Greek world of Macedonia.

Using the language of "colony," Paul was in effect saying that you (the ekklesia in Philippi) are a colony of heaven, reflecting the culture of heaven in a foreign land (the Roman Empire). Jesus, who is in heaven, is your Savior and Lord (not Caesar).

If a person living in Philippi said, "I'm a citizen of Rome," he wouldn't be saying "I'm looking forward to living in Rome." No. By living in Philippi, it was as if he were already living in Rome. Because Philippi was a Roman colony—a miniature of Rome.

Caesar didn't want people in Philippi—and other Roman colonies—returning to Rome. Instead, the purpose of being a citizen of a Roman colony was to bring the culture and rule of Rome to the colony. It was to expand Roman influence in the world.

That is what Paul was communicating in Philippians 3:20.

The ekklesia is a colony of heaven on earth. Therefore, she has the responsibility of bringing the life and rule of heaven to earth. (Recall the Lord's prayer, "On earth as it is in heaven.") Jesus will eventually return to set up His kingdom on earth. (Recall also that the New Jerusalem descends to earth.)

The Culture of Heaven

• • •

God's eternal purpose is to bring the culture of heaven to earth and bring us back to the garden, the overlap of man's space and God's space, of the heavenlies and the earthlies.

Paul's words in Philippians 3:20 are subversive. He was posing a powerful challenge to the believers in Philippi, that they give their full allegiance, not to Rome, but to heaven. To Jesus Christ, not to Caesar. Our citizenship is in heaven. We are a colony of the heavenly realm. We look forward to our Savior who dwells in heaven—Jesus Christ—returning to earth.

In the Roman Empire, the terms "savior" and "lord" were titles for Caesar. By using them to refer to Jesus of Nazareth, Paul was saying, "Jesus is Lord, and Caesar isn't."

So Philippi was a colonial outpost of Caesar's empire. The empire of Jesus Christ (the kingdom of God)—of which the church in Philippi was a colonial outpost—was the reality.

Therefore, the point of being a citizen—or a colony—of heaven is not that we will eventually go to heaven. Instead, the point is that the true emperor (Jesus) will one day return from the mother city to liberate His loyal followers and transform them into His full image. That's what the next verse says:

> He will take our weak mortal bodies and change them into glorious bodies like his own, using the same power with which he will bring everything under his control. (Philippians 3:21 NLT)

The ekklesia, then, is not a holding place where we wait to go home to our "heavenly mansion." It's actually the opposite.

The ekklesia is an outpost of heaven on this earth to embody the life of heaven and express the rule and reign of Jesus Christ, right here, right now.

As Jesus-followers living in this world, we are resident aliens, present pilgrims, native sojourners, heavenly foreigners, earthly strangers from another realm who stand on this earth for the Lord's rights.

Live out your time as foreigners here in reverent fear. (1 Peter 1:17 NIV)

Beloved, I urge you as aliens and strangers to abstain from fleshly lusts which wage war against the soul. (1 Peter 2:11 NASB)

These all died in faith, not having received the promises, but having seen them afar off were assured of them, embraced them and confessed that they were strangers and pilgrims on the earth. (Hebrews 11:13 NKJV)

Our Savior, Jesus the Christ and the King, will one day return from heaven to the earth to change the present age, bringing forth a new heaven and a new earth. He will transform our bodies to be like His glorious body and free the creation from its bondage to the curse, transforming the entire universe (Romans 8).

The ekklesia is the true nation of God, ruled by the heavens. While Satan may rule the kingdoms of this world, he cannot rule the ekklesia. Through the ekklesia, the kingdom of God stands in this earth as a colony from heaven.

The Less Fortunate

Perhaps you're incredibly fortunate and the church to which you belong *is* operating like the ekklesia I've described. It's living as a powerful signpost of the kingdom of God.

If that's the case, maybe your church will use this book to go deeper and higher in enjoying the kingdom and seeing its advancement.

But suppose that you are less fortunate and cannot find such a church in your area. You're also not able to relocate in order to be part of one.

What do you do then?

This may sound trite, but it's not. You can begin by regularly touching the throne of God in prayer. I'd suggest beginning small in your prayers rather than large. Ask the Lord for just *one person* to come into your life who has a heart for God's kingdom. Then begin looking for opportunities to meet new people.

Consider starting a book-reading group in your town to discuss the kingdom of God with others who are interested.

If you can find just one or two people who are interested in seeking the kingdom with you, you can use this book as a springboard, going through the "Taking Action" sections together and exploring ways of implementing the lessons collectively.

Perhaps out of that two or three, the Lord will add to your number. So prayerfully consider inviting others to join you.

Let the Lord lead you step by step. Elsewhere I've provided ideas for how small groups can begin to create community and have a shared life. That instruction may be of help to you at some point.*

---

* See Frank Viola, *Finding Organic Church* (Colorado Springs: David C. Cook, 2009), part 3.

Other Spheres

· · ·

As you wait on the Lord for others to join you in seeking the kingdom first, you can still be an agent of God's kingdom even while you're without a believing community.

You can embody and demonstrate the kingdom in your home. You can embody and demonstrate the kingdom in your workplace. You can embody and demonstrate the kingdom in your friendships. You can find organizations in your city that are alleviating human suffering and support them.

Conducting yourself as a kingdom citizen in your home, at your workplace, and in your relationships makes your teaching about God and His kingdom attractive to unbelievers (Titus 2:9–10; 1 Thessalonians 4:11–12; 1 Peter 3:1).

> And this gospel of the kingdom will be preached in the whole world as a testimony to all nations, and then the end will come. (Matthew 24:14 NIV)

According to the Weymouth New Testament translation, the word "testimony" in Matthew 24:14 is translated "set the evidence."

Jesus said that the gospel of God's royal reign shall be proclaimed in the whole inhabited world for a testimony—to "set the evidence" before all nations.

The good news of the kingship of Jesus must be embodied in concrete action or else it's just a theological talking point. When Christ's kingship is embodied, it constitutes the proof and evidence of its reality.

Yes, you can "set forth the evidence" that Jesus is enthroned by the righteousness, peace, and love you display in your home, work, and friendships. By so doing, you bear witness to the reality of God's kingdom.

So it all begins with honest prayer. If your heart is given to seeking the Lord's kingdom first in your life, He will show you the next steps on how to make it a living reality right where you are.

What the Early Christians Did Not Do

. . .

The followers of Jesus in the first century were completely different from the other revolutionary groups during the same time period. For example,

> The Zealots employed violence, coercion, and force to overthrow the Roman Empire.
>
> The Sadducees collaborated with Roman overlords and their puppets.
>
> The Essenes withdrew from the empire entirely and lived their lives in the wilderness.
>
> The Pharisees tried to remain separate and pure, but they kept themselves away from those they deemed to be "sinners," and proved themselves to be hypocrites in the process.

Both Jesus and His body—the ekklesia—took a completely different approach.

They didn't use the power of the sword to try to defeat the rulers of the world, like the Zealots did.

They didn't try to grab political power, like the Sadducees did.

They didn't withdraw from society, like the Essenes did.

They didn't keep those who weren't part of their company at arm's length, like the Pharisees did. In fact, according to Jesus, the self-righteous Pharisees didn't enter the kingdom of God while the so-called sinners did.

The Pharisees scapegoated the prostitutes, the drunkards, and the other "sinners" while refusing to see themselves as sinners.

Only sinners are permitted entrance into the kingdom. So if you can't admit that you're a sinner, you're out of luck with God.

The early Christians also weren't involved in acts of mercy and social activism *apart* from Jesus Christ and the power and leadership of the Holy Spirit.

No, whatever the early Christians did was in, by, and through Jesus Christ Himself, the King of His kingdom, advancing it on earth as it is in heaven.

Unfortunately, there are Christian versions of the Zealots, Sadducees, Essenes, and Pharisees today. And God's people should not adopt any of these approaches.

The kingdom comes by and through the cross. The first-century believers understood this all too well. But today, many Christians do not.

Scripture is clear that we share the inheritance of the kingdom if we share in our Lord's sufferings.

> Therefore, among God's churches we boast about your perseverance and faith in all the persecutions and trials you are enduring. All this is evidence that God's judgment is right, and as a result you will be counted worthy of the kingdom of God, for which you are suffering. (2 Thessalonians 1:4–5 NIV)

The ekklesia are the people of the kingdom; therefore, they are a cross-bearing people.

It is through bearing the cross—the laying down of our lives—that God advances His kingdom. When you are a follower of the King, the cross of Jesus Christ is to be worked out in your own life (Mark 8:34–37; Luke 9:23–25).

The cross, then, is the lynchpin of the insurgence.

Nationalism and Politics

• • •

God has called the ekklesia to be the place in which the kingdom of God finds its expression, not the political process.

God's kingdom can never be implemented at the political level. One key reason is that the political system is part of the world system. That doesn't mean that the political system can't be a force for good in the world. It can. But it can never bring in or replace the kingdom of Jesus Christ. For that reason, we should never place our hope in it.

In the same way, nationalism is a form of idolatry. Nationalism says, "My country right or wrong." It also asserts, "My country embodies the kingdom of God" or something close to that statement.

A nation cannot be the kingdom of God unless it submits to Jesus as King. Your allegiance, therefore, is to a King and His kingdom. It's not to a country, a flag, a political party, or a fallen man or woman who is in power.

We—God's people—are called to be salt and light, not by coercing people with political or military power, but by living out an alternative reality. As citizens of the kingdom of God, we don't seek to influence the State. The State is part of the world system and God's kingdom is never a tool of the State.

As the body of Christ, we instead proclaim, embody, and demonstrate the kingdom—a kingdom that comes from another realm.

Like ancient Israel, the ekklesia is called to be a microcosm of the kingdom of God. It's designed to be a visible expression of the kingdom in the world.

By observing her life together, people witness a new social order, a new kind of justice, a new kind of peace, forgiveness, reconciliation, love, and mutual care in the ekklesia. Within her walls, there is no racism, sexism, bigotry, social prejudice, or discrimination (Colossians 3:11; Galatians 3:28).

Jesus was clear that those who follow Him do not belong to this world system just as He doesn't belong to it:

- Jesus is not of (from) this world. (John 8:23)
- You do not belong to the world. Jesus chose you to be out of the world. That's why the world hates you. (John 15:19)
- Jesus doesn't pray for the world. (John 17:9)
- You are not of (from) the world, even as Jesus isn't of (from) the world. (John 17:16)

Those who are part of the insurgence understand their true identity and live accordingly.

Cyanide and Grape Juice

. . .

Mixing Christianity with partisan politics is like mixing cyanide with grape juice. It won't harm the cyanide, but it makes the grape juice toxic.

To be blunt, you cannot be wrapped up and consumed with today's political system and be useful to the kingdom of God. You cannot embrace nationalism and embrace God's kingdom.

I was born in the United States, so that makes me an American citizen. But to a real degree, I'm not an American citizen. I belong to another kingdom. My citizenship is in the heavenly realm, and my allegiance belongs to that realm.

So if my country asks me to do something that's at variance with my citizenship in God's kingdom, the choice is easy. I settled it a long time ago. I belong to God's kingdom, and I renounce my American citizenship for God's true kingdom.

Many Christians are completely sold out to the political system—nationalism—as well as the religious system, not knowing that all of these systems are part of the world.

In speaking of the ekklesia as an alternative to the fallen order ruled by the state, I love how John Nugent put it:

> We pray for the state because we are well aware of its potential to do great good and to inflict great harm. Moreover, the state creates the conditions and context in which we live out our distinct role. . . . Neither warm embrace, nor hostile resistance will do; instead, our mission requires a stance of respectful disengagement. Christians who choose not to get deeply entangled in the political affairs of their host nations are not simply lazy, unloving, or irresponsible. Nor are they attempting to dishonor the blood that was shed by those who fought to establish the various nations we live in today. They are honoring the blood that Christ shed, as well as those Christian martyrs who followed his steps. These martyrs traded worldly domination for the reign of God and, by refusing to worship the rulers of the nations, bore witness to the transterritorial eternal kingdom of which we are now a part.[21]

Paul's exhortation to Timothy is fitting:

Join with me in suffering, like a good soldier of Christ Jesus. No one serving as a soldier gets entangled in civilian affairs, but rather tries to please his commanding officer. (2 Timothy 2:3–4 NIV)

Tragically, any political or religious system that is threatened by the radical vision of God's kingdom will crucify Jesus Christ all over again, even if that system flies the flag of His name. This fact is woven into the fabric of church history.

Many of God's servants spilled their blood at the hands of political and religious systems that labored under the name of Jesus.

We really don't know how much the systems of this world—political and religious—hold us until God opens our eyes.[*]

---

[*] For further thoughts on politics, see my online article "A Word About Political Elections" at InsurgenceBook.com.

The Mystery of Suffering

No one wants to hear about it. So few people talk about it. But suffering is in the DNA of divine life. And it's part of the fabric of God's kingdom.

Paul warned the Galatian believers, all of whom were brand-new converts, "We must suffer many hardships to enter the Kingdom of God" (Acts 14:22 NLT).

Entering, enjoying, and advancing the kingdom of God—the sovereign rule of Jesus Christ—comes through *many* afflictions.

You see, Jesus' victory over the usurping power of the world came through means of His cross. In the same way, Jesus-followers today implement the Lord's victory by bearing the Lord's cross.

In other words, it comes about by suffering.

We obviously don't suffer to atone for sin, for only Jesus has done that. But by losing our lives, denying ourselves, laying our lives down to benefit others at the expense of ourselves, we gain more ground for God to work in and through us.

> Not only so, but we also glory in our sufferings, because we know that suffering produces perseverance; perseverance, character; and character, hope. (Romans 5:3–4 NIV)

Giving Jesus Christ His rightful place in our lives means that His character begins to take shape in us (Galatians 4:19). This is where the cost comes in, because the process is often painful.

Throughout the book of Acts, we find the ekklesia growing and becoming more powerful as persecution starts and spreads. This is also the story of church history. And it's a critical feature of the insurgence.

So suffering and dying to ourselves is the way in which the kingdom of God advances. The cross of Jesus launched the insurgence. And His cross, as it's borne by the followers of Christ, is the means by which the insurgence increases.

Don't Waste Your Sufferings

．．．

There are many things in life that contradict God's kingdom. But the Lord doesn't annihilate those things. He allows and even uses them to establish His kingdom in our lives.

In Matthew 20, we see James and John, two of the Lord's disciples, nudging their mother to ask Jesus to give them the top jobs when Jesus comes into His kingdom.

Jesus responds by saying that they must drink the cup He must drink to have those positions. The cup He spoke about was the cup of suffering.

Point: There is no kingdom without the cross. And there is no reign without suffering.

> If we endure hardship,
>   we will reign with him. (2 Timothy 2:12 NLT)

And since we are his children, we are his heirs. In fact, together with Christ we are heirs of God's glory. But if we are to share his glory, we must also share his suffering. (Romans 8:17 NLT)

To the one who is victorious and does my will to the end, I will give authority over the nations. (Revelation 2:26 NIV)

To him that overcometh will I grant to sit with me in my throne, even as I also overcame, and am set down with my Father in his throne. (Revelation 3:21 KJV)

It is when we are emptied of ourselves through suffering that we experience the power and victory of Christ. Suffering also enables us to implement that power and victory in the earth. Christians who don't know how to surrender their sufferings to the Lord end up wasting them.

So my word to you is simple: *Don't waste your sufferings.* They are designed to give the Lord more ground in your life so that His kingdom may advance in and through you. Your sufferings, hardships, and tribulations are your training for reigning, equipping you to bear God's image and exercise His authority, the fulfillment of His eternal purpose.

Those who enter the kingdom and then step out of it due to the suffering it brings are not fit to serve.

> Jesus replied, "No one who puts a hand to the plow and looks back is fit for service in the kingdom of God." (Luke 9:62 NIV)

Don't let yourself be part of that number.

The Greatest Suffering

. . .

The kind of insurgence that Jesus Christ launched is not accomplished by a sprint. It's a marathon. As participants of God's kingdom, we have been called to share in the sufferings of our Lord.

Denying the false gods and resisting the temptations they bring constitutes suffering.

When we deny Kratos, the god of power, we suffer.

When we deny Plutus, the god of wealth, we suffer.

When we deny Aphrodite, the god of lust, we suffer.

Therefore, since Christ suffered in his body, arm yourselves also with the same attitude, because whoever suffers in the body is done with sin. As a result, they do not live the rest of their earthly lives for evil human desires, but rather for the will of God. (1 Peter 4:1–2 NIV)

Because he himself suffered when he was tempted, he is able to help those who are being tempted. (Hebrews 2:18 NIV)

. . . let us throw off everything that hinders and the sin that so easily entangles . . . In your struggle against sin, you have not yet resisted to the point of shedding your blood. (Hebrews 12:1, 4 NIV)

Resisting temptation and "struggling against sin" is certainly a form of suffering. Sometimes extremely painful suffering. But as someone once said, "If you're going through hell, keep going." Resist the devil and he will eventually flee from you (James 4:7).

Some who have tasted "the fleeting pleasures of sin" have initially felt as though they've surrendered themselves to a boring life. Indeed, living a life absent of the tantalizing spice that the world so attractively offers is a form of suffering. But note that the pleasures of sin are always temporary.

. . . choosing rather to be mistreated with the people of God than to enjoy the fleeting pleasures of sin. (Hebrews 11:25 ESV)

However, the greatest suffering that you will ever experience will come to you at the hands of your brothers and sisters in the Lord. Yes, it will come from other Christians.

Consider this statement which is a prophetic word regarding Jesus, the Messiah:

I was wounded in the house of my friends. (Zechariah 13:6 NKJV)

It was the pagan Romans who drove the nails into His hands, but it was God's own people who ordered the Lord's death.

Those who live by the Lord's life will be led up a hill to die. That is the direction in which divine life flows. If you don't believe me, look at your Lord and ask the question, Where did divine life lead Him?

His Father led Him up a hill to die.

Setting aside His atoning death and His coronation as Lord above all, whatever happened to Jesus Christ will happen to you. You are in Christ. Therefore, His experience is your destiny.

What did Jesus Christ suffer? He suffered being misunderstood. He suffered being lied about. He suffered false rumors. He suffered betrayal. He suffered having to put up with followers who rarely understood what He was talking about. He suffered and agonized over Jerusalem who had hardened its heart against Him.

He suffered being hated by His own people. He suffered rejection from His own family members as well as denial and betrayal by some of His closest followers.

Beyond all that, He suffered the pain of the cross—the most inexplicable, unfathomable, brutal, barbaric, savage, horrific, painful punishment ever invented by the human mind.

Yes, Jesus suffered. That's where divine life led Him. And that's where it will lead you also. Why? So that He might gain more ground in your life and His kingdom might advance.

But thank God, all who are crucified are also resurrected. And there is no power that can touch a resurrected person.

Those who are part of the insurgence relive the death and resurrection of Christ in their own lives.

Accusations

. . .

Jesus of Nazareth was no politician, yet He was subject to a continuous stream of smears. Here are eleven accusations that were laid at our Lord's feet during His day. He was called

- an illegitimate child
- a drunkard, a glutton
- a false prophet
- a deceiver
- a blasphemer
- mentally ill
- demon possessed
- a law-breaker ["unbiblical"]
- Beelzebub [Satan incarnate]
- a temple-destroyer

Strikingly, the Lord never defended Himself against any of these allegations. That's just how divine life rolls.

Those of you who have given—or will give—your life utterly to the Lord may see God using you powerfully. If and when that happens (or if it's already happening), take heed. False accusations are not far away.

Stirring up the kingdom of darkness will bring them to your door. The enemy's name is "slanderer," and accusing the brethren is among his most effective weapons (Revelation 12:10).

> Remember what I told you: "A servant is not greater than his master." If they persecuted me, they will persecute you also. If they obeyed my teaching, they will obey yours also. (John 15:20 NIV)

So don't be surprised when you see mud slung your way. It was so then, and it is so today. But discover the uncommon secret of how to react to the accusations, as did your Lord (1 Peter 2:21–23; Matthew 26:57–63).

It's profoundly different from the way virtually all politicians—and many Christians—react.

Those who are part of the insurgence have learned the power of these words:

> Do not resist the one who is evil. But if anyone slaps you on the right cheek, turn to him the other also. And if anyone would sue you and take your tunic, let him have your cloak as well. And if anyone forces you to go one mile, go with him two miles. Give to the one who begs from you, and do not refuse the one who would borrow from you. (Matthew 5:39–42 ESV)

> When he [Jesus] was reviled, he did not revile in return; when he suffered, he did not threaten, but continued entrusting himself to him who judges justly. (1 Peter 2:23 ESV)

These admonitions are not a command to be a doormat for everyone who would like to wipe his or her feet on you. A Jew offering his left cheek to a Roman who just backhanded him was a way of exposing the Roman's violence and defying it without responding with violence.

Offering the left cheek said, "If you're going to be violent toward me, you'll have to treat me like an equal. You can't just backhand me like you would a slave. Hit me with your fist, the way you would fight with another Roman."

This approach is different from fighting back with a dagger, running away, or cowering in fear. It is neither violent nor cowardly.

Life in God's kingdom is about denying ourselves without reacting or retreating.

The insurgence is marked by the denial of oneself and the resurrection of that which is of Christ.

Implementing the Victory

. . .

So what does it practically mean for Jesus of Nazareth to be the Lord of the world? *In practical terms, it means that Jesus Christ rules the world through His body, the ekklesia of God.*

It is you and me—and all of God's people—who make the Lord's rule in the world active and effective.

That's why in Genesis 3:15, we are told that the seed of the woman will bruise the head of the serpent. The seed of the woman is Jesus. Yet this promise is fulfilled in Romans 16:20 where Paul says that the head of the serpent will be crushed under the feet of the ekklesia.

After the fall, the serpent was made to "eat dust" (Genesis 3:14). Man was made from dust. Consequently, the deeper meaning is that the devil has power over ("consumes") fallen man ("dust").

However, he has no power over those who have come into Christ. We who are in Christ are part of a new race, a new creation, a new humanity who has power over the enemy.

So Jesus, the second Adam, came to do what the first Adam failed to do. He lived by the life of God (symbolized by the tree of life), He bore God's image, and He exercised God's authority in the earth. And then at His resurrection, He was fruitful and He multiplied.

> Most assuredly, I say to you, unless a grain of wheat falls into the ground and dies, it remains alone; but if it dies, it produces much grain. (John 12:24 NKJV)

Though principalities and powers have been defeated at the cross, they still exist to enslave people and thwart God's purpose. But Satan's power has been broken at the cross, so all are free to respond to the Lord's grace and implement it in their lives. *Including you.*

Because of Christ's work on the cross, Satan has no legal claim on anyone who is in God's kingdom.

The fulfillment of God's eternal purpose is centered on implementing the victory that Jesus Christ won on the cross. Consequently, the only power the enemy has over you and me is the power we give him. This is why it's essential that we give him no ground in our lives.

In Ephesians 4:27, Paul says, "Do not give the devil a foothold" (NIV). It's possible for a believer, who has victory over the devil, to give him a foothold or a loophole to operate. Jesus stated that Satan had no ground or foothold in Him when He said that "he [the prince of this world] has nothing in me" (John 14:30 NASB).

Fear is Satan's calling card. Surrendering to the powers of the world system, which is the enemy's turf, also gives him ground. Such compromises invite the devil to operate in our lives and give him power over us.

Sometimes "love" clothed in "tolerance" toward evil deceives God's people and gives the enemy power. The root here is often fear as well. On this score, A. W. Tozer wrote,

> The fashion now is to tolerate anything, lest we gain the reputation of being intolerant. The tender-minded saints cannot bear to see Agag slain, so they choose rather to sacrifice the health of the Church for years to come by sparing error and evil; and this they do in the name of Christian love.[22]

The shared sufferings of the cross of Christ is what keeps our hearts open to God and shuts them off from the enemy. Hence, we can say with our Lord, "The ruler of this world has approached me, but he has no claim on or power over me."*

It is the ekklesia of God who wears God's armor and knocks down the gates of hell. The armor that Paul lists in Ephesians 6 is worn by a woman, the bride of Christ. She is the one who storms the gates of hell, as Jesus put it in Matthew 16.

> Simon Peter replied, "You are the Christ, the Son of the living God." And Jesus answered him, "Blessed are you, Simon Bar-Jonah! For flesh and blood has not revealed this to you, but my Father who is in heaven. And I tell you, you are Peter, and on this rock I will build my church, and the gates of hell shall not prevail against it. (vv. 16–18 ESV)

* I share more about the dethroning of Satan and why God leaves him on the earth during this present age in my online article "The Mission of the Insurgence" at InsurgenceBook.com.

The "rock" that Jesus builds His ekklesia upon is not Peter. It is the revelation that Jesus is "the Christ, the Son of the living God." Peter confessed that revelation in this passage.

Gates are defensive structures. So the ekklesia is on the advance, pushing back the gates of Hades by the power of the Holy Spirit who indwells her.[*]

This is the work of the insurgence.

---

[*] Michael Heiser gives an excellent defense for the idea of the church pushing down the gates of hell in *The Unseen Realm*, 281–85.

Filling Up His Sufferings

· · ·

If you don't have something for which to die, you don't have anything for which to live.

In Colossians 1:24, Paul makes an earth-shaking statement. It reads,

> Now I rejoice in my sufferings for your sake, and in my flesh I do my share on behalf of His body, which is the church, in filling up what is lacking in Christ's afflictions. (NASB)

This text says that the sufferings of Christ were not complete when Jesus was on the earth as a man.

That's an amazing statement.

Jesus did not complete His sufferings on the cross. He has left the rest of that suffering to His body—the ekklesia—to complete.

What on earth does that mean?

It means that there will be those in the body of Christ (like Paul) who will stand on the front lines of the kingdom and take the brunt of the Lord's sufferings into themselves. And God's people will receive life from it.

Speaking about this very thing, Paul says,

> We are afflicted in every way, but not crushed; perplexed, but not driven to despair; persecuted, but not forsaken; struck down, but not destroyed; always carrying in the body the death of Jesus, so that the life of Jesus may also be manifested in our bodies. For we who live are always being given over to death for Jesus' sake, so that the life of Jesus also may be manifested in our mortal flesh. So death is at work in us, but life in you. (2 Corinthians 4:8–12 ESV)

Both Peter and Paul speak about the mystery of sharing in the sufferings of Jesus and the glory that follows:

> But rejoice inasmuch as you participate in the sufferings of Christ, so that you may be overjoyed when his glory is revealed. (1 Peter 4:13 NIV)

I consider that our present sufferings are not worth comparing with the glory that will be revealed in us. (Romans 8:18 NIV)

For as the sufferings of Christ overflow to us, so through Christ our comfort also overflows. (2 Corinthians 1:5 HCSB)

I want to know Christ—yes, to know the power of his resurrection and participation in his sufferings, becoming like him in his death. (Philippians 3:10 NIV)

For you have been given not only the privilege of trusting in Christ but also the privilege of suffering for him. (Philippians 1:29 NLT)

The sufferings of Christ that we share have nothing to do with redemption. Where redemption is concerned, Christ's sufferings are fully complete. Nothing can be added to or subtracted from them.

But there are sufferings that we participate in and absorb which bring life to others. These are the sufferings that Christ has not yet completed. And they are the means by which the insurgence advances.

The Work of God on Earth

* * *

If you ever see a work of God that is living, powerful, and transformational, stand back and know this: Someone went into the earth and died to produce that bountiful harvest. Someone was taking the sufferings of Christ into themselves.

The supreme lordship of Jesus Christ—His kingdom displayed—is manifested to the whole cosmic realm in and through a body of believers in whom the divine meaning of the cross of Christ—in all of its shared sufferings—is a reality.

Every true follower of Jesus will face suffering. And those sufferings are what allows God to advance His kingdom in the earth.

In addition, in some mysterious way, what we do for the kingdom of God in this life will not be wasted in the next. Rather, it will go into the final establishment of God's kingdom.

> Therefore, my dear brothers and sisters, stand firm. Let nothing move you. Always give yourselves fully to the work of the Lord, because you know that your labor in the Lord is not in vain. (1 Corinthians 15:58 NIV)

God's call for us who have eyes to see and ears to hear is to submit to the lordship of Jesus Christ and live under His domain, knowing full well that it will entail suffering.

Through the eyes of faith, we see that Jesus of Nazareth is the rightful Lord of the world. It is our journey to act accordingly.

So the ekklesia is called to implement the victorious rule of Jesus Christ by entering, enjoying, proclaiming, embodying, and demonstrating the kingdom of God.

To enter the kingdom means to repent and believe the gospel of God's royal rule.

To enjoy the kingdom means to live abundantly in its blessings and riches.

To proclaim the kingdom means to bear witness to the rule of God's domain and its demands.

To embody the kingdom means to showcase its unique life before a watching world.

And to demonstrate the kingdom means to bless others with the manifestation of God's ruling presence.

This is how the insurgence works.

The Power of the Spirit

. . .

Unfortunately, some movements in the Christian family today have abused the power of the Holy Spirit and turned it into a toy, wielding it immaturely to get one's own selfish desires met.

This is tragic, because the power of God is a very real thing. But it's not to be taken lightly or used selfishly.

God's intention is for the body of Christ to exercise His authority in the world. Not through political or military power. But through spiritual power against the forces of evil.

> For our struggle is not against flesh and blood, but against the rulers, against the authorities, against the powers of this dark world and against the spiritual forces of evil in the heavenly realms. (Ephesians 6:12 NIV)

All authority has been given to Christ. And that authority has been placed in His body to wield in heavenly realms.

When the members of the body of Christ are laying down their lives, allowing the cross of Jesus Christ to work in them, the life of Christ grows within them. And God's power is contained in that life.

Together, they can exert God's power through prayer, pulling down strongholds in heavenly realms.

But such prayers won't reach above the ceiling if God's people are living for themselves, giving themselves over to bickering, petty jealousy, disunity, conflict, unforgiveness, and so forth. These things give ground to the enemy and deplete spiritual power.

However, the cross—which puts to death the deeds of the flesh—and the exercise of God's power working through the ekklesia work hand in hand. You cannot have one without the other.

When God's people mean business with the Lord and learn the art of losing, forfeiting, and letting go, they begin to touch the heavenly throne with their prayers. And the kingdom of God begins to impact the kingdoms of this world.

So self must be put out of the way in order for the kingdom to come with God's power.

Recall that the Lord could not get His people into the promised land until they completely repudiated Egypt in their hearts.

This difficulty should not be underestimated. There were only two people who came out of Egypt and made it into the promised land. And it was much harder to get Egypt out of the children of Israel than it was to get the children of Israel out of Egypt.

All told, the kingdom doesn't advance when we hold on to that which the Lord has asked us to forfeit. Again, you won't get very far in the Lord's kingdom until you learn to be violent toward the things of the world that have captured your heart.

Thankfully, the promised Holy Spirit has been given to us to make this possible.

The Blessed Hope

· · ·

God's intention is to raise up colonial outposts all over the world that serve as signposts of the divine insurgence. Outposts that are embodying the life of the kingdom of the Lord Jesus Christ and demonstrating its power. Not perfectly, and sometimes quite muddled, but they are bearing witness to the kingdom nonetheless.

These subversive groups wave the banner of the insurgence as a visible sign that there is a new King, a new Lord, and a new kingdom that the physical eye cannot see. But the eyes of faith cannot help but notice them.

The people of the insurgence are "occupying until He comes," advancing the kingdom until Jesus Christ—this world's true Lord—returns in glory and "the kingdom of the world has become the kingdom of our Lord and of his Christ, and he shall reign forever and ever" (Revelation 11:15 ESV).

> For the grace of God has appeared that offers salvation to all people. It teaches us to say "No" to ungodliness and worldly passions, and to live self-controlled, upright and godly lives in this present age, while we wait for the blessed hope— the appearing of the glory of our great God and Savior, Jesus Christ, who gave himself for us to redeem us from all wickedness and to purify for himself a people that are his very own, eager to do what is good. (Titus 2:11–14 NIV)

Notice the words of Titus, "while we wait for the blessed hope." Our blessed hope is that Jesus will return to earth and set all things right. The dead in Christ will be raised and those living will be translated.

Christ will reign over all things until all enemies are put under His feet, including the last enemy—death. Then He will turn over the absolute authority that He has attained, handing the kingdom back to His Father, and God will be all in all (1 Corinthians 15:23–28).

> Then the end will come, when he hands over the kingdom to God the Father after he has destroyed all dominion, authority and power. (1 Corinthians 15:24 NIV)

Plato longed for a philosopher-king. Jesus of Nazareth is the ultimate Wisdom-King. His kingdom is spiritual, but it's also a geopolitical kingdom on this earth, just as Isaiah prophesied:

> Of the greatness of his government and peace
>> there will be no end.
> He will reign on David's throne
>> and over his kingdom,
> establishing and upholding it
>> with justice and righteousness
>> from that time on and forever.
> The zeal of the LORD Almighty
>> will accomplish this. (Isaiah 9:7 NIV)

Until the time comes when Christ returns in glory—and our blessed hope arrives—the mighty power of the Holy Spirit is working the energy of the kingdom of God in and through all who yield to Him.

Living in the Conscious Presence of Christ

. . .

The taproot behind everything I've written in this book is the privilege of living in the presence of Jesus Christ.

God's presence walked in the Garden of Eden (Genesis 3:8). His presence also walked in the tabernacle and then later the temple (Deuteronomy 23:14; 2 Samuel 7:6).

> In your presence there is fullness of joy;
> at your right hand are pleasures forevermore. (Psalm 16:11 ESV)

We've already seen the deep connection between God's presence and His rule. As a spiritual priest, you have been given access to God's presence. *This means that God is really present with you in an intimate way.* When Jesus died, the veil of the temple was ripped in two from top to bottom, opening God's presence to all who believe (Matthew 27:51).

> Therefore, brethren, having boldness to enter the Holiest by the blood of Jesus, by a new and living way which He consecrated for us, through the veil, that is, His flesh, and having a High Priest over the house of God, let us draw near with a true heart in full assurance of faith. (Hebrews 10:19–22 NKJV)

Living in the Lord's presence doesn't mean seeking a feeling or even a "sense." It's rather the deliberate awareness that the Lord is present in your life.

To live in the Lord's presence is to set your mind on Him, to remember Him, and to live the intentional awareness of His abiding life.

> The mind set on the Spirit is life and peace. (Romans 8:6 NASB)

> Since you have been raised to new life with Christ, set your sights on the realities of heaven, where Christ sits in the place of honor at God's right hand. (Colossians 3:1 NLT)

Abide in Me, and I in you. As the branch cannot bear fruit of itself unless it abides in the vine, so neither can you unless you abide in Me. (John 15:4 NASB)

One of the most remarkable biblical portrayals of what it looks like when the kingdom of God comes to earth is found in the tabernacle of David in the Old Testament. Time and space prevent me from rehearsing the story here, but I've shared it elsewhere.*

I've also discussed how to practically live in the Lord's presence elsewhere, but living in the kingdom of God means living in the Lord's presence.†

---

* For details, listen to the audio message "The Tabernacle of David" at InsurgenceBook.com.

† See my book *Jesus Speaks* with Leonard Sweet as well as my online article "Aware of His Presence" at InsurgenceBook.com.

Inheriting the Kingdom

When Jesus ushered in the kingdom of God, He did so as the "Son of Man," a favorite self-title of His.

Those who have been faithful to the Lord will inherit the kingdom in the next life when Christ returns and this world receives her King. The throne of God, which is seated in heaven, will descend from heaven to earth (Isaiah 66:1; Revelation 22:1, 3). And God will dwell with His people (Revelation 21:1–4).

In this respect, it is the Father's good pleasure to give us the kingdom of God as an inheritance (Luke 12:32).

Those who consistently reject the lordship of Christ through the way they live will not inherit the kingdom (1 Corinthians. 6:9–10; Galatians 5:21; Ephesians 5:5).

Flesh and blood cannot inherit this kingdom. Rather, the kingdom is inherited by resurrected bodies, bodies that will be just like our Lord's resurrected body (1 Corinthians 15:50). It is the resurrected body that allows us to live in the overlap between heaven and earth.

By His grace and mercy, the Father has qualified His children to inherit the kingdom (Colossians 1:12–13). Those who are poor in the eyes of the world, but rich in faith and love for Christ, will inherit it.

> Listen, my beloved brothers, has not God chosen those who are poor in the world to be rich in faith and heirs of the kingdom, which he has promised to those who love him? (James 2:5 ESV)

Friends Yet Separate

. . .

No doubt, when John the Baptist proclaimed the new King, he expected Jesus to be just as sober, somber, and serious as John was. Shockingly, the reputation that Jesus got for Himself was that He ate and drank too much. The gossip around Galilee was that "Jesus is a glutton and a drunkard."

That should encourage you. Jesus Christ, the spotless Son of God, enjoyed being a human. Of course, He was neither a glutton nor a drunkard, but He was a specialist in eating in people's homes, enjoying both food and wine.

Yet Jesus also experienced Gethsemane, crucifixion, abandonment from God, and death.

And that's what the Christian life holds for you and me. It is a life full of joy and sorrow, eating and drinking, death and resurrection.

John withdrew from society. But Jesus lived in the midst of it.

Christians today seem to fall off one side of the horse or the other on this point. Some are like John. They get as far away from society as they can, throwing rocks at it from a distance. (Some of them suffer from rapture fever. They are just waiting for Jesus to return and take them home. So they have very little to do with the culture.)

Others get so close to society that they end up being defiled by and becoming part of the world system.

Jesus was the friend of sinners (Matthew 11:19), yet He was also separate from them (Hebrews 7:26).

That is, Jesus befriended sinners, but He did not adopt their values or lifestyle. In that regard, He was separate from the world. Jesus mingled with society. He didn't curse the darkness from the outside. He struck a match right in the midst of it.

Watchman Nee was correct when he wrote that "separation is the first principle of Christian living."[23]

The way of Jesus is our way.

As You sent Me into the world, I also have sent them into the world. (John 17:18 NASB)

"Come out from among them and be separate" (2 Corinthians 6:17 HCSB) is still God's word for us today.

In that regard, Jesus has but one word for you and me. It was the same word He uttered to His first disciples,

Come, follow me. (Matthew 4:19 NIV)

This Corrupt Generation

For far too long, the kingdom of God has been shrunken and reduced to mean either individual salvation or social transformation. But to define the kingdom this way is to distort what it means.

When Jesus said, "The kingdom is at hand," He meant that the world was about to have a new king. It was also about to see a new reign on the earth in and through a new people.

There is no kingdom outside of Jesus, the King. And there is no kingdom outside the ekklesia, the people who are governed by the King.

For this reason, there is a close connection between the kingdom and the ekklesia. In both places in the Gospels where Jesus refers to the ekklesia, He ties it into the kingdom (see Matthew 16:16–19 and 18:15–18). Binding and loosing is kingdom language.

No kingdom exists without a king. The same is true for the kingdom of God. Caesar was called "the son of God." When people called Jesus the Son of God, they were claiming that He was a king. In the Old Testament, both the terms "Messiah" and "Son of God" carry the meaning of "king."

When Peter preached the gospel of the kingdom on the day of Pentecost,[*] he ended his message with these sober words:

Save yourselves from this corrupt generation. (Acts 2:40 NIV)

My word to you is to save yourself from this corrupt generation. How? By coming under the rule of the realm of the kingdom of God.

As Tozer once put it,

We need men and women who have fought their way to endure scorn and may even have been called fanatics—scoffed at and called everything but a

---

[*] Peter's message in Acts 2 was in fact a presentation of the gospel of the kingdom. Even though Peter didn't use the word "kingdom," he was talking about David's continued reign in the earth through Jesus of Nazareth.

Christian. We need men and women today who are willing to push in and bear their way past the flesh, the world, and the devil, and cold Christians and deacons and elders. They will have to push themselves until they are fascinated by what they see in Christ. Those who have truly seen Christ in His glory have eyes for nothing else.[24]

Forsaking All

• • •

When the Lord's first disciples heard Jesus say, "Come, follow me," they left everything and followed Him.

To follow Jesus today means to leave everything and follow Him wherever He leads. It means and requires cross-bearing. It means and requires self-denial. It means and requires self-sacrifice. It means climbing on the altar as a living sacrifice to God and leaving the world behind.

Sin, with its selfishness, idolatry, pride, and independence, can be juiced down to our desire to be king, to be in control, usurping the place of Jesus as King. Entering and enjoying the kingdom, then, means surrender.

As Jesus-followers, our calling is to live in the world without being captured by its spirit. We are the people who live in the divine parenthesis, living between the end of one age and before the age to come. We are those "on whom the culmination of the ages has come" (1 Corinthians 10:11 NIV).

The insurgence doesn't square with the idea that Christians should retreat from the culture and throw rocks at it from afar. Neither does it square with the idea that Christians should try to fix the problems of the world through political power and activism.[*]

Instead, the insurgence is about living in a different kingdom and putting that kingdom life on display before principalities and powers as well as before fallen women and men.

The insurgence is marked by radical generosity. That is, using our material goods for the good of others, not just for ourselves.

The insurgence looks toward God's final judgment, which is about adjusting what's wrong in the world and making everything right.

When Jesus said, "My kingdom is not of this world," He was referring to a new way to live (John 18:36 NIV). The way that Jesus orders our social life is radically different from the top-down pecking order that's found everywhere in human civilization. The way of Jesus is a completely

---

[*] I take dead aim at these two reactions in *Jesus Manifesto* with Leonard Sweet.

different way to live, be human, and interact socially (Matthew 20:25–28; Luke 22:25–26).

The kingdom of God is a social order in this world that's a stark alternative to the kingdom of Caesar (the empires of the world).

The insurgence calls us to model the true "radicalization," one that's in and for God's already-but-not-yet kingdom. A kingdom of which we are called to be faithful witnesses.

The call of the insurgence is to forsake all and follow the new King and His peaceable kingdom, which is here now but will come in full someday.

Everlasting Domain

* * *

As we follow the Lord Jesus Christ in this life, we can look forward to an "everlasting kingdom" (Daniel 4:3 NIV) where "there will be no end" (Isaiah 9:7 NIV).

The LORD will reign forever and ever! (Exodus 15:18 NLT)

He was given authority, glory and sovereign power; all nations and peoples of every language worshiped him. His dominion is an everlasting dominion that will not pass away, and his kingdom is one that will never be destroyed. . . . But the holy people of the Most High will receive the kingdom and will possess it forever—yes, for ever and ever. (Daniel 7:14, 18 NIV)

But to the Son he says,

"Your throne, O God, endures forever and ever.
    You rule with a scepter of justice." (Hebrews 1:8 NLT)

For a child will be born to us, a son will be given to us;
And the government will rest on His shoulders;
And His name will be called Wonderful Counselor, Mighty God,
Eternal Father, Prince of Peace. (Isaiah 9:6 NASB)

And for that everlasting kingdom, our hearts are full of worship and awe.

The Lord will rescue me from every evil attack and will bring me safely to his heavenly kingdom. To him be glory for ever and ever. Amen. (2 Timothy 4:18 NIV)

All of this was foretold prophetically by Daniel the prophet. Consider the words of his remarkable prophecy:

I saw in the night visions, and, behold, one like the Son of man came with the clouds of heaven, and came to the Ancient of days, and they brought him near before him.

And there was given him dominion, and glory, and a kingdom, that all people, nations, and languages, should serve him: his dominion is an everlasting dominion, which shall not pass away, and his kingdom that which shall not be destroyed. . . .

Until the Ancient of days came, and judgment was given to the saints of the most High; and the time came that the saints possessed the kingdom. . . .

And the kingdom and dominion, and the greatness of the kingdom under the whole heaven, shall be given to the people of the saints of the most High, whose kingdom is an everlasting kingdom, and all dominions shall serve and obey him. (Daniel 7:13–14, 22, 27 KJV)

Take heart, dear child of God. The Lord has given you the kingdom, and you are destined to rule and reign with Him forever. So remain faithful.

This is where the insurgence eventually leads.

Mary's Song

It's known as "the Magnificat." It is the song of Mary, the mother of Jesus, after she was told by the angel Gabriel that she would be carrying the King of Israel, the Messiah of the world.

Her words vividly portray what the kingdom of God looks like when it comes in its fullness. Mary had prophetic insight into the future. Here's an excerpt from it:

> He has done mighty deeds with His arm;
> He has scattered those who were proud in the thoughts of their
>   heart.
> He has brought down rulers from their thrones,
> And has exalted those who were humble.
> HE HAS FILLED THE HUNGRY WITH GOOD THINGS;
> And sent away the rich empty-handed.
> He has given help to Israel His servant,
> In remembrance of His mercy,
> As He spoke to our fathers,
> To Abraham and his descendants forever. (Luke 1:51–55 NASB)

Hundreds of years earlier, Isaiah also described what the earth would look like when God's kingdom comes in its fullness. Here are his words:

> And the wolf will dwell with the lamb,
> And the leopard will lie down with the young goat,
> And the calf and the young lion and the fatling together;
> And a little boy will lead them.
> Also the cow and the bear will graze,
> Their young will lie down together,
> And the lion will eat straw like the ox.
> The nursing child will play by the hole of the cobra,
> And the weaned child will put his hand on the viper's den.
> They will not hurt or destroy in all My holy mountain,

For the earth will be full of the knowledge of the LORD
As the waters cover the sea.

Then in that day
The nations will resort to the root of Jesse,
Who will stand as a signal for the peoples;
And His resting place will be glorious. (Isaiah 11:6–10 NASB)

Paul tells us that all creation will be liberated from the curse of the fall and reconciled to Christ (Romans 8:18–25; Colossians 1:20).

Those who are part of the insurgence find in these words a vision worth living and dying for.

A Farewell to Kings

. . .

So far in this book, we've explored the stunning beauty of the King; how to enter the kingdom; enjoy its riches; and proclaim, embody, demonstrate, and inherit it.

The kingdom of God is the true empire, and it stands against all other empires, allegiances, lords, and kings.

The only kingdom that will stand in the end is the royal domain of Jesus Christ. All other kings will be displaced. All other rulers will be uprooted.

While you and I are citizens of our own country, our higher citizenship is in the kingdom of the heavens.

This doesn't mean that we must renounce our earthly citizenship, but our first and full allegiance is always to our citizenship in God's kingdom.

That may mean disloyalty to our own country at times. (Paul didn't renounce his Roman citizenship, but he often went against the rule of Rome when it collided with God's rule.)

The New Testament contains an unvarnished witness to never compromise our allegiance to Jesus Christ and His kingdom. Instead, it exhorts us to refuse to be part of the world system and choose the path of suffering for our stance.

The divine promise is that we will receive a reward for our suffering, a surpassing glory where we will eventually share the throne of our Lord in the age to come.

The reward of the kingdom and the details concerning our training for reigning are themes that are beyond the scope of this book. But to simplify it, the reward of the kingdom is to be part of the family of God and enjoy eternal life now and in the future (Mark 10:28–30). It also includes the promise to rule and reign with Christ.

The kingdom of God confronts you. The future has invaded the present. The life of the age to come stands before you, calling you to enter and enjoy it. The words "Lord Jesus" and "Jesus is Lord" imply entrusting ourselves to Christ's lordship, and this is what saves us (Romans 10:9; Acts 16:31).

The kingdom demands a radical decision. So radical that it's put in terms of "pressing in" and "taking it with violence." I urge you, therefore, to become like a little child, poor in spirit, taking up your cross, denying yourself, following Jesus Christ in His kingdom.

This is the true "radicalization" to the true "empire." All other allegiances are counterfeits.

Coming Full Circle

So we come full circle. The gospel of the kingdom is designed to wreck your life. It will set you free on the one hand, but provoke misunderstanding and even get you in trouble on the other.

Many evangelicals have been taught to believe that the kingdom of God is only relegated to heaven and the future, making it our job to get as many souls ready for the afterlife.

On the flip side, many progressive Christians have been taught that the world system is a legitimate entity on the earth. And Christians should come alongside it, using it to make the world a better place.

The gospel of the kingdom calls us to stand against the world system for the world's sake.

The world system was conceived in the fall of humans in Genesis 3. At that time, the seed of the woman and the seed of the serpent went to war. The rest of the Bible is the unfolding saga of the seed of the woman (Jesus Christ and His body) versus the seed of the serpent (the principalities and powers of this present evil age). That battle rages all the way through Revelation when we see the seed of the woman overcoming the serpent himself.

Today, you and I live in the middle of that saga.

Let us stand on the banks of the Jordan, and let us believe. Let us not harden our hearts, but walk into the land and possess the fullness of Christ, obeying and then proclaiming the glorious gospel of the kingdom of God.

The God of peace will soon crush Satan under your feet. The grace of our Lord Jesus be with you. (Romans 16:20 NIV)

Meet Jennifer

. . .

I met Jennifer many years ago. She was tremendously gifted. A loving soul as well. Most people who knew her loved and respected her.

Unfortunately, one individual whom Jennifer graciously helped turned against her. This individual's heart was filled with jealousy, and it quickly turned into hatred toward Jennifer.

At the hands of this individual, Jennifer became the subject of the worst kind of slander the human mind can imagine. But like Mary of Bethany in the Gospels, Jennifer never responded in kind.

She kept silent.

Jennifer was able to take the high road in Jesus Christ because she had heard the gospel of the kingdom and had been "radicalized." She went through three years of hell, watching friends believe the slander and disassociate from her. She lived under the agony of betrayal from lying words.

Jennifer learned the lessons of suffering with Christ and bearing His cross.

Three years later, the Lord vindicated her. Terrible judgment fell on the woman who launched the smear campaign, and she was publicly exposed as being a dishonest soul void of any credibility.

Many who believed the lies apologized to Jennifer, and relationships were mended.

Jennifer was a great example to me of what it means to live in the insurgence and hand oneself completely over to the Lord, trusting Him with one's life.

Meet Two Uncommon Communities

● ● ●

Many years ago, I was involved with a beautiful expression of the ekklesia. This community was made up of a group of believers who had seen the kingdom and given their lives fully to it. These believers had hot hearts for Jesus Christ, and they pressed their way into His kingdom with aggressive desperation.

As the fellowship grew, people from all over the world came to visit them. Some of these visitors sold their homes and quit their jobs, relocating to be a part of the community and share in its collective life.

The community practically lived in common. While they didn't live out of a common purse, each person recognized that his or her possessions belonged to Christ and His body. Thus those who possessed more helped those who possessed less. The result was that no one lacked in the community.

Some years later, I introduced a similar community of believers to a new spiritual season of outreach.

The season was marked by breaking the church up into small groups, each with a defined kingdom outreach mission.

Some of the groups in the church had a burden for the poor. Others had a burden for the widows and fatherless. Others had a burden for pregnant teens. Others had a burden for drug addicts. Others had a burden for those caught in the sex trafficking industry, and so on.

Each month, these "kingdom cells" would investigate what the Lord was already doing in their city with respect to these specific ministries.

I encouraged them to embrace the principle of "cooperation without compromise." In other words, with respect to the work of the kingdom, each group in the church could display Jesus Christ by joining arms with others who were already engaged in helping the hurting. But that didn't mean they had to compromise their own specific values and beliefs in doing so.

As an example, an evangelical Christian could join arms with a Catholic organization to help the poor without compromising their specific evangelical views. A charismatic can lock arms with a Methodist church in helping drug addicts and pregnant teens without compromising their charismatic beliefs.

A great deal of fruit can emerge by finding out what the Lord is already doing in a particular city and joining arms with that work, and at the same time, displaying the kingdom of God in your own unique way.

Cooperation can be accomplished without compromise.

The Insurgency Has Begun

. . .

The insurgency began and you missed it
I looked for it and I found it . . .
Let's begin again.[25]

R.E.M.

So the sword has fallen. The curtain has been raised. If you made it this far in the book, you've heard the gospel of the kingdom. Perhaps for the first time.

The lyrics above come from R.E.M., an American rock band that started in the twentieth century. While this song has nothing to do with the theme of this book, the lyrics give language for a tragedy that's befallen multitudes of Christians in our generation.

The insurgency began and they missed it.

It is because of this wholesale ignorance among Christians today that I've written this book. To open their eyes—to open *your* eyes—to the insurgency.

And if you look for it, you will find it.

Yes, the insurgence that Jesus Christ began 2,000 years ago when He rose again from the dead is here. Now. But it must be implemented in and through the Lord's true followers.

We are not simply the beneficiaries of the insurgence; we are called to be its agents. In the weeks to come, there will be tremendous pressure on you to become distracted from all the challenges contained in this book.

There will be pressure to turn your attention to other things.

There will be pressure to forget the message.

Don't be deceived. Busyness is a myth. We all make time for what matters to us.

If you take a stand for God's kingdom, you will be tested over it. But if you resolve to stand firm and resist the enemy, he will eventually flee (Ephesians 6:14; James 4:7).

To implement the full extent of the victory that Christ won on the cross, you'll have to sink your feet deep into the sand and declare, "I am going to leave this world behind! I am going on with the Lord, moving deeper and higher into Him and His kingdom, no matter what it costs. By God's mercy, I refuse to let anything stop me."

This is the attitude I leave you with.

I also want you to know something else. It's going to hurt. So I can offer you nothing but tears and blood. But out of it God will gain His kingdom, and He will obtain some women and men who have learned to live under His rule.

Before the Lord, I have sought to be faithful in sharing what's been placed on my heart. This book represents a single message. And I hope that I've delivered it by the Holy Spirit.

If you've read this far, it is your journey to continue the message in your own life. And in time, you will know whether or not you've received the message.

On that note, I invite you to be a part of the present insurgence. The one that began in Century One and that's being reclaimed today.

So if you wish to go deeper—as well as connect with other insurgents who are standing for the kingdom in our time—go to this website:

InsurgenceBook.com

On the website, you will gain access to the following resources:

- Complimentary audio messages that expand the themes explored in this book.
- Supplemental articles that go along with the book.
- An opportunity to join my UNFILTERED email list where I share short, timely articles that are not "religiously correct" once a week.
- An opportunity to connect with other insurgents through a special online network.
- An opportunity to attend a conference designed to equip and connect you with other insurgents.
- A list of the other books I've written that explore other aspects of the insurgence.

- A Master Class called *Everlasting Domain: Restoring the Kingdom Message*. The class contains spoken conference messages that are a supplement to this book.
- A Question & Answer feature where you can ask me questions about any of the material presented in this book.

The final "Taking Action" section follows this chapter. I encourage you to read it, then take action on it.

I've sought my best to set forth a vision of the kingdom of God in these pages, through admittedly weak and feeble words. May the Holy Spirit bring the rest of this message to you.

To quote R.E.M. once more, *let's begin again.*

Your brother in the costly but glorious quest,

Frank

TAKING ACTION »

1. Listen to "The Tabernacle of David" at InsurgenceBook.com.

   Spend some time praying over the points in the message that stirred your heart.

2. Listen to "The Ultimate Issue" at InsurgenceBook.com.

   Spend some time praying over the points in the message that stirred your heart.

3. Listen to "Living in the Divine Parenthesis" at InsurgenceBook.com with at least one friend who lives near you. You can even listen to it with a small group.

   After you finish hearing the message, consider forming a "kingdom cell" with two, three, or four other believers. Create a plan to begin meeting together regularly. I suggest you do four things in your meetings:

   a. Tell your stories. This will help you to get to know each other better.

   b. Spend time in the Lord's presence. You may also want to go through volume 2 of *Jesus Speaks* and then read my online article "Aware of His Presence."[26]

   c. Discuss ways that you can take care of each other as well as the other members of the body of Christ whom you know.

   d. Discuss ways of plotting good deeds that show forth the beauty of Christ to the poor, the afflicted, the hurting, and the oppressed where you live. Ask the Lord to give your "cell" ideas on how to practically carry out this work together.

4. Now that you have finished the book, I recommend that you reread it with a friend (or with your new "kingdom cell"). In my experience, the gospel of the kingdom needs to be heard more than once and lived out with others—even if it's only one, two, three, or four others—before you'll begin to see its full fruit in your life.

Notes

Introduction

1. Frank Viola, *From Eternity to Here* (Colorado Springs: David C. Cook, 2009).
2. John Bright, *The Kingdom of God* (New York: Abingdon-Cokesbury Press, 1953), 7, 197.

A Warning Before You Read Further

1. Taken from Sizoo's "Unsung Heroes."

Part I Three Different Gospels

Recovering a High-Octane Gospel

1. T. Austin-Sparks, *The Gospel of the Kingdom* (Austin-Sparks.net, 2012); George Eldon Ladd, *The Gospel of the Kingdom* (Grand Rapids: Eerdmans, 1959); E. Stanley Jones, *The Unshakable Kingdom and the Unchanging Person* (Nashville: Abingdon Press, 1972); Watchman Nee, *The Collected Works of Watchman Nee*, set 3, vol. 59 (Anaheim: Living Stream Ministry, 1994); and Witness Lee, *The Kingdom* (Anaheim: Living Stream Ministry, 1980)—this book is based on messages delivered in 1972.

Complicating Factors

2. J. I. Packer, *Keep in Step with the Spirit* (Grand Rapids: Baker Publishing Group, 2005), 93.

Part II Unveiling the King's Beauty

Alive to Beauty

1. Jonathan Edwards, *The Works of Jonathan Edwards* (New Haven, CT: Yale University Press, 1957–2008), 25:635.

Recasting the Gospel Stories

2. P. T. Forsyth, *Work of Christ* (Blackwood, South Australia: New Creation Publications, 1994), 41.

The Untold Secret to Loving Christ

3. From the hymn "Hast Thou Heard Him, Seen Him, Known Him?" by Miss Ora Rowen.

Captured for Christ

4. T. Austin-Sparks, *The Gospel According to Paul* (Pelham: AL: Testimony Book Ministry, 1988), 70–71.

Part III The Gospel of the Kingdom

Israel's Calling

1. John Howard Yoder, *The Original Revolution* (Scottdale, PA: Herald Press), 28.

The Time Has Come!

2. Leonard Sweet and Frank Viola, *Jesus: A Theography* (Nashville: Thomas Nelson, 2012), 127. In chap. 7 of *Jesus: A Theography*, Jesus' wilderness temptation is explored in detail.

The King Declares His Kingdom

3. Michael Heiser, *The Unseen Realm* (Bellingham, WA: Lexham Press, 2015), 273.

Manifesting God's Rule

4. Alva McClain, *The Greatness of the Kingdom* (Winona Lake, IN: BMH Books, 1959), 17.

A Clash of Kingdoms

5. Frank Viola and George Barna, *Pagan Christianity* (Carol Stream, IL: Tyndale, 2008), 244–45.

Part IV Entering and Enjoying the Kingdom

Surpassing Devotion

1. https://www.lastdaysministries.org/Groups/1000086201/Last_Days_Ministries/Articles/By_Keith_Green/Total_Commitment/Total_Commitment.aspx.
2. A. W. Tozer, *The Pursuit of God* (Camp Hill, PA: Christian Publishers, 1982), 67.

Getting Into the Kingdom

3. F. F. Bruce, *The Message of the New Testament* (Grand Rapids: Eerdmans, 1973), 85.

Public Confession

4. F. F. Bruce, *Answers to Questions* (Grand Rapids: Zondervan, 1973), 189.

Spiritual Violence

5. T. Austin-Sparks, *Prophetic Ministry* (Pelham, AL: Testimony Book Ministry, 1989), 93–94.

What Holds Us to the Altar?

6. Watchman Nee, *A Living Sacrifice* (New York: Christian Fellowship Publishers, 1972), 54–55.

Part V Our Glorious Liberty

Fully Accepted, Fully Freed

1. Frank Viola, *Revise Us Again* (Colorado Springs: David C. Cook, 2011).

A Liberated Captive

2. Quoted in Andy Zubko, *Treasury of Spiritual Wisdom* (Delhi: Motilal Banarsidass, 2004), 172.

The Works of the Law

3. Quoted in Scot McKnight, *The Blue Parakeet* (Grand Rapids: Zondervan, 2008), 207.

Sin Metrics

4. Candace Chellew-Hodge, "Amazed by Grace: An Interview with Author Philip Yancey," *Whosoever*, 2004, http://www.whosoever.org/v8i6/yancey.shtml.

Freedom From the Law

5. Attributed to either English writer and Puritan preacher John Bunyan or English revivalist and hymnist John Berridge.

The Battle of the Ages

6. A. W. Tozer, *My Daily Pursuit* (Minneapolis: Bethany House, 2013), 13.

Sin Remixed

7. William Blake, *The Marriage of Heaven and Hell* (Oxford, UK: Oxford University Press, 1975), xviii.

A Tale of Two Kingdoms

8. *A Greek-English Lexicon of the New Testament and Other Early Christian Literature (BDAG)*, 3rd ed., s.v. "kosmos," 2000, 561–62.
9. Watchman Nee, *Love Not the World* (Fort Washington, PA: CLC Publications, 2004), 12–13.
10. F. F. Bruce, *The Message of the New Testament* (Grand Rapids: Eerdmans, 1973), 89.
11. John Howard Yoder, *The Royal Priesthood* (Scottdale, PA: Herald Press, 1998), 56.
12. Clinton Arnold, *Powers of Darkness* (Downers Grove, IL: InterVarsity Press, 1992), 203–4.
13. A. W. Tozer, *The Pursuit of Man* (Camp Hill, PA: Christian Publications, 1950), 116.

The Birth of the World System

14. Jacque Ellul, *Anarchy and Christianity* (Grand Rapids: Eerdmans, 1988), 58.
15. John Nugent, *Polis Bible Commentary, Genesis 1–11*, vol. 1 (Skyforest, CA: Urban Loft Publishing, forthcoming), Genesis 4:17–24.

Fallen Human Civilization

16. John C. Nugent, *The Politics of Yahweh* (Eugene, OR: Cascade Books), 34.
17. Nugent, *Polis Bible Commentary*, Genesis 4:17–24.

False Security

18. Jacques Ellul, *The Subversion of Christianity* (Grand Rapids: Eerdmans, 1986), 21.

Detaching Yourself

19. Nee, *Love Not the World*, 30–31.
20. Bruce, *Message of the New Testament*, 89–90.

Dealing With the World
21. Quoted in George Sweeting, *Who Said That?* (Chicago: Moody Publishers, 1995).

The Deceitfulness of Riches
22. From Ellul's article "Anarchism and Christianity," published in *Katallagete*, Fall 1980, 20.
23. Watchman Nee, *Love Not the World*, 113, 117.

The Story of Money
24. A. W. Tozer, *The Pursuit of God* (Camp Hill, PA: Christian Publishers, 1982), 27–28.

A Disturbing Observation
25. Nee, *Love Not the World*, 78–79.

The Witness of Church History
26. Respectively—Lucian, *The Death of Peregrine*, 13 (also called *The Passing of Peregrinus*); Aristides, *Apology*, 15; Tertullian, *The Apology*, 39; quoted in Rodney Stark, *The Rise of Christianity* (Princeton: Princeton University Press, 1966), 82.; Julian, *Letter to Arsacius*.

Taking Action
27. St. John Chrysostom, Hom. in Lazaro 2, 5: PG 48, 992.
28. Loose translation from St. Basil the Great, Homily on the saying of the Gospel According to Luke, "I will pull down my barns and build bigger ones," and on greed, §7 (PG 31, 276B–277A).

Part VI Advancing the Kingdom

Another Brand of Worldliness
1. H. Richard Niebuhr, *The Kingdom of God in America* (Middletown, CT: Wesleyan University Press, 1988), 193.
2. Tozer, *My Daily Pursuit*, 25.

The Cross and the Insurgence
3. Taken from "When I Survey the Wondrous Cross" by Isaac Watts.

The Collective Expression of Christ
4. Bruce, *Message of the New Testament*, 116.

The Better Place
5. John Nugent, *Endangered Gospel* (Eugene, OR: Cascade Books, 2016), 166–67, 175.

The Centrality of the Ekklesia
6. Frank Viola, *From Eternity to Here* (Colorado Springs: David C. Cook, 2009), 240.

The Authority of the Believer
7. T. Austin-Sparks, *Four Greatnesses of Divine Revelation* (Pelham: AL: Testimony Book Ministry, 1994), 64.

The Fellowship of the Reconciled

8. Bruce, *Message of the New Testament*, 40.
9. Bruce, *Message of the New Testament*, 40.
10. Bruce, *Message of the New Testament*, 42.
11. John Howard Yoder, *The Politics of Jesus* (Grand Rapids: Eerdmans, 1994), 150–51.

Dethroning Principalities and Powers

12. Arnold, *Powers of Darkness*, 123.

The Powers Behind the Actors

13. Yoder, *The Politics of Jesus*, 201–2.
14. Jacques Ellul, *The Subversion of Christianity* (Grand Rapids: Eerdmans, 1986), 179–80.

The Cosmic Story

15. Viola, *From Eternity to Here*, chap. 17.

More Tragedy

16. Heiser, *The Unseen Realm*, 121, 329.

Eden Restored

17. Heiser, *The Unseen Realm*, 298.
18. Craig Keener, *Acts: An Exegetical Commentary*, vol. 1 (Grand Rapids: Baker Academic, 2012), 843.
19. Keener, *Acts*, 841.

To the End of the Earth

20. *New Bible Dictionary*, 2nd ed. (Wheaton: Tyndale House Publishers, 1982), 1165; *Nelson's Illustrated Bible Dictionary* (Nashville: Thomas Nelson, 1986), 1030.

Cyanide and Grape Juice

21. Nugent, *Endangered Gospel*, 186, 189.

Implementing the Victory

22. A. W. Tozer, quoted in James Snyder, *In Pursuit of God* (Camp Hill, PA: Christian Publications, 1991), 128.

Friends Yet Separate

23. Nee, *Love Not the World*, 46.

This Corrupt Generation

24. Tozer, *My Daily Pursuit*, 68.

The Insurgency Has Begun

25. R.E.M., "Begin the Begin," *Lifes Rich Pageant*, I.R.S. Records, 1986. A word to the peevish: It should go without saying that I don't endorse every word of this song nor this band or its individual members.

Taking Action

26. Leonard Sweet and Frank Viola, *Jesus Speaks* (Nashville: Thomas Nelson, 2016); and Frank Viola, "Aware of His Presence," at InsurgenceBook.com.

Acknowledgments

This book would not have been possible if it were not for the countless people who have blazed the trail before me. My views on the kingdom of God have been shaped over three decades of seeking, studying, and sitting at the feet of others. The many influences on my thinking are too numerous to even recall.

Consequently, this volume is the product of everything I've learned from the Lord as well as from scores of other servants of God who have written and spoken on the kingdom of God over decades.

Even so, the four major influencers who have given me my foundation in understanding God's kingdom have been T. Austin-Sparks, Watchman Nee, A. W. Tozer, and F. F. Bruce. In addition, the people I've cited in the footnotes and endnotes have also helped me put various pieces of the kingdom puzzle together.

I also want to thank John Nugent and Tim Oslovich for going through the unedited manuscript and giving me their critical feedback. These men have made this a better book.

Finally, I'm grateful to the Baker team and my agent, Greg Daniel, for believing in this book and launching it into the world.

May God use it to further foment the insurgence.

Frank Viola has helped thousands of people around the world to deepen their relationship with Jesus Christ and enter into a more vibrant and authentic experience of church. He has written many books on these themes, including *God's Favorite Place on Earth* and *From Eternity to Here*. His blog, frankviola.org, is ranked in the top ten of all Christian blogs on the Web today.

Join

FRANK VIOLA

at Beyond Evangelical

Blog: frankviola.org

——— JOIN ———

THE DEEPER
CHRISTIAN
LIFE NETWORK

An online community for virtual mentoring and connection into the deeper things of God.

 THE DEEPER CHRISTIAN LIFE NETWORK

THEDEEPERCHRISTIANLIFE.COM

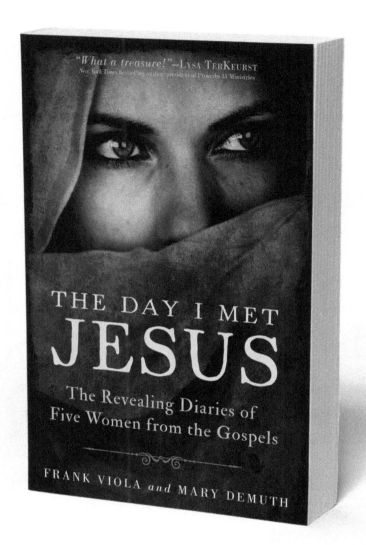

"What a treasure! The way Mary and Frank portray their stories will help any woman who has experienced heartbreak, loneliness, and rejection step right into the extravagant grace and love of Jesus."

—Lysa TerKeurst,

New York Times bestselling author of *The Best Yes*; president of Proverbs 31 Ministries

CPSIA information can be obtained
at www.ICGtesting.com
Printed in the USA
LVHW031249101218
599881LV00010B/56